Artificial Intelligence in Hospitality and Tourism in Africa

HOSPITALITY, TOURISM, CREATIVE AND CULTURAL (HTCC) INDUSTRIES IN AFRICA

Series Editors: Ishmael Mensah, Esi Akyere Mensah, Abena Aidoo Hewton and Robert E. Hinson

Hospitality, Tourism, Creative and Cultural (HTCC) Industries in Africa explores the dynamic intersections of hospitality and tourism within Africa's socio-cultural and political economy. With centuries of embedded relevance, the HTCC sector has evolved into a vital contributor to the global tourism landscape, driven by Africa's rich cultural assets, progressive government policies, and the transformative impact of digitisation. The series highlights the continent's growing prominence in international tourism, underscored by rising tourist arrivals, expanding infrastructure, and increasing foreign exchange contributions. It also examines country-specific developments – from adventure tourism in South Africa to hotel expansion in Nigeria and coastal tourism in Kenya – demonstrating the sector's potential to drive sustainable economic growth and community development.

Despite this momentum, the management of emerging frontiers in HTCC industries remains underexplored, particularly in the context of Africa's resource constraints and institutional challenges. The series addresses that gap by inviting scholarly contributions that apply contemporary management theories to the African HTCC context, providing a platform for innovative research, policy dialogue, and strategic insights.

Artificial Intelligence in Hospitality and Tourism in Africa: Prospects, Opportunities and Challenges

EDITED BY

ESI AKYERE MENSAH
International University of Grand Bassam, Cote D'Ivoire

AARON YANKHOLMES
Nottingham Trent University, UK

FRANK BADU-BAIDEN
University of Central Florida, USA

AND

NII LONGDON SOWAH
University of Ghana, Ghana

emerald PUBLISHING

United Kingdom – North America – Japan – India – Malaysia – China

Emerald Publishing Limited
Emerald Publishing, Floor 5, Northspring, 21-23 Wellington Street, Leeds LS1 4DL

First edition 2026

British Library Cataloguing in Publication Data
A catalogue record for this book is available from the British Library

ISBN: 978-1-80686-170-5 (Print)
ISBN: 978-1-80686-169-9 (Online)
ISBN: 978-1-80686-171-2 (Epub)

Printed and bound by CPI Group (UK) Ltd, Croydon, CR0 4YY

INVESTOR IN PEOPLE

Contents

About the Editors

Dr Esi Akyere Mensah is a Senior Lecturer in Tourism Management with over 10 years of teaching and research experience in Ghana, the United Kingdom and Ivory Coast. She teaches tourism, business management and sustainability at undergraduate and postgraduate levels. Her research interests are at the intersection of tourism marketing, sustainability and development. She has co-edited 2 books with works published in journals such as *Tourism Geographies, Tourism Management Perspectives and International Journal of Tourism Cities*. She serves on the editorial board of Tourism Planning and Development.

Dr Aaron Yankholmes is an Associate Professor in Marketing at Nottingham Business School, Nottingham Trent University, with a PhD from The Hong Kong Polytechnic University. He has held academic roles in Macau, the Netherlands and the United Kingdom. His research focuses on generational perspectives in sustainability and responsible AI, with broader interests in tourism, culture and social issues. His has published in top journals, including *Tourism Management, Journal of Cleaner Production* and *Tourism Recreation Research*. Dr Yankholmes serves as Book Reviews Editor for the Journal of Heritage Tourism and Associate Editor for Frontiers in Sustainable Tourism.

Dr Frank Badu-Baiden is a scholar in hospitality and tourism management and currently serves as an Assistant Professor at the Rosen College of Hospitality Management, University of Central Florida. He earned his PhD from The Hong Kong Polytechnic University. His expertise spans tourism management, consumer behaviour and the application of emerging technologies and innovations in tourism and hospitality. Dr Badu-Baiden has an impressive record in both teaching and research, with publications in leading academic journals and contributions to successfully funded international research projects. He is also a member of the Infectious Disease and Travel Health research cluster at the University of Central Florida. A Certified Hospitality Educator, he is actively involved in professional associations, including the Travel and Tourism Research Association (TTRA) and the International Council on Hotel, Restaurant, and Institutional Education (ICHRIE).

Dr Nii Longdon Sowah is a Senior Lecturer in Computer Engineering at the University of Ghana, with more than 12 years of teaching experience and a strong research background in artificial intelligence and computer vision. With a proven track record of instructing over 3,000 students at both undergraduate and graduate levels, he is recognised for his commitment to academic excellence and integrity. Dr Sowah is part of a team of experts developing the Ghana AI Practitioners Guide, funded by GIZ. He is also lending his expertise to the review of the National AI Policy Strategy being led by RAIL and funded by GIZ. Dr Sowah is the Lead Instructor for the SES STEM Academy at the University of Ghana. He currently is part of the Local Language Accelerator Programme by UNDP Ghana Digital Office as an AI Consultant. He believes that Africans must write their narrative when it comes to artificial intelligence.

About the Contributors

Benedict Jojo Afful – Front-end developer with a BSc in Computer Science (University of Cape Coast). Specialises in UI/UX design, front-end technologies and data visualisation.

Stephen Owusu Afriyie – Lecturer, Department of Accounting, Banking and Finance, Ghana Communication Technology University. Research interests include corporate finance, fintech, corporate governance, microfinance, entrepreneurship and sustainability. Has published in SCI, SSCI, Scopus, PubMed, DOAJ and other indexed journals.

John Agyekum Addae is a PhD researcher at LUT University, Finland, and a Lecturer in Banking and Finance at Ghana Communication Technology University (GCTU). He holds an MSc in Microfinance and an MSc in Development Finance and is a Chartered Banker (ACIB). His research interests span FinTech, central bank digital currencies (CBDC), risk governance, banking risk-taking behaviour, microfinance, development finance, digital finance and multichannel banking systems. His scholarly work has been published in several reputable peer-reviewed journals, including *Journal of Hospitality and Tourism Insights, Managerial Finance, International Journal of Bank Marketing, The Learning Organization, International Journal of Entrepreneurship & Innovation* and *International Journal of Quality & Reliability Management,* among others.

Sheraz Ahmed is an Associate Professor of Finance and the Director of the Master's degree programme in Strategic Finance and Analytics at LUT Business School, LUT University, Finland. He earned his doctoral degree in Economics and Business Administration from the Hanken School of Economics, Finland. His research interests encompass market microstructure, factor investing, asset pricing, portfolio performance evaluation, Fintech development and adoption under uncertainty and corporate governance. He has published extensively in esteemed journals such as the *International Review of Financial Analysis*, *North American Journal of Economics and Finance*, *The European Journal of Finance*, *Empirical Economics*, *Algorithmic Finance* and *Emerging Markets Finance and Trade*.

Gertrude Amoakohene – Senior Lecturer, Department of Accounting, Banking and Finance, Ghana Communication Technology University. Research interests include accounting, corporate finance, investment, green hydrogen financing and development finance.

Anna Arthur-Amissah – Assistant Lecturer, Department of Ecotourism, Recreation and Hospitality, University of Energy and Natural Resources, Sunyani, Ghana. Research interests include organisational behaviour in the hospitality industry, hospitality and tourism entrepreneurship and education, waste management in tourism sites, technology adoption and usage in hospitality and sustainability in the hospitality and tourism industry.

Maame Gyamfua Asante-Mensah – Lecturer, Department of Computer Science and Information Technology, University of Cape Coast. Holds a PhD in Computational and Data Science and Engineering (Skoltech, Russia). Research focuses on deep learning, tensor completion, computer vision and randomised algorithms.

Michael Ashun – Holds a BSc in Computer Science (University of Cape Coast). Expertise includes database administration, forex and cryptocurrency trading and AI tools for financial markets.

Reginald Olympas Akua Awusiedu – Assistant Lecturer, Department of Hospitality and Tourism Management, Ho Technical University. Over 23 years of teaching experience, 12 at tertiary level. Research interests include ICT, food production, accommodation and restaurant operations and front office management.

Desmond Tutu Ayentimi – Senior Lecturer of Management at the Tasmanian School of Business and Economics, University of Tasmania, Hobart. Holds a PhD in Management from Curtin University, Western Australia. Research interests include multinational enterprises HRM, technology and employment relations, cross-cultural management, diversity, equality and inclusion and HRD in sub-Saharan Africa. Has published extensively in reputable international journals including *Industrial Relations Journal, Personnel Review, Journal of Industrial Relations, International Journal of Project Management, Education + Training, Asia Pacific Journal of Human Resources, Thunderbird International Business Review, Technology Analysis and Strategic Management* and *Journal of Social Entrepreneurship*.

Sarah Blankson-Stiles-Ocran – Holds an MPhil in Hospitality Management from the University of Cape Coast. Former Assistant Lecturer at Ho Technical University, Ghana; currently Clinical Associate with Bancroft, USA. Research interests include technology in hospitality, employee well-being, gender studies, food tourism, service quality and psychological issues in tourism.

Nandipha David is a Lecturer in Tourism at the University of South Africa (Unisa) with extensive industry and academic experience. She earned her undergraduate and honours degrees in Tourism from the University of Pretoria, followed by a Master's in Tourism while working in the sector, and is currently pursuing a PhD in Tourism. Before joining academia, she spent a decade in the travel industry, working for travel management companies (TMCs) and an outbound tour operator, gaining expertise in customer relationship building, strategic planning, leadership and operational management. She is recognised for her adaptability to change, strong budget and time management skills and ability to deliver results under pressure while maintaining a strong commercial focus.

Eudora Hagan – Senior Lecturer and Head of Department of Tourism Management, Takoradi Technical University, Ghana. Holds a PhD and MPhil in Tourism (University of Cape Coast). Research focuses on service quality, ecotourism, sustainable tourism, food and culture, AI in tourism and hospitality technology.

Charles Roland Haruna – Senior Lecturer, Department of Computer Science and Information Technology, University of Cape Coast. Holds a PhD and MEng in Computer Science (University of Electronic Science and Technology of China). Research areas include AI in Big Data, network security, XR, distributed databases and systems development.

Victor Anderson Hodibert – Senior Lecturer, Department of Tourism Management, Takoradi Technical University, Ghana. Holds a PhD and MPhil in African Studies (University of Ghana) and an MA in Cultural Projects for Development (University of Turin, Italy). Research interests include community tourism development, cultural heritage, tourism livelihoods and AI in African tourism.

Abdul Bashiru Jibril – Assistant Professor of Marketing, School of Management and Economics, University of Kurdistan Hewlêr (UKH), Erbil, Kurdistan Region, Iraq. Holds a PhD in Marketing Management from Tomas Bata University, Czech Republic. Teaches digital marketing, relationship marketing, brand management and related modules. Research areas include technology adoption, social media analytics, brand management and sustainable e-entrepreneurship, with a focus on data mining for business intelligence. Has led several external projects, including a recent grant collaboration between the International University of Rabat and the University of Oxford on Morocco's gig economy. Published in ABS/ABDC-listed journals and presented at international conferences in the United States, the United Kingdom, Germany, Czech Republic, France and Saudi Arabia.

Peter Yao Lartey – Visiting Research Scholar, Niagara Community Observatory, Brock University, Canada. Holds a PhD in Finance and Economics (Jiangsu University, China), MBA in Finance (Cardiff Metropolitan University, UK) and diplomas in Accounting and Business Studies. Research areas include corporate governance, CSR, knowledge management and internal control.

Joseph Akwasi Nkyi – Lecturer, Department of Accounting, Banking and Finance, Ghana Communication Technology University. Holds a PhD in Business Administration (CASS European Institute, France), MBA (University of Leicester, UK) and BCom (University of Cape Coast). Over 20 years in banking before academia.

Ricky Yao Nutsugbodo – Senior Lecturer, Department of Ecotourism, Recreation and Hospitality, University of Energy and Natural Resources, Sunyani, Ghana. Research focuses on hospitality and tourism education, women's participation in ecotourism destinations, tourism transportation and waste management at tourism sites, entrepreneurship and technology usage in the hospitality and tourism industry.

Boamah Charles Ofosu Ofori – Holds a BSc in Computer Science (University of Cape Coast). Interests include software development, cybersecurity and emerging technologies.

Frederick Pobee – Lecturer, Department of Business Administration, University of Professional Studies, Accra, Ghana. Holds a PhD in Business Administration and an MPhil in Management Information Systems. Research interests: financial technology, e-commerce, innovative entrepreneurship and ICT4D. Recently part of a research team for a project between the International University of Rabat (Morocco) and the University of Oxford (UK) on enhancing working conditions in Morocco's gig economy. Has published in peer-reviewed ABS/ABDC-listed journals and presented at conferences in the United States, the United Kingdom, Hungary and Vietnam.

Richmond Sakyi – Lecturer, Department of Hospitality and Tourism Management, Ho Technical University, Ghana. Holds an MPhil in Tourism Management from the University of Cape Coast (2018) and is pursuing a PhD in Hospitality and Tourism Management at Kwame Nkrumah University of Science and Technology. Research interests include sustainable tourism development, eco-tourism, human resource management, hospitality and tourism marketing, corporate social responsibility, customer service and travel intermediaries.

Nyamekesse Samuel – Software Engineer at Bosonit. Holds a BSc in Computer Science (University of Cape Coast). Research interests include AI applications in emerging economies, cloud infrastructure and healthcare AI systems.

Cornelius Tengan – Lecturer, Department of Hospitality Management, Bolgatanga Technical University, Ghana. PhD candidate in Tourism Management, University of South Africa. Research focuses on service quality, organisational behaviour, attraction management, tourism interpretation and sustainable tourism development.

Foreword

By
Kwaku Adutwum Ayim Boakye
Professor of Tourism and Hospitality, Vice Chancelor Cape
Coast Technical University, Ghana

The conversation about AI has transitioned from the philosophical 'whys' to the practical 'hows'. But are African countries ready? As with every new technology or phenomenon, adoption and use by the developing world has been relatively slower and, sometimes more problematic because of contextual differences between the generating society and the adapting one. By producing this potentially seminal piece set in the African context, the authors have drawn us into the policy space – an area that regrettably does not appear to be popular among managers of destinations.

It is against background that I find this book a timely guide to our adoption of AI. Assembling a coterie of fine emerging authors, this volume carefully navigates both the broad issues affecting implementation (such as challenges, bottlenecks and opportunities) as well as the specialised topics which address AI's use in robotics fintech, the customer experience, to mention a few.

Technology has a way of hastening the bridging of the North–South developmental divide, and this book clearly articulates how AI plays such a role in the hospitality and tourism space. The authors and editors outline some very bold and audacious interventions which can help the continent to, as they succinctly put it, 'leapfrog' into competitiveness.

Acknowledgements

This book would not have been possible without the dedicated contributions of an extraordinary team of scholars, practitioners and researchers who generously shared their expertise, time and insights on the intersection of artificial intelligence, hospitality and tourism across Africa.

We extend our deepest gratitude to the following authors and collaborators, whose chapters form the backbone of this book: Richmond Sakyi, Frederick Pobee, Abdul Bashiru Jibril, John Agyekum Addae, Sheraz Ahmed, Desmond Tutu, Ricky Yao Nutsugbodo, Anna Arthur-Amissah, Sarah Blankson-Stiles-Ocran, Cornelius Tengan, Reginald Olympas Akua Awusiedu, Victor Anderson Hodibert, Eudora Hagan, Nandipha David, Stephen Owusu Afriyie, Joseph Akwasi Nkyi, Gertrude Amoakohene, Peter Yao Lartey, Charles Roland Haruna, Maame Gyamfua Asante-Mensah, Michael Ashun, Nyamekesse Samuel, Benedict Jojo Afful and Boamah Charles Ofosu Ofori.

We are immensely thankful for the collegiality, patience and support of all contributors. Their diverse perspectives and case studies add remarkable depth to this project and highlight the global and African realities of AI adoption in hospitality and tourism.

Above all, we celebrate the spirit of collaboration and knowledge-sharing that has guided this journey. It is our hope that the collective efforts captured in these chapters will inspire new pathways for research, practice and policy in AI-driven hospitality and tourism across Africa.

Chapter 1

The Adoption of Artificial Intelligence in Hospitality and Tourism in Africa

Esi Akyere Mensah[a], *Aaron Yankholmes*[b], *Frank Badu-Baiden*[c] *and Nii Longdon Sowah*[d]

[a]International University of Grand Bassam, Cote D'Ivoire
[b]Nottingham Trent University, UK
[c]University of Central Florida, USA
[d]University of Ghana, Ghana

Abstract

While Artificial Intelligence (AI) has revolutionised the world of business globally, its adoption in hospitality and tourism across sub-Saharan Africa (SSA) remains limited. This introductory chapter explores the global proliferation of AI and its specific implications for the hospitality and tourism sector, with a focused lens on Africa. It presents a detailed regional analysis of Africa's diverse tourism economies, highlighting stark disparities in performance, digital infrastructure and AI readiness. This chapter argues that while AI presents a significant opportunity for efficiency, personalisation and sustainable development in tourism, its adoption in Africa is constrained by foundational challenges, including data inconsistencies, skills gaps and uneven digital infrastructure.

Keywords: AI adoption; Africa; AI opportunities; AI challenges; technology adoption

Overview

For the foreseeable future, the discourse on Artificial Intelligence (AI) and its opportunities, prospects and challenges will remain a source of contention for all industries and regions of the world. AI is at the threshold of transforming

Artificial Intelligence in Hospitality and Tourism in Africa, 1–18

Published under exclusive licence by Emerald Publishing Limited
doi:10.1108/978-1-80686-169-920261001

industries, societies and redefining the very concept of intelligence. At its core, AI is a multidisciplinary field within computer science that seeks to create systems capable of performing tasks that traditionally require human-like intelligence, such as learning, reasoning, problem-solving and decision-making (Davenport & Ronanki, 2018; Russell & Norvig, 2016). In the realm of cognitive science, AI strives to replicate human cognitive processes like perception and problem-solving through computational models and algorithms (Boden, 2006). Beyond mere data processing, AI also encompasses autonomous systems that adapt to dynamic environments and make real-time decisions without human intervention (Goodall, 2014).

In what has been referred to as the third wave of AI, many countries around the world have moved beyond narrow, task-specific applications and are now integrating AI into broader socio-economic systems, including governance, industry, education, health and finance (see Fig. 1). Historically, the first wave of AI (1950s–1980s) was characterised by symbolic systems and expert rules, where research focused on logic, reasoning and knowledge representation. The second wave (1990s–2010s) was marked by the emergence of machine learning and deep learning, driven by the availability of big data, increased computing power and advances in neural networks (UNCTAD, 2025). The third wave, which began in the early 2020s, was defined by generative and systemic AI, as large language models (LLMs) and multimodal systems were integrated into multiple sectors such as governance, health, education, finance and creative industries (Cristofaro & Giardino, 2025; UNCTAD, 2025). This wave was distinguished by its generative capabilities, cross-sector adoption and the global policy debates it evoked.

It is therefore not surprising that AI has been a major topic in both academic and political circles, evoking both excitement and fear in equal measure (Kumawat et al., 2025; UNCTAD, 2021; World Bank, 2021). On one hand, the prospects of greater efficiency, medical breakthroughs and new opportunities for economic growth were celebrated. On the other hand, fears arose due to concerns about large-scale job displacement, widening inequality, ethical dilemmas and the risks of surveillance and misuse of AI technologies (PwC, 2023).

This tension between optimism and apprehension provides a critical backdrop for examining how AI is unfolding within specific sectors of the global economy. Nowhere is this more evident than in hospitality and tourism, a highly service-oriented industry that is deeply sensitive to technological change. As global competition intensifies, countries and corporations have begun embedding AI into core tourism and hospitality operations, from customer service and pricing strategies to destination management and sustainability planning.

Global Trends in AI Adoption in Hospitality and Tourism

Ever since OpenAI launched ChatGPT in November 2022, awareness and applications of AI have multiplied across industries and sectors worldwide. The so-called AI race between developed countries has seen intense competition between the United States, China, Japan, South Korea and the European Union,

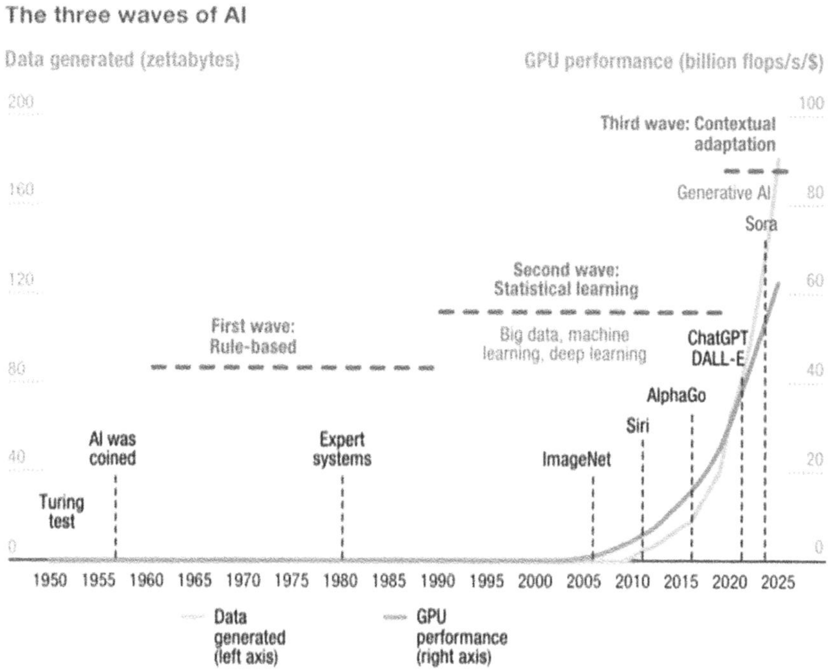

Fig. 1. The Three Waves of the Evolution of AI. *Source:* UNCTAD (2025).

each vying for technological dominance, regulatory influence and market leadership (see Fig. 1). At the corporate level, the leading companies at the forefront – Apple, Nvidia and Microsoft – each now have a market capitalisation of more than US$3 trillion, a figure close to the entire gross domestic product (GDP) of the African continent (UNCTAD, 2025). Indeed, this concentration of market power underscores the geopolitical and economic significance of AI, as leadership in this domain is increasingly equated with global competitiveness and future economic security.

In developed markets such as the United States, the United Kingdom, China and the European Union (EU), as well as in emerging economies like India, Brazil, Indonesia, Vietnam and Turkey, AI applications are now mainstream. Its applications in hospitality and tourism range from hotel guest services and revenue optimisation to personalised trip planning and destination management.

Hotels and travel companies have widely adopted AI-driven tools to enhance guest interaction. In the United States, major chains such as Hilton and Marriott use AI chatbots to handle inquiries, manage bookings and deliver personalised recommendations (Bulchand-Gidumal et al., 2023). Hilton's robot concierge 'Connie', powered by IBM Watson, provides local tips to guests, while Marriott uses machine learning to tailor services based on customer preferences (Hall & Cooper, 2025). Wyndham has similarly deployed AI assistants through its mobile app, enabling real-time responses and upselling of local services (Bulchand-Gidumal et al., 2023).

Quantitative benefits are evident in travel platforms. Trip.com in China launched TripGenie, an AI travel assistant capable of crafting itineraries and resolving queries. The platform doubled its booking conversion rate and achieved over 70% automated resolution of flight and hotel inquiries, thanks to high semantic recognition accuracy (Parulis-Cook, 2025).

Revenue Management and Operational Efficiency

AI has become integral to dynamic pricing and revenue optimisation. Algorithms analyse booking patterns, competitor rates and seasonal demand to adjust prices in real time (Hall & Cooper, 2025). Wyndham was among the first global brands to implement a fully AI-driven revenue management system, allowing franchisees to optimise occupancy and maximise yield (Amadeus Hospitality, 2025). Case studies show hotels using such systems have achieved revenue per available room (RevPAR) increases of around 20–30% within months of deployment.

In the United Kingdom and Europe, hotels are also adopting AI for automation and cost reduction. Service robots now handle check-ins, luggage and room service delivery, freeing staff for higher-value interactions (Tuomi & Passos Ascenção, 2023). Analyses suggest that automating routine tasks can reduce hotel operating costs by 15% and boost revenues by 10% (Gössling & Mei, 2025). In Vietnam, Vias Hotel introduced an AI concierge that increased direct bookings by 10% while allowing a 30% reduction in staffing needs. Airlines are also benefiting. Delta Air Lines in the United States applies AI-driven predictive maintenance to anticipate aircraft issues, reducing delays and unscheduled downtime (Hall & Cooper, 2025). Such operational efficiencies translate directly into better customer experiences and cost savings across the sector. These examples highlight AI's role in addressing labour shortages while maintaining service quality.

AI is also being harnessed to address sustainability and overtourism. Venice, Italy, employs an AI monitoring system that analyses real-time foot traffic via sensors and cameras, allowing authorities to redirect flows and prevent overcrowding in fragile heritage zones (Singh & Kaunert, 2025). Spain's Iberostar Hotels uses predictive analytics to monitor water and energy usage, identifying anomalies and reducing wastage across resorts (Hall & Cooper, 2025). These initiatives show AI's potential not only for efficiency and marketing but also for environmental and social sustainability.

Consumer-Level Adoption

From the traveller's perspective, AI has become embedded in nearly every stage of the journey. Surveys suggest that 80% of travellers now use some form of AI tool for trip planning, and over half would allow AI to fully plan and book their trips. Adoption is particularly high in emerging economies: more than 90% of travellers in India and China say they are willing to use AI assistants for trip planning.

Consumer-facing platforms such as Expedia and Booking.com have integrated generative AI into their apps, enabling users to ask open-ended questions like '*plan me a three-day family trip to Istanbul*' and receive customised itineraries (Szpilko et al., 2023). This functionality saves travellers time and provides tailored suggestions, increasing loyalty to these platforms. However, research indicates that while many customers appreciate AI convenience, around 60% still prefer human interaction for complex travel needs. Indeed, no where is the balance between technological innovation and the human touch more critical than in Africa—a continent with deeply rooted traditions of hospitality. A balance that is especially critical in Africa, where technological innovation must be woven into the continent's deeply rooted traditions of welcome.

Africa In Context

Africa is the world's second-largest continent, covering more than 30 million km^2 and home to 54 countries and about 1.4 billion people. The continent is divided into five regions: North, West, East, Central and Southern Africa. North Africa (Egypt, Morocco, Algeria, Tunisia, Libya) has around 250 million people, West Africa over 400 million (with Nigeria nearly half of this number), East Africa about 440 million, Central Africa ~180 million and Southern Africa 70 million. Africa's geographic and cultural diversity – ranging from the Sahara Desert to the Congo Basin and from over 1,000 languages to varied colonial legacies – shapes its economies, technology adoption and tourism potential.

Regional Economic Diversity

Africa's economies differ markedly across regions. North Africa benefits from proximity to Europe, with economies built on oil and gas exports (Algeria, Libya) and diversified sectors in Egypt and Morocco, including tourism and manufacturing. West Africa is resource-rich, led by Nigeria's oil and Ghana's gold, while also producing cocoa, bauxite and other commodities. However, infrastructure deficits and currency instability limit growth despite dynamic hubs in Lagos and Accra (World Bank, 2021). East Africa remains agriculture-based (coffee, tea, horticulture), yet countries like Kenya, Tanzania and Ethiopia have diversified into technology, services and tourism, with Nairobi recognised as a 'Silicon Savannah' for Fintech and mobile innovation (GSMA, 2024). Central Africa is dominated by extractive industries, such as oil (Angola, Gabon) and mining (DRC's cobalt and copper), but weak governance and instability constrain broader development (UNCTAD, 2021). Southern Africa is comparatively more advanced, with South Africa's diversified industrial base, Botswana's diamond wealth and Mauritius' services sector standing out.

Digitalisation and Technology Adoption

Africa's digital transformation has accelerated since 2000, driven by mobile telephony. Mobile subscriptions rose from 2 per 100 people in 2000 to 83 by 2020 (ITU, 2024). Mobile money, pioneered by Kenya's M-Pesa, expanded financial inclusion across the continent (GSMA, 2024). In West Africa, similar platforms have flourished. MTN MoMo operates in Ghana and Côte d'Ivoire, offering millions of users access to savings, transfers and bill payments via mobile phones. In Côte d'Ivoire, Senegal, Burkina Faso and Mali, Wave gained popularity with its low-cost, user-friendly services, quickly becoming one of the fastest-growing Fintech companies in the region (GSMA, 2024). These platforms illustrate how African markets have adapted digital tools to address local needs, particularly in contexts where traditional banking infrastructure is limited.

Alongside financial inclusion, internet access has expanded rapidly. Internet penetration grew from 6% in 2010 to 36% in 2022, though rural-urban and gender gaps persist (World Bank, 2021, 2024). North and Southern Africa enjoy higher connectivity due to fibre-optic links and better infrastructure, while Central Africa lags behind (ITU, 2024). Affordability remains a barrier, with 1 GB of data costing 7% of monthly income compared to 1–2% globally (GSMA, 2024).

Despite challenges, Africa's digital hubs – Nairobi, Lagos, Cape Town and Cairo – have nurtured startups and attracted over $2 billion in venture capital in 2021, mostly in Fintech and e-commerce. Governments are also prioritising digital strategies, with the African Union (AU) Digital Transformation Strategy (2020–2030) aiming for universal access by 2030 (African Union, 2024). Global companies (e.g. Google's Equiano cable, Meta's 2Africa project, Microsoft's and AWS's data centres in South Africa, Nigeria, Kenya and Egypt) are further strengthening infrastructure (GSMA, 2024).

Hospitality and Tourism in Africa

Tourism is unevenly distributed but critical to many African economies. This distribution is not merely a matter of visitor numbers but reflects complex intersections of geopolitical stability, historical legacies, infrastructure development and the strategic packaging of hospitality experiences (Saarinen et al., 2022). The sector's growth is often framed within the context of the UN Sustainable Development Goals, though achieving equitable and sustainable outcomes remains a challenge.

North Africa leads in arrivals and revenue, a status solidified by the data as shown in Table 1. Egypt (with 13 million arrivals in 2019, generating $4.9 billion in 2020) and Morocco (2.8 million arrivals in 2020, generating $4.5 billion) are the continent's clear leaders. Next, Tunisia's Mediterranean resorts attracted 2 million arrivals and generated $1 billion in receipts in 2020 (UNWTO, 2023). The hospitality model of North Africa is deeply influenced by the region's long history of international travel. However, scholars note that this often involves the 'commodification of culture', where hospitality is packaged for a Western gaze,

Table 1. International Tourist Arrivals Versus Receipts Based on Available Data.

Country	International Tourist Arrivals (Year)	Tourism Receipts in US$ (Year)
Algeria	591,000 (2020)	$50,000,000 (2020)
Angola	218,000 (2019)	$19,000,000 (2020)
Benin	337,000 (2019)	$240,860,001 (2019)
Botswana	1,830,000 (2018)	$217,000,000 (2020)
Burkina Faso	67,000 (2020)	$173,000,000 (2019)
Burundi	299,000 (2017)	$3,700,000 (2011)
Cabo Verde	180,000 (2020)	$169,000,000 (2020)
Cameroon	1,021,000 (2019)	$437,000,000 (2020)
Central African Republic	87,000 (2019)	$15,600,000 (2013)
Chad	10,399 (2020)	$25,000,000 (2002)
Comoros	7,000 (2020)	$18,500,000 (2020)
Congo, Rep.	158,000 (2018)	$42,900,002 (2016)
Congo, Dem. Rep.	351,000 (2016)	$60,500,000 (2018)
Côte d'Ivoire	668,000 (2020)	$200,000,000 (2020)
Djibouti	20,100 (2000)	$57,000,000 (2018)
Egypt	13,026,000 (2019)	$4,874,000,000 (2020)
Equatorial Guinea**	—	$14,000,000 (2001)
Eritrea	142,000 (2016)	$48,000,000 (2016)
Eswatini	345,299 (2020)	$7,300,000 (2020)
Ethiopia	518,000 (2020)	$2,282,000,000 (2020)
Gabon	230,000 (2000)	$28,700,001 (2015)
Gambia, The	246,000 (2020)	$53,000,000 (2020)
Ghana	897,000 (2015)	$191,000,000 (2020)
Guinea	99,000 (2017)	$1,290,000 (2020)
Guinea-Bissau	52,400 (2019)	$18,920,000 (2019)
Kenya	2,049,000 (2019)	$1,762,000,000 (2019)
Lesotho	1,142,000 (2019)	$23,100,000 (1999)
Liberia	63,000	$123,000,000 (2009)
Libya	963,000 (2000)	$170,000,000 (2010)
Madagascar	87,099 (2020)	$202,000,000 (2020)

(Continued)

Table 1. *(Continued)*

Country	International Tourist Arrivals (Year)	Tourism Receipts in US$ (Year)
Malawi	871,000 (2018)	$35,000,000 (2020)
Mali	217,000 (2019)	$231,000,000 (2018)
Mauritania	30,000 (2000)	$6,400,000 (2020)
Mauritius	316,000 (2020)	$518,000,000 (2020)
Morocco	2,802,000 (2020)	$4,514,000,000 (2020)
Mozambique	2,033,000 (2019)	$113,000,000 (2020)
Namibia	187,100 (2020)	$155,000,000 (2020)
Niger	85,000 (2020)	$130,000,000 (2019)
Nigeria	5,265,000 (2016)	$321,000,000 (2020)
Rwanda	1,634,000 (2019)	$212,000,000 (2020)
São Tomé and Príncipe	*10,786 (2020); 15,100 (2021)*	*$25,000,000 (2020)*
Senegal	1,376,000 (2017)	$557,000,000 (2018)
Seychelles	124,500 (2020)	$228,000,000 (2020)
Sierra Leone	71,000 (2019)	$39,000,000 (2018)
*Somalia	—	—
South Africa	3,886,600 (2020)	$2,716,000,000 (2020)
**South Sudan	—	$12,000,000 (2018)
Sudan	836,000 (2018)	$1,043,000,000 (2018)
Tanzania	1,527,000 (2019)	$2,624,500,000 (2019)
Togo	482,000 (2020)	$264,000,000 (2019)
Tunisia	2,012,000 (2020)	$1,007,000,000 (2020)
Uganda	473,000 (2020)	$518,000,000 (2020)
Zambia	502,000 (2020) 1.2 million (2025)	$820 million (2019)
Zimbabwe	639,000 (2020)	$66,000,000 (2020)

Source: UNWTO (2025) https://www.unwto.org/tourism-data/un-tourism-tourism-dashboard; World Bank (2025) https://databank.worldbank.org/metadataglossary/world-development-indicators/series/ST.INT.ARVL; Knoema (2019), World Bank (2024a).

Notes: *Data not available for Somalia due to political instability; **Partial data available.

sometimes reinforcing stereotypical 'Orientalist' narratives to market the destination. The recovery post-Arab Spring further highlights the critical link between perceived political stability and hospitality investment (Groizard et al., 2022).

Southern Africa is another dominant hub. South Africa welcomed millions of visitors (3.9 million in 2020, generating $2.7 billion), supported by its strong infrastructure and diverse offerings from urban luxury to wildlife experiences (WTTC, 2024). The region, including high-value island destinations like Mauritius (with 316,000 arrivals in 2020 and $518 million in receipts) excels in a luxury hospitality model. This aligns with the concept of the 'experience economy', where success is tied to creating premium, memorable and exclusive experiences for high-yield tourists (Pine & Gilmore, 1999). However, this model has been critiqued for providing limited benefit to local communities.

East Africa is a globally renowned region for its wildlife and safari tourism, with a few spots for luxury (such as Seychelles, which had 24,500 arrivals in 2020 and $228 million in receipts. Kenya and Tanzania remain major destinations, with Kenya recording 2 million arrivals in 2019 and $1.8 billion in receipts. Tanzania recorded 1.5 million arrivals in 2019, generating $2.6 billion in receipts). Meanwhile, Rwanda had 1.6 million arrivals in 2019, with $212 million in receipts. Uganda, with its growing niches in eco- and conference tourism, on the other hand, had 473,000 arrivals in 2020 and $518 million in receipts (UNWTO, 2023). The hospitality industry in East Africa appears to be linked to conservation and community-based tourism (CBT) models.

West Africa features emerging markets, though arrivals remain modest compared to other regions. Senegal (1.4 million arrivals in 2017, $557 million in receipts in 2018) shows a healthy sector, while Ghana's highly successful 'Year of Return' (YoR) campaign (recorded 897,000 arrivals in 2015, $191 million in receipts in 2020). The success of the YoR campaign underscores a powerful trend in diaspora tourism. This form of hospitality is less about luxury and more about facilitating profound emotional and heritage experiences (Adu-Ampong & Dillette, 2024). The case of Nigeria (5.3 million arrivals in 2016, $321 million in receipts in 2020) presents a paradox, suggesting a large volume of travel is for business or visiting friends and relatives (VFR), which generates less direct tourism revenue.

Central Africa remains the least developed in tourism due to persistent challenges with conflict, political instability and poor infrastructure. The data reflects this profound underdevelopment, with countries like Chad (10,399 arrivals in 2020) and the Democratic Republic of Congo (351,000 arrivals in 2016) recording minimal figures. Niche eco-tourism exists in countries like Gabon and Cameroon (1 million arrivals in 2019, $437 million in receipts in 2020), but it operates on a limited scale. The literature on tourism in post-conflict regions suggests that rebuilding a hospitality sector requires first establishing safety and security, as the perception of risk is the primary barrier to visitation. The development here is often tied to complex models of 'peace through tourism', which aim to use tourism as a tool for economic stabilisation and cross-cultural understanding, though its efficacy is widely debated.

The mismatch in years between arrivals and receipts reflects gaps in Africa's tourism data. Many countries report arrivals more frequently, while receipts depend on irregular surveys or balance-of-payments data.

AI Adoption in Sub-Saharan Africa (SSA)

Comparatively, AI adoption in many African countries, especially those south of the Sahara, has been slow. As previously noted, developing regions often face challenges such as limited access to advanced technologies, inadequate infrastructure and insufficient training for personnel, which hinder the seamless integration of AI. Many African countries have most of their labour employed in primary, informal and non-knowledge-intensive sectors, which have fewer opportunities for AI applications. In addition, challenges with the availability of relevant data to train AI models are a constraint, especially considering that the best data sets are often controlled by global corporations. In fact, the pervasiveness of data inconsistencies, generally and in the hospitality and tourism industry, can be seen in Table 1.

Tourism data for many African countries suffers from inconsistencies and reporting gaps, which explains why Table 1 often shows different years for arrivals and receipts. In some cases, national statistical offices or ministries report visitor arrivals more frequently, while tourism receipts – which depend on surveys of expenditure, banking records or balance-of-payments data – are updated less often or only captured when international partners like the World Bank or IMF assist.

Political instability, limited statistical capacity and reliance on donor-funded surveys further compound the problem. For example, Zambia's last verifiable receipts figure is from 2019 (USD 820 million), while arrivals are available up to 2025 from the Ministry of Tourism. Similarly, countries like Burundi, Chad and Lesotho have receipts recorded a decade or more apart from arrivals, reflecting how fragmented the reporting systems are. These challenges in data availability not only complicate tourism planning and investment but also have broader implications for research and innovation. Where traditional statistics fall short, there is growing interest in how emerging technologies, particularly AI, can help bridge these gaps by improving data collection, validation and analysis. This shift aligns with wider discussions in SSA about leveraging AI as a tool for development, creating new opportunities to strengthen evidence-based decision-making across sectors.

In SSA, the literature highlights the opportunities that AI can present for development (Arakpogun et al., 2021). Indeed, the adoption of AI in SSA has gained some traction in recent years, especially in media spaces and public discourse.

AI Readiness

AI readiness remains uneven across the continent. Mauritius, South Africa, Rwanda, Kenya and Egypt rank among the highest, supported by stronger digital infrastructure, governance frameworks and skills development (Oxford Insights, 2024; UNCTAD, 2025). North Africa, as a region, outperforms SSA, while Central Africa remains at the bottom of readiness indices. By 2024, at least 15 African countries had published or drafted national AI strategies – including

Mauritius, Egypt, Tunisia, Rwanda, Nigeria, Ethiopia and South Africa – demonstrating growing recognition of AI's developmental role (African Union, 2024). Nonetheless, gaps in infrastructure, data availability and specialised skills continue to act as barriers for many developing economies (OECD, 2024, 2025; UNCTAD, 2025).

As shown in Table 2, the disparities between regions are stark. North and Southern Africa score relatively high in terms of digitalisation, infrastructure and

Table 2. Regional Indicators of Tourism, Technology, Infrastructure and AI Readiness in Africa.

Region	Tourism Prominence	Technology & Digitalisation	Infrastructure Maturity	AI Readiness
North Africa	Egypt remains a continental leader with ~13m international arrivals (2019). Morocco and Tunisia are also strong tourism markets.	High levels of ICT integration in education; Tunisia leads with 71% ICT skills integration; strong developer density (Tunisia: 4,120 per million; Morocco: 1,345; Egypt: 1,224).	Relatively advanced infrastructure, especially electricity access and internet penetration; regional average higher than sub-Saharan peers.	Highest regional average (38.2/100). Egypt, Morocco, Tunisia, Algeria all in top 10 of AI readiness. Libya lags due to conflict.
West Africa	Strong cultural and heritage tourism (e.g., Ghana, Senegal, Nigeria). Nigeria has a large diaspora-driven market but inconsistent reporting.	Growing startup ecosystem (Fintech, AgriTech, EdTech). Digital uptake is uneven across the region.	Infrastructure gaps (electricity, transport, connectivity) persist, slowing digital growth.	Mid-tier average (27.6/100). Ghana (rank 7) leads the region; Nigeria (rank 18) has strong potential but underperforms given its economic size.

(Continued)

Table 2. *(Continued)*

Region	Tourism Prominence	Technology & Digitalisation	Infrastructure Maturity	AI Readiness
East Africa	Safari tourism dominates (Kenya, Tanzania, Uganda). Rwanda is rising in conference tourism.	Dynamic mobile-first innovation (M-Pesa, eGov). ICT is embedded in schools across Kenya and Rwanda.	Strong regional mobile penetration; yet electricity access uneven, especially in rural areas.	Fastest growth region (32.7/100). Rwanda ranks #1 in governance readiness; Kenya (rank 4), Mauritius (5), Rwanda (6) among continental leaders.
Central Africa	Limited international tourism except in Cameroon and DR Congo; conflict dampens the sector.	Weak technology adoption; very low ICT integration in schools; minimal AI-related institutions.	Regional avg. lowest in electricity and internet coverage (over 50% lack access to power).	Weakest region (19.4/100). Only Cameroon (rank 11) shows competitive readiness; others (e.g., DRC, Chad, CAR) at the bottom.
Southern Africa	South Africa leads with diverse tourism (safari, cultural, urban). Strong regional destinations: Namibia, Botswana, Mauritius.	Strong digital ecosystem anchored by South Africa's universities and research hubs; Mauritius has advanced ICT integration.	Better transport, electricity and connectivity than other regions, but disparities remain between urban and rural areas.	Strongest performer: South Africa ranks #1 overall (52.15/100). Mauritius (rank 5) also strong. Regional avg. = 35.3/100.

Source: Authors based on data from African Union (2024), GSMA (2024), Oxford Insights (2020, 2024), UNCTAD (2025), UNWTO (2023), WTTC (2024) and World Bank (2021).

AI policy development, while East Africa shows promising momentum led by Kenya and Rwanda. By contrast, West Africa lags due to infrastructure and policy gaps despite Nigeria and Ghana's emerging ecosystems, and Central Africa remains at the lowest tier, constrained by instability and poor digital infrastructure.

A central pillar of this readiness is the human talent required to drive the AI revolution. This is captured by the AI Talent Readiness Index for Africa, published by Oxford Insights (2024), which evaluates all 54 African nations on their capacity to develop, retain and deploy AI talent (Fig. 2). The framework is built on three interdependent pillars, designed to reflect the continent's unique context: digital skills (40% weight), data and infrastructure (35% weight) and government readiness (25% weight). The structure of the AI Talent Readiness Index, with its heaviest weighting on digital skills, implies that the primary bottleneck for AI development in Africa is not a lack of government strategy or infrastructure alone, but a fundamental deficit in the human capital capable of creating and implementing AI solutions. This suggests that even with improved

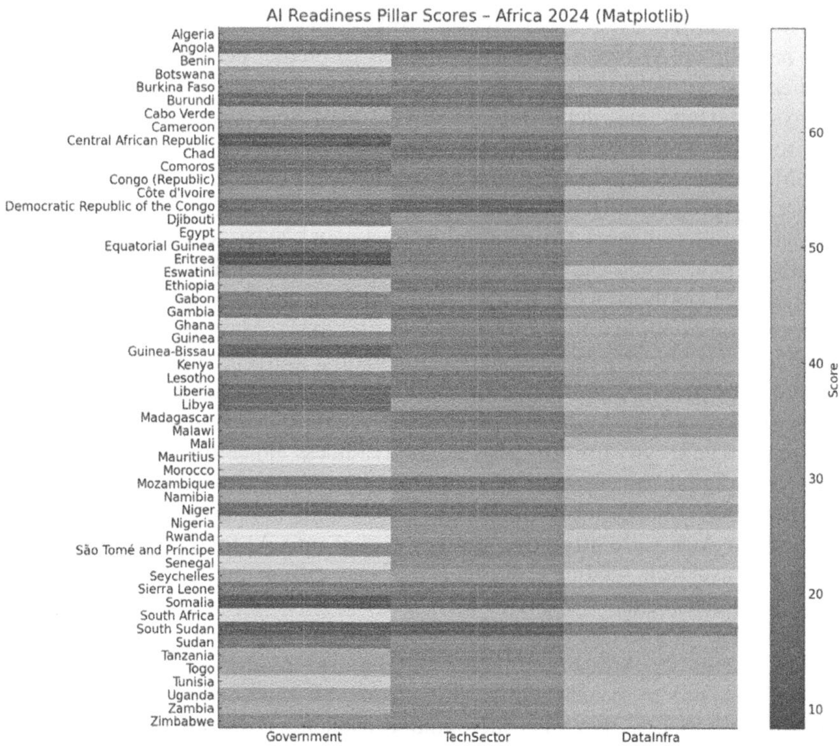

Fig. 2. Africa's AI Readiness (GAR 2024). *Source:* Oxford Insights (2024).

infrastructure (35%) and government policy (25%), progress will be critically limited without a concerted focus on building a skilled workforce first and foremost.

Beyond readiness, practical applications of AI are gradually emerging across sectors. In agriculture, AI is being tested to enhance productivity and climate resilience, with precision farming tools using machine learning to optimise crop yields and forecast weather patterns (Shaikh et al., 2022). Platforms such as PlantVillage Nuru, which applies image recognition to diagnose crop diseases, are gaining traction among smallholder farmers (Selvaraj et al., 2019). In healthcare, AI-based telemedicine platforms are bridging gaps in remote areas where access to professionals is limited (Ibeneme et al., 2021; Owoyemi et al., 2020). In education, AI integration in digital learning environments is beginning to reduce disparities, with natural language processing (NLP) tools translating content into local African languages to overcome linguistic barriers (Kiemde & Kora, 2022).

In tourism and hospitality, adoption is nascent but visible. As summarised in Table 2, Ghana, Kenya, Rwanda, South Africa and Mauritius are among the early movers experimenting with AI to streamline operations, reduce costs and enhance customer experiences (World Bank, 2021). Ghana's Ministry of Tourism has piloted AI-based forecasting models to predict peak travel seasons and manage crowd flows at heritage sites (Ministry of Tourism Ghana, 2024). In Kenya, startups are deploying AI-driven platforms that recommend rural eco-tourism experiences and are testing dynamic pricing tools for domestic travel (GSMA, 2024). Rwanda's national AI strategy supports the integration of AI in smart city projects in Kigali, enabling applications in tourism mobility, visitor analytics and transport (Munanura & Backman, 2025; Ndayisaba, 2023). In South Africa, hotel chains in Cape Town and Johannesburg have trialled AI-powered chatbots, while Kruger National Park employs AI-driven drones to support conservation tourism (Nnamdi et al., 2024). Mauritius has positioned itself as a leading African destination for luxury tourism, supported by strong digital infrastructure and targeted marketing initiatives led by the Mauritius Tourism Promotion Authority (MTPA). These initiatives across the continent are reinforced by government policies and readiness indicators (see Table 2) that prioritise digital transformation, supported by public–private partnerships and international collaboration. Importantly, tech hubs in countries such as Kenya and South Africa are attracting venture capital into AI-focused startups, especially in travel tech, seeding ecosystems that may diffuse innovations more widely across the continent.

However, numerous questions remain regarding the trajectory of AI advancements in Africa and other developing countries. While developing countries stand to benefit significantly from AI applications in tourism and hospitality services, they also face unique challenges. As such, understanding how AI can be equitably and sustainably implemented in these contexts remains a critical area for future research. This introductory chapter sets the stage for the book by exploring trends in the adoption of AI in tourism and hospitality. The chapter continues by outlining the key contributions of each chapter in the book.

Contributions in This Book

Following the introductory chapter, Richmond Sakyi, Federick Pobee and Abdul Bashiru Jibril (Chapter 2) dive into the heart of the customer experience, asking the question of whether or not AI has truly transformed the way we travel? From chatbots that talk like seasoned concierges to predictive analytics that anticipate tourists' every need, this chapter explores the technology already shaping guest experiences – and maps out where research needs to go next. In Chapter 3, John Agyekum Addae and Sheraz Ahmed explore how Fintech innovations such as crowdfunding can open new doors for the visitor economy. Their systematic literature review reveals untapped opportunities for tourism growth in emerging markets, as well as the tools needed to unlock them.

Chapter 4 (by Desmond Tutu, Ricky Yao Nutsugbodo and Anna Arthur-Amissah) delves into issues specifically related to how AI technologies like service robots and intelligent devices are used to delight guests, even where infrastructure and resources are scarce. In Chapter 5, Sarah Blankson-Stiles-Ocran, Cornelius Tengan, Richmond Sakyi and Reginald Olympas Akua Awusiedu weigh the promise of AI for tourism and hospitality service providers against the potential clients' mistrust, fear and worries about privacy, safety and security. The authors asked if AI can truly boost satisfaction, revenue and efficiency in emerging economies, given the insatiable customer expectations and demands on the tourism and hospitality service providers. Chapter 6 (by Ricky Yao Nutsugbodo, Anna Arthur-Amissah, Desmond Tutu) widens the lens to AI and robotics, exploring biometric check-ins, automation and other innovations that can help the industry adapt in an age of pandemics, climate change and shifting traveller expectations. Chapter 7, written by Victor Anderson Hodibert and Eudora Hagan, examines the awareness, preparedness, expectations and concerns of hotel managers of the emerging technologies, with a particular focus on hotel industry players in the Western Region of Ghana. In the context of sustainable tourism development, Nandipha David (Chapter 8) describes AI's potential to drive responsible and sustainable tourism that connects the environmental, social and economic aspects. Following David's contribution, Chapter 9 (Stephen Owusu Afriyie, Joseph Akwasi Nkyi, Gertrude Amoakohene and Peter Yao Lartey) investigates practitioners' perceptions about the role of AI in transforming Ghana's tourism industry and the key drivers of sustainability in the industry. Chapter 10 by Charles Roland Haruna, Maame Gyamfua Asante-Mensah, Michael Ashun, Nyamekesse Samuel, Benedict Jojo Afful and Boamah Charles Ofosu Ofori examines the use of pre-trained AI models in the tourism and hospitality industries in emerging economies, showing how pre-trained models like BERT can power sentiment analysis, personalised recommendations and conversational bots that elevate the travel experience.

The concluding chapter by Esi Akyere Mensah, Aaron Yankholmes, Frank Badu-Baiden and Nii Longdon Sowah summarises the key issues explored throughout this book and proposes a forward-looking agenda by addressing the future needs in research, policymaking, the cultivation of robust partnerships and strategic investments to bridge the AI gap between advanced countries and the developing economies. With the aim of enabling hospitality and tourism practitioners in sub-Saharan Africa not only to catch up but also to establish their own benchmarks for an AI-driven future.

References

Adu-Ampong, E. A., & Dillette, A. (2024). Commemoration and commodification: Slavery heritage, Black travel and the #YearofReturn2019 in Ghana. *Tourism Geographies*, *26*(1), 120–139. https://doi.org/10.1080/14616688.2023.2275731

African Union. (2024). *Continental digital transformation strategy 2024–2030*. AU Commission.

Amadeus Hospitality. (2025). *Amadeus Demand360: Unrivaled depth and breadth of data to drive demand*. https://www.amadeus.com. Accessed August 20th, 2025.

Arakpogun, E. O., Elsahn, Z., Olan, F., & Elsahn, F. (2021). Artificial intelligence in Africa: Challenges and opportunities. In A. A. Elragal (Ed.), *The fourth industrial revolution: Implementation of artificial intelligence for growing business success* (pp. 375–388). Springer. https://doi.org/10.1007/978-3-030-62796-6_22

Boden, M. A. (2006). *Mind as machine: A history of cognitive science*. Oxford University Press.

Bulchand-Gidumal, J., William Secin, E., O'Connor, P., & Buhalis, D. (2023). Artificial intelligence's impact on hospitality and tourism marketing: Exploring key themes and addressing challenges. *Current Issues in Tourism*, *27*(14), 2345–2362. https://doi.org/10.1080/13683500.2023.2229480

Cristofaro, M., & Giardino, P. L. (2025). Surfing the AI waves: The historical evolution of artificial intelligence in management and organizational studies and practices. *Journal of Management History*. https://doi.org/10.1108/JMH-01-2025-0002

Davenport, T. H., & Ronanki, R. (2018). *Artificial intelligence for the real world*. Harvard Business Review.

Goodall, N. J. (2014). *Machine learning and autonomous vehicles: The intersection of AI and transportation*. IEEE Intelligent Systems.

Gössling, S., & Mei, X. Y. (2025). AI and sustainable tourism: An assessment of risks and opportunities for the SDGs. *Current Issues in Tourism*, 1–14.

Groizard, J. L., Ismael, M., & Santana-Gallego, M. (2022). Political upheavals, tourism flight, and spillovers: The case of the Arab spring. *Journal of Travel Research*, *61*(4), 921–939.

GSMA. (2024). *The mobile economy sub-Saharan Africa 2024*. https://www.gsma.com/solutions-and-impact/connectivity-for-good/mobile-economy/sub-saharan-africa/. Accessed August 1, 2025.

Hall, C. M., & Cooper, C. (2025). Making tourism smart in the age of artificial intelligence. *Current Issues in Tourism*, *28*(1), 1–5. https://doi.org/10.1080/13683500.2025.2460922

Ibeneme, S., Okeibunor, J., Muneene, D., Husain, I., Bento, P., Gaju, C., Housseynou, B., Chibi, M., Karamagi, H., & Makubalo, L. (2021). Data revolution, health status transformation, and the role of artificial intelligence for health and pandemic preparedness in the African context. *BMC Proceedings*, *15* (1), 1–12.

ITU. (2024). *AI policy and regulation in developing countries.* International Telecommunication Union.

Kiemde, S. M. A., & Kora, A. D. (2022). Towards an ethics of AI in Africa: Rule of education. *AI and Ethics*, *2*(1), 35–40.

Knoema. (2019). *Liberia - International tourist arrivals.* World Data Atlas. https://knoema.com/atlas/Liberia/topics/Tourism/Key-Tourism-Indicators/Number-of-arrivals. Accessed on November 11, 2025.

Kumawat, E., Datta, A., Prentice, C., & Leung, R. (2025). Artificial intelligence through the lens of hospitality employees: A systematic review. *International Journal of Hospitality Management*, *124*, 103986.

Ministry of Tourism Ghana. (2024). *National tourism digital strategy*. Government of Ghana.

Munanura, I. E., & Backman, K. F. (2025). Rwanda. In *Encyclopedia of tourism* (pp. 892–893). Springer Nature Switzerland.

Ndayisaba, J. (2023). Ecological sustainability in urban landscapes and smart cities: Case study Kigali City, Rwanda. In *Proceedings of the 11th IALE World Congress.* https://www.researchgate.net/profile/Joel-Ndayisaba-2/publication/373629657_Ecological_sustainability_in_urban_landscapes_and_smart_cities_Case_study_Kigali_city_Rwanda/links/64f37b6f8270743 13ff2500c/Ecological-sustainability-in-urban-landscapes-and-smart-cities-Case-study-Kigali-city-Rwanda.pdf

Nnamdi, J., Akinola, T., & Dlamini, M. (2024). Afrocentric innovation in AI applications: Lessons from Africa. *Technology in Society*, *78*, 102553. https://doi.org/10.1016/j.techsoc.2024.102553

OECD. (2024). *Training supply for the green and AI transitions: Equipping workers with the right skills, getting skills right.* OECD Publishing. https://doi.org/10.1787/7600d16d-en

OECD. (2025). *Bridging the AI skills gap: Is training keeping up?* OECD Publishing. https://www.oecd.org/en/publications/bridging-the-ai-skills-gap_66d0702e-en.html

Owoyemi, A., Owoyemi, J., Osiyemi, A., & Boyd, A. (2020). Artificial intelligence for healthcare in Africa. *Frontiers in Digital Health*, *2*, 6.

Oxford Insights. (2020). *Government AI readiness Index 2020.* Oxford Insights.

Oxford Insights. (2024, December 20). *Government AI readiness Index 2024.* Oxford Insights.

Parulis-Cook, S. (2025). *How AI is transforming Chinese tourism.* https://dragontrail.com/resources/blog/ai-for-chinese-tourism-2025?utm_source=chatgpt.com. Accessed August 17, 2025.

Pine, B. J., & Gilmore, J. H. (1999). *The experience economy: Work is theatre & every business a stage.* Harvard Business School Press. https://archive.org/details/experienceeconom00pine

PwC. (2023). *2023 Global artificial intelligence study: Sizing the prize.* https://www.pwc.com/gx/en/issues/data-and-analytics/publications/artificial-intelligence-study.html

Russell, S., & Norvig, P. (2016). *Artificial intelligence: A modern approach.* Pearson.

Saarinen, J., Fitchett, J., & Hoogendoorn, G. (Eds.). (2022). *Climate change and tourism in Southern Africa.* Routledge. https://doi.org/10.4324/9781003102618

Selvaraj, M. G., Vergara, A., Ruiz, H., Safari, N., Elayabalan, S., Ocimati, W., & Blomme, G. (2019). AI-powered banana diseases and pest detection. *Plant Methods*, *15*, 1–11.

Shaikh, T. A., Rasool, T., & Lone, F. R. (2022). Towards leveraging the role of machine learning and artificial intelligence in precision agriculture and smart farming. *Computers and Electronics in Agriculture*, *198*, 107119.

Singh, B., & Kaunert, C. (2025). Embracing virtual reality (VR) for environmental conservation in tourist spots. In *Redefining tourism with AI and the metaverse* (pp. 279–300). IGI Global Scientific Publishing.

Szpilko, D., Jimenez Naharro, F., Lăzăroiu, G., Nica, E., & de la Torre Gallegos, A. (2023). Artificial intelligence in the smart city—A literature review. *Engineering Management in Production and Services*, *15*(4), 53–75.

Tuomi, A., & Passos Ascenção, M. (2023). Intelligent automation in hospitality: Exploring the relative automatability of frontline food service tasks. *Journal of Hospitality and Tourism Insights*, *6*(1), 151–173. https://doi.org/10.1108/JHTI-07-2021-0175

UNCTAD. (2021). *Digital economy report 2025: Inclusive artificial intelligence for development*. United Nations Conference on Trade and Development.

UNCTAD. (2025). *Technology and innovation report 2025: Inclusive artificial intelligence for development*. https://unctad.org/publication/technology-and-innovation-report-2025

UNWTO. (2023). *Artificial intelligence and the future of tourism*. World Tourism Organization.

World Bank. (2021). *Harnessing artificial intelligence for development in the post-COVID-19 era: A review of national AI strategies and policies*. The World Bank.

World Bank. (2024a). *International tourism, number of arrivals - Liberia*. World Development Indicators. https://data.worldbank.org/indicator/ST.INT.ARVL?locations=LR. Accessed May 21, 2024.

World Bank. (2024b). *Digital development in Africa: Progress and prospects*. The World Bank.

World Bank. (2024c). *International tourism, receipts (current US$) - Liberia*. World Development Indicators. https://data.worldbank.org/indicator/ST.INT.RCPT.CD?locations=LR. Accessed May 21, 2024.

WTTC. (2024). *Travel & tourism economic impact 2023*. World Travel & Tourism Council.

Chapter 2

Has AI Revolutionised Customer Experience in the Tourism and Hospitality Industry? A Review of the Future Research Agenda

Richmond Sakyi[a], *Frederick Pobee*[b] *and Abdul Bashiru Jibril*[c]

[a]Ho Technical University, Ghana
[b]University of Professional Studies, Ghana
[c]Westminster International University in Tashkent, Uzbekistan

Abstract

The advent of Artificial Intelligence (AI) has sparked a transformative revolution across numerous industries, and the tourism and hospitality sector is no exception. This paper delves into the profound impact of AI on customer experience within tourism and hospitality, aiming to elucidate the extent to which AI technologies have reshaped various facets of customer interactions, service delivery and overall satisfaction within this domain. This study seeks to uncover insights into how AI has revolutionised the customer journey in tourism and hospitality through an exhaustive review of existing literature encompassing peer-reviewed articles, conference papers, white papers and reports published between 2017 and 2024. In the authors' quest of synthesising key findings, identifying emerging trends and highlighting challenges and opportunities, this review not only provides valuable insights for industry practitioners seeking to adapt to the AI-driven landscape but also serves as a roadmap for researchers and policymakers keen on understanding the implications of AI adoption within the tourism and hospitality industry. From personalised recommendations and AI-driven chatbots to predictive analytics and robotics, the study explores how AI technologies have redefined customer experiences, offering unparalleled innovation and efficiency optimisation opportunities. Through a critical examination of the existing literature, this review sets the stage for

Artificial Intelligence in Hospitality and Tourism in Africa, 19–37

doi:10.1108/978-1-80686-169-920261002

future research endeavours, identifying gaps in knowledge and proposing a comprehensive research agenda to further elucidate the transformative potential of AI in shaping the future of tourism and hospitality.

Keywords: Artificial Intelligence; customer experience; tourism; hospitality; service delivery; technology; review

Introduction

The tourism and hospitality industry stands at the forefront of technological innovation, continually evolving to meet travellers' dynamic needs and expectations (Buhalis et al., 2023; Buhalis & Foerste, 2015). In recent years, this evolution has been propelled by groundbreaking technological advancements, fundamentally reshaping the customer experience landscape. Among these transformative technologies, Artificial Intelligence (AI) emerges as a dominant force, wielding unprecedented capabilities to enhance service delivery, personalise interactions and optimise operational efficiency within the tourism and hospitality sector (Gursoy, 2025). Integrating AI technologies, encompassing machine learning, natural language processing and robotics, has revolutionised how businesses engage with customers and manage their operations (Buhalis et al., 2024; Xiang & Gretzel, 2010). Through sophisticated algorithms and predictive analytics, AI empowers organisations to analyse vast volumes of data, glean actionable insights and anticipate customer preferences with remarkable precision (Li et al., 2019). This analytical prowess enables businesses to tailor their offerings to individual needs, delivering personalised experiences that resonate deeply with travellers.

One of the most prominent manifestations of AI in tourism and hospitality is the proliferation of AI-driven chatbots and virtual assistants (Wang et al., 2012; Zhou et al., 2024). These intelligent systems utilise natural language processing algorithms to engage customers in real-time conversations, offering personalised recommendations, responding to queries and facilitating bookings with unparalleled efficiency. With this development, such as automating routine enquiries and tasks, chatbots enhance customer convenience and free up human resources to focus on more complex and value-added activities, thereby driving operational efficiency and cost savings. Furthermore, AI-powered recommendation engines have emerged as invaluable tools for curating personalised travel experiences (Vallabhaneni et al., 2024). By analysing past behaviour, preferences and contextual factors, these recommendation systems can suggest tailored itineraries, accommodations, and activities that align with individual interests and preferences. This personalisation enhances customer satisfaction and fosters loyalty and repeat business, as travellers feel understood and catered to on a profoundly personalised level.

In addition to enhancing customer-facing interactions, AI technologies have revolutionised backend operations within the tourism and hospitality industry (Bilgihan & Ricci, 2024; Buhalis et al., 2023). From revenue management and demand forecasting to supply chain optimisation and resource allocation, AI-driven algorithms drive efficiency gains and cost savings across various business facets. For example, predictive analytics models can accurately forecast demand patterns, enabling enterprises to optimise pricing strategies, allocate resources effectively and maximise revenue generation. Moreover, integrating robotics and automation technologies has further augmented the capabilities of AI in hospitality operations (Ali et al., 2025; Nanu, 2025). From robotic concierges and luggage handlers to automated check-in kiosks and room service delivery robots, these innovative solutions are reshaping the guest experience and redefining traditional notions of hospitality service. Therefore, in the quest to automate routine tasks and minimise human intervention, robots enhance operational efficiency, reduce labour costs and improve service consistency.

Despite the transformative potential of AI in tourism and hospitality, its adoption is not without challenges and considerations (Bulchand-Gidumal et al., 2023; Gretzel et al., 2015). Ethical and privacy concerns regarding data collection, usage and algorithmic biases necessitate careful attention and regulatory oversight to ensure responsible and ethical AI deployment. Moreover, the rapid pace of technological change requires organisations to continuously adapt and evolve their capabilities to harness the full potential of AI while mitigating risks and challenges.

In light of these developments, this review aims to provide a comprehensive examination of the multifaceted impact of AI on customer experience within the tourism and hospitality industry. Hence, by synthesising recent research findings, identifying emerging trends and highlighting key challenges and opportunities, this review seeks to inform industry practitioners, researchers and policymakers alike about the transformative potential of AI in shaping the future of tourism and hospitality.

Literature Review

AI in Tourism and Hospitality

The Fourth Industrial Revolution, as a result of these advancements, has seen notable advances in robots and AI systems (Bulchand-Giddumal, 2022). All facets of the travel and tourism sector are currently developing and testing AI applications, such as voice recognition, natural language processing, robots, personal travel assistants, personalisation and recommender systems, prediction and forecasting systems, and language translation applications (Bulchand-Gidumal, 2022). For several reasons, travel and tourism are particularly crucial to AI. Travellers must decide on some items for their upcoming travels, including where to go, how to get there, where to stay and what to do. These choices will greatly impact the tourists' level of enjoyment during with their trip. However, the variety of locations, modes of transportation, lodging and activities that are currently offered offers a nearly limitless number of alternatives that call for assistance.

The Global Distribution Systems (GDSs), an advancement of Computer Reservation Systems (CRS) and the legacy of systems supporting a range of information technology-based services are the most well-known digital systems for tourism operators, according to Mich (2020). When users gained access to digital services via the Internet and the Web, intermediaries and other operators in the tourism industry were either eliminated or had their roles altered. Those systems underwent a significant transformation (Buhalis & Licata, 2002). AI advanced that process even further by providing fresh methods for interaction and online strategy assistance. Enhancing personalisation and customising suggestions are the inherent objectives of AI applications in the tourism industry, and this also holds for the next generation of GDSs (Mich, 2020). In all their information systems solutions, businesses and organisations in the tourism sector utilise AI technologies. AI solutions are available for all parties involved, including visitors, operators, destination managers, online travel agencies and travellers (Gajdosik, 2019; Ivanova, 2019; Katsanakis et al., 2025). By utilising AI technology, companies may better utilise information systems to alter their business models by incorporating customers into their strategies, saving time and money, and enhancing the quality of their operations and services. After arriving at their destination, travellers must navigate a foreign environment marked by various factors, including different customs, languages, cuisine and habits.

Impact of AI on Customer Experience in the Tourism and Hospitality Industry

AI systems have numerous uses in the travel industry. From the standpoint of the customer, AI facilitates the discovery of more accurate and pertinent information, increases mobility, enhances decision-making and, in the end, improves the travel experience (Bulchand-Gidumal, 2022; Grundner & Neuhofer, 2021; Tsaih & Hsu, 2018). AI applies to practically every facet of management from a business standpoint (Buhalis et al., 2019), particularly in productivity and promotion (Tussyadiah & Miller, 2019). According to Tussyadiah and Miller (2019), AI is also anticipated to promote more environmentally friendly travel by persuading patrons to adopt a more socially conscious viewpoint. In the travel and tourism sector, AI technologies can be integrated into pre-existing applications and systems or used independently. Conversational systems (chatbots and voice assistants), predictive analytics forecasting tools, devices and integrated systems (robotics), augmented and virtual reality (VR), smart tourism and data-driven marketing personalisation are some of the systems that have affected the traveller experience (Buhalis et al., 2019; Irawan, 2023).

Conversational Systems (Chatbots and Voice Assistants)

Customers can have conversations with conversational systems, mainly about finding information. These discussions may take a while and entail multiple steps (Biancofiore et al., 2025; Lipani et al., 2021). Virtual agents or chatbots are other terms for conversational systems. In the hospitality sector, using chatbots and virtual assistants driven by AI has wholly changed customer service (Buhalis & Moldavska, 2022). In the tourism industry, these automated systems give travellers immediate assistance by answering questions, making reservations and providing advice around the clock (Vashishth et al., 2024). According to research, chatbots increase overall guest happiness, decrease response times and boost operational efficiency (Rossmann et al., 2020).

Forty percent of Millennials use chatbots daily, per a recent survey (De Cicco et al., 2020). There are various types of chatbots: voice chatbots, such as those found in virtual assistants (like Alexa, Cortana, Google Assistant or Siri); textual chatbots, which typically operate in social media platforms or instant messaging services; and robot chatbots, which are considerably more sophisticated systems that facilitate in-person interactions (Adam et al., 2021). Consumers are far more familiar with the features and advantages of these devices – which include the top three systems, Alexa, Google Assistant and Siri – than they are (Brill et al., 2022). As a result, they value the innovation and simplicity they provide and encounter fewer issues while using them in motels. Even though they were not designed with tourism in mind, the emergence of some major AI projects is crucial for the industry. One of the most useful of these projects is Google Translate, which can reportedly translate 345 source languages into 345 target languages, which is especially helpful for travellers who need to communicate in various languages (Mich, 2020).

Predictive Analytics Forecasting Tools

Using historical and contextual data, forecasting is a technique that generates future forecasts based on present trends. It is employed in several economic industries to help decision-making where forecasting future events is necessary. According to Buhalis et al. (2019), the systems assess how customers relate (e.g. trust) and react to implementations, both with and without the mental agility required to grasp the macro-level concerns being addressed. They also assess how data is further integrated into predictive systems. With the use of big data, forecasting is especially well adapted for AI algorithms (Adadi, 2021; Duan et al., 2019). The five kinds of AI methods in forecasting are as follows: support vector machines (SVMs), fuzzy time series, rough sets approach, grey theory and artificial neural networks (ANNs) (Masood & Ahmad, 2021).

For organisations in the hospitality industry, AI-driven predictive analytics is essential to optimise demand forecasts and revenue management. AI algorithms can precisely forecast changes in demand and adjust pricing strategies by examining past data and market trends (Masood & Ahmad, 2021). Hotels can use predictive analytics to optimise resource allocation, reduce inventory costs and increase revenue (Kaul, 2023). By putting in place a tourism analytics network (STAN) to collect and analyse visitor data from mobile phones, transportation, traffic and safety systems, the majority of destinations are currently spearheading efforts in smart tourism. Customising tourism products at certain times, locations and price points is the goal of the data-driven strategy (Chen et al., 2021).

According to Buhalis and Jun (2011), companies in the tourism industry, such as Amadeus, Sabre and Travelport, use AI technologies to assist e-commerce and e-marketing, anticipate demand, identify tourist profiles, detect fraud, monitor internal systems and automate agency operations. AI approaches are employed to forecast ticket prices or identify the most efficient detour in the event of a disruption (e.g. extracting information for travellers from rail operators' tweets). Travel agencies and other businesses can provide new services that are accessible through mobile apps by exchanging data. Travel agencies may, for instance, work with weather forecasting agencies to manage traffic and unfavourable weather conditions, and they could employ AI technologies to provide real-time weather notifications.

Devices and Integrated Systems (Robotics)

An autonomous robot is a physical device with AI and environmental sensing capabilities that enable it to act and make decisions. Greek, Egyptian and Babylonian traditions first introduced the idea of human-like robots (Ivanov et al., 2022). More recently, science fiction literature from the 1800s to the early 1900s is where robots were first mentioned (Murphy et al., 2021). Robots can be divided into two main categories according to their tasks: industrial and service robots (Lu et al., 2020; Murphy et al., 2021). Manufacturing, assembly, inspection, packing and transportation are just a few industrial robot applications (Murphy et al., 2021). Typically, service robots help humans by carrying out useful activities. These robots can be found in a variety of service industries, such as retail and different hospitality and tourist sectors, as well as assisting with personal care, domestic chores, health care and ageing care (Ivanov et al., 2022; Reis et al., 2020; Zeng et al., 2020).

Robots in Hotels

The hotel industry has seen examples of recruiting robots as front desk agents, concierges, delivery robots, porters and housekeepers (Ivanov et al., 2022; Ivanov & Webster, 2019), interacting with the guests at the arrival, stay and departure stages of their journeys (Lukanova & Ilieva, 2019). Hilton Worldwide introduced Connie, a robotic concierge designed to answer guest questions (Lu et al., 2019; Tussyadiah & Park, 2018), as well as Aloft Hotels pioneered the use of the robotic butler 'Relay' developed by Savioke. These robots later spread to such brands as Residence Inn by Marriott and Holiday Inn Express. Robots such as NAO and Relay check-in guests assist hotel staff in running deliveries to hotel guests, respectively (Tussyadiah & Park, 2018). From pillows to toothbrushes, the robots can carry anything from these. They can operate the elevators, navigate the hotel floors independently and even call the rooms to let them know a delivery is coming. These robots charge at their designated station when they're not running errands. Recently, most hotels have added robots to their staff rosters to cut labour costs and eliminate pointless interactions between staff and guests.

Robots in Restaurants

With the use of robotics and AI, technological disruption is already having an operational impact on the restaurant industry (Buhalis et al., 2019). Most fast-food restaurants and eateries have implemented robots to promote efficient service delivery and ensure uniformity in food service. Numerous uses of robotic technologies have also been found in the restaurant business (Berezina et al., 2019). These applications include meal delivery, complete restaurant automation, front-of-house and back-of-house operations. Robots aid cooks in the back of the house by flipping burgers, preparing sushi, chopping noodles and even baking pizzas (Berezina et al., 2019; Collins, 2017). Burger patties and French fries may be fried by the robot Flippy (Berezina et al., 2019). Some restaurants, such as Spyce Robotic Kitchen and Creator Burger Robot, have completely automated their kitchen operations. Robots have taken over front-of-house roles such as bartenders, hosts, wait staff and food runners (Ivanov et al., 2022; Berezina et al., 2019; Collins, 2017). For instance, Pizza Hut and Tanuki restaurant in Dubai, UAE, have employed robotic hosts (Berezina et al., 2019; Ivanov et al., 2022) to welcome guests and entertain them. On the other hand, Pepper combines the duties of a waiter and a host by helping customers place orders and submit payments.

Robots at Attraction Sites

There isn't much scientific research on the employment of robots in attractions like theme parks and museums. However, to streamline operations and improve the visitor experience, attractions – like other segments of the tourism and hospitality industries – have begun utilising robots (Ivanov et al. 2019). Gyeongnam Masan Robot Land, South Korea, is the world's first robot-themed park, while Disneyland in Anaheim, California, has been using robots like Spider-Man for guest entertainment since 2020 (Bogue, 2022; Coates, 2020). Besides robots used as information agents and tour guides, housekeeping robots can efficiently clean expansive open areas on museum floors (Ivanov et al., 2022). The National Museum of African American History and Culture, the Hirshhorn Museum and Sculpture Garden, the National Museum of African Art and the Smithsonian Castle are just a few of the museums that have used Pepper Robots' services (Fuentes-Moraleda et al., 2021). In addition to reading stories and taking selfies, these robots entertain guests and offer information about museums and their collections.

Robots in Travel

Airports use robots with varying degrees of autonomy, sophistication and interaction, just as other segments of the tourist and hospitality business (Christou et al., 2020). Airport robots carry out a range of functions, including cleaning, baggage drop-off, passenger check-in and customer assistance (Karanam et al., 2024). In customer service, robots can make travel more comfortable by giving instructions, providing real-time flight information and even conversing with customers in multiple languages. The use of these robots in airports can be seen in the following examples: a robot valet at Düsseldorf Airport; a bag-drop robot at Geneva International Airport; a robot named Pepper at Munich Airport; bilingual Bots and US robots serving clients at Gatwick Airport in London, UK (Duvall et al., 2022). This list is not exhaustive.

Robots will also likely impact air travel since self-driving, or autonomous, vehicles are expected to alter how passengers perceive their journeys significantly (Duncan et al., 2015). Self-driving cars may benefit travellers and car rental companies by removing the need to confirm driver's licences, examine drivers' physical conditions and sobriety, and reduce accident rates and insurance costs (Ivanov et al., 2022). In addition, self-driving cars could be used for tourist tours, taxi services and airport transfers (Cohen & Hopkins, 2019; Perrine et al., 2020). Self-driving cars have the potential to reduce travel expenses by doing away with the driver entirely or in part.

Methodology

This study employs a systematic approach to comprehensively review existing literature on the influence of AI on customer experience within the tourism and hospitality industry. Firstly, a thorough search was conducted across scientific databases such as Web of Science, Scopus and Google Scholar, targeting studies published between 2017 and 2024. Keywords, including variations of 'Artificial Intelligence', 'AI', 'customer experience', 'tourism', 'hospitality', 'service delivery' and 'satisfaction', were utilised, with Boolean operators (AND, OR) used to refine search queries and ensure inclusivity.

Secondly, the screening and selection process involved evaluating titles and abstracts to assess relevance to the research topic. Only peer-reviewed articles, conference papers, white papers and reports published in English and meeting the inclusion criteria were considered. Any discrepancies or uncertainties regarding study eligibility were resolved through consensus among the research team. Thirdly, data extraction and synthesis were performed to identify common themes, emerging trends and notable insights across the literature. Thematic analysis was employed to integrate findings from individual studies, providing a comprehensive overview of the impact of AI on customer experience in tourism and hospitality.

Lastly, a quality assessment was conducted to evaluate the methodological rigour of included studies, considering established criteria appropriate for their respective study designs. Studies with methodological limitations or biases were critically evaluated, and their implications were considered in interpreting findings. Through this systematic methodology, the review aims to offer valuable insights into the transformative impact of AI on customer experience within the tourism and hospitality industry. Additionally, it identifies gaps in the existing literature and proposes a future research agenda to advance knowledge and inform strategic development for scholars and practitioners alike.

Review Findings

The systematic review of journal articles revealed the impact of AI on customer experience, the impact of AI on conversational systems and robots in hotels, restaurants, attraction sites and travel. Our review suggests that AI significantly enhances the quality and accessibility of tourist information. AI-driven systems, such as chatbots and virtual assistants, utilise natural language processing to accurately understand and respond to customer enquiries (Bulchand-Gidumal, 2022; Grundner & Neuhofer, 2021). These systems can access vast databases to provide accurate and tailored information to the customer's preferences. For example, AI can suggest personalised travel recommendations based on past behaviour, preferences and real-time data. Moreover, AI enhances real-time communication, which is crucial in managing expectations and improving customer satisfaction (Buhalis et al., 2019). For instance, AI can send immediate updates about travel itinerary changes, weather conditions or even local events, ensuring that tourists have all the necessary information to make informed decisions. Furthermore, AI plays a crucial role in increasing the mobility of tourists by making transportation more accessible and efficient. AI-driven applications can optimise routes in real time, predict transportation needs and integrate different modes of transport to provide a seamless travel experience (Hsu, 2018; Irawan, 2023). AI algorithms used by ride-sharing services can optimise pick-ups and drop-offs, adjust traffic conditions and improve shared rides' efficiency. AI can facilitate easier navigation in unfamiliar places through augmented reality (AR) and other location-based services, thereby enhancing the mobility of tourists and allowing for a more immersive exploration experience. The literature review reveals that AI empowers tourists with information to make better decisions regarding their travel plans. AI can forecast future trends in tourism, such as price fluctuations in flights and accommodations, allowing tourists to book at optimal times. Decision-making is also enhanced by AI's ability to analyse vast amounts of data to provide insights that would be difficult for humans to calculate, such as identifying the least crowded times to visit particular attractions (Brill et al., 2022; Tussyadiah & Miller, 2019). Moreover, AI-driven platforms can aggregate reviews and ratings from various sources, presenting these insights to help tourists make informed choices about accommodation and attractions, thus enhancing the decision-making process for tourists.

Another interesting finding from our systematic review is AI's revolutionisation of conversational systems. In hospitality and tourism, AI-powered conversational systems, such as chatbots and voice assistants, have revolutionised how customers interact with service providers (Buhalis & Moldavska, 2022; Lipani et al., 2021). Research shows that these systems are pivotal in enhancing the overall customer experience by offering prompt assistance, facilitating travel reservations and providing valuable advice around the clock (De Cicco et al., 2020; Rossmann et al., 2020; Sigala et al., 2019). AI-powered conversational systems excel in answering queries promptly and efficiently. Tourists can ask about hotel amenities, transportation options and local attractions. The instantaneous support by AI enhances customer satisfaction by eliminating long lead times and ensuring accurate information is readily available. The reviewed articles also show that AI-powered conversational systems streamline the travel reservations process (Adam et al., 2021; Brill et al., 2022). Whether booking a hotel room or scheduling airport transfers, these systems simplify the booking process through intuitive interfaces and seamless integration with booking platforms. Tourists can make reservations anytime, even outside traditional business hours, enhancing convenience and accessibility.

Another astounding finding from our review is how integrating AI into the hospitality industry has led to significant transformations, particularly in customer experience. According to the literature (Ivanov et al., 2022; Lukanova & Ilieva, 2019; Lu et al., 2019), one pivotal aspect of this transformation is the utilisation of AI in robotics, which has revolutionised various sectors within the hospitality industry, including hotels, restaurants and attraction sites. Research by Tussyadiah and Park (2018) indicates that, in hotels, AI-driven robots are reshaping the guest experience in numerous ways. For instance, they show that the robotics concierge assists guests with check-in procedures, provides hotel amenities information and even delivers room service items directly to guests' doors. These AI-manned robots enhance efficiency and contribute to a futuristic and innovative ambience, appealing to tech-savvy travellers. Extant research (Buhalis et al., 2019; Berezina et al., 2019; Collins, 2017) also shows that AI-driven robotics are streamlining operations and enhancing the restaurant dining experience. Berezina et al. (2019) indicate that automated servers and waitstaff robots can efficiently take orders, serve food and handle basic customer enquiries, reducing the workload on human staff and minimising wait times.

The Use of VR and AR in the Stages of Travel

To investigate the points at which VR/AR is integrated into tourist travel, we break down the stages of travel into three key phases, as described by Google (2016) and Leiper (1979). Phases pre-travel (dreaming, organising and scheduling); phases during travel (transit, experiencing and sharing); and phases after travel (sharing) (Fig. 1).

Pre-Travel Phase

The initial travel stage, known as the pre-visit phase, is crucial to the entire experience because it's at this time that travellers form their expectations for the trip and begin to make decisions (Eletxigerra et al., 2021; Kochling, 2021). Since the nature of tourism products and services is intangible, it would be beneficial to provide tourists with any information that would help them better comprehend what to expect from these offerings. Pre-travel involves dreaming, organising and making reservations. Travellers begin to think about their destinations and the things they will do and see, and stay in those places when they dream. Travellers formulate their expectations for the trip and start the decision-making process

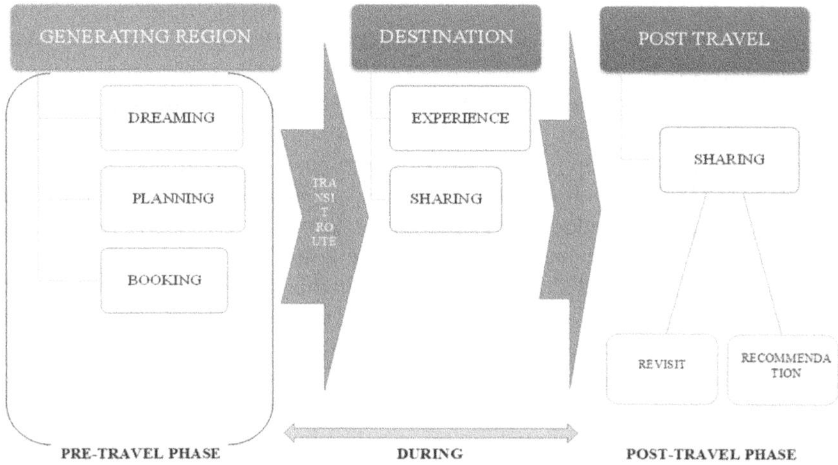

Fig. 1. Stages of Travel. *Source:* Adapted from Leiper (1979).

during this phase (Fang & Pan, 2024). VR can give travellers a first impression of the location and the accessible activities to entice them to come while dreaming (Bulchand-Gidumal & William, 2022; Tussyadiah et al., 2019). Several operators of tourist destinations have developed their online counterparts of Second Life (Yung & Khoo-Lattimore, 2019). Enhancing information about a destination can also be accomplished through AR (Park & Stangl, 2020).

According to Centamor et al. (2017), planning is the process by which travellers choose a place and the range of activities they will partake in. They then manually or automatically create their schedule for the trip. By using VR to get a preview of the experiences that are accessible at the destination, travellers can lessen the intangibility feature of tourism items and associated risks (buying before use). This will likely lead to a more satisfying decision process.

Booking is the initial interaction between the service providers and travellers when they decide to buy a product that they will use right away or later. During this stage, travellers can utilise VR to verify certain needs for the lodging and activities they intend to reserve, resulting in a more individualised experience that enhances the customer's journey. It is also possible to create immersive distribution platforms using VR.

During the Trip

Transit, experiencing and sharing are the three primary phases that take place throughout a tourist's visit to the location. Travellers use transit, which entails using designated routes, to get from their typical residence to their destination. Often, it can be a tedious and drawn-out procedure, but this can be lessened by using VR for amusement to explore the destination and preview the offered activities. VR can be utilised to replace any missing or vulnerable portions of a site, while AR can provide visitors with more information (Guttentag, 2010). Visitors can enjoy a place with expanded knowledge about its sites thanks to AR, which enhances the whole experience (Zaifri et al., 2023).

AR may guide travellers through airports, showing them where gates, bars, baggage claim areas, public transportation stops and vehicle rental desks are and how to get there. To help tourists have an experience or to show people what a certain place looks like at a different moment in history, AR can be used, for instance, as a tourist guide to provide information on the sites and to generate an adventure in a real-life game while tourists visit a site. In particular, Boletsis and Chasanidou (2018) and Ketchell et al. (2019) highlight Pokémon Go as an AR smartphone application with significant potential as a travel aid. After the experience, sharing occurs, which may happen while travellers are at their destination or after returning to their home region. Users can exchange content they have created, such as VR and 360-degree photos and films, during this process (Buhalis et al., 2019). Social media platforms like Facebook, Instagram, Twitter, Snapchat and WhatsApp allow people to share these experiences, which add to the knowledge about VR and AR.

Post-Travel Phase

Travellers' post-behavioural intentions are influenced by their emotions, both positively and adversely, when they share their experiences at the location. In the post-travel period, VR has also been demonstrated to be beneficial (Santoso et al., 2022; Cunha, 2019). Users can create VR material and share it after their vacations, just like they can with social media, where they can share their experiences in text, image and video formats (Buhalis et al., 2019; Munar & Jacobsen, 2014). To supplement the information on VR and AR, several platforms have allowed users to share their experiences on social networks like Facebook, Instagram, Twitter, TikTok, Snapchat and WhatsApp, as well as video platforms like Vimeo and YouTube. These communal experiences are linked to electronic word-of-mouth (eWOM). They will utilise virtual and AR for immersive social media and post-behavioural intention (return or suggest to friends and family).

Data-Driven Marketing and Personalisation

AI systems can provide individualised offers that appeal to specific travellers by examining client data and behaviour patterns through big data analysis (Han et al., 2021). According to Choi et al. (2020), data-driven marketing improves consumer engagement, spurs revenue development and cultivates enduring relationships with visitors. A lesser-known but no less significant use of AI tools for automated asset management is found in businesses and organisations. Destination Management Organizations (DMOs) can now store, sort, retrieve, annotate, alter and share their assets differently thanks to cloud computing and AI-based solutions (Becerra-Fernandez et al., 2024; Mich, 2020). Additionally,

AI algorithms support the annotation of multimedia documents, photos and videos.

Mainly employed by social networking platforms, which record and examine every contact, targeted advertising (or adverts) also makes use of language technology, big data and AI analytics tools (Haleem et al., 2022). A major revenue stream and essential part of the business plan for many Internet businesses is targeted advertisements. Facebook, for instance, uses DeepText to identify potential marketing targets and automatically select ads based on information gleaned from user chats. These aid in creating tourism-related goods and services that cater to the unique requirements and tastes of travellers, providing individualised care through positive client encounters.

Future Research Directions

Opportunities exist for researchers to expand AI in tourism and hospitality research in developing countries to provide governments, organisations, individuals and policymakers with enough information for well-informed decisions. To further enhance the understanding of AI's transformative role in the tourism and hospitality industry, future research could pivot towards several promising directions. While most cross-sectional studies' findings show the benefits of AI integration in hospitality, longitudinal studies could provide deeper insights into the long-term effects of AI on customer satisfaction. Such studies would help understand how the perception and effectiveness of AI-powered tools evolve over time. Another interesting area to focus on is investigating how AI adoption in hospitality varies across cultural contexts. Cultural idiosyncrasies might influence the effectiveness and acceptance of AI technologies like chatbots, voice assistants and service robots. A multicultural perspective on this could offer valuable insights.

Conclusion

The exploration of AI within the tourism and hospitality sector marks a significant stride towards redefining customer experience paradigms. This review has unearthed AI's various roles in enhancing service and operational efficiency in the tourism and hospitality industry. Our study achieved this by reviewing extant scholarly literature in tourism and hospitality. The findings demonstrate that AI-driven technologies significantly contribute to a seamless, personalised and responsive customer experience. These technologies optimise human resource allocation and enrich customer interactions and satisfaction by providing 24/7 assistance and tailored recommendations. Chatbots and voice assistants, powered by sophisticated AI algorithms, have shown their capability to handle a wide range of tourist enquiries and requests with remarkable speed and accuracy. This enhances tourist satisfaction through immediate responsiveness and allows human staff to focus on more complex guest needs. The literature also demonstrates that AI in robots for tasks such as room service delivery and cleaning has introduced an element of novelty and innovation that enhances the guest experience.

Despite the numerous benefits, adopting AI technologies in tourism and hospitality also presents challenges, including the need for continuous learning and adaptation of AI systems to keep pace with the evolving expectations of guests and concerns related to privacy. Ensuring that AI implementations enhance rather than detract from human interaction remains critical. In conclusion, as AI continues to evolve and integrate more deeply into the fabric of hospitality services, it can profoundly transform the tourism industry by enhancing customer experience. If managed wisely, this transformation promises greater efficiency, satisfaction and a new era of innovation and customer service.

References

Adadi, A. (2021). A survey on data-efficient algorithms in big data era. *Journal of Big Data*, *8*(1), 24.

Adam, M., Wessel, M., & Benlian, A. (2021). AI-based chatbots in customer service and their effects on user compliance. *Electronic Markets*, *31*(2), 427–445.

Ali, I., Warraich, N. F., & Butt, K. (2025). Acceptance and use of artificial intelligence and AI-based applications in education: A meta-analysis and future direction. *Information Development*, *41*(3), 859–874.

Becerra-Fernandez, I., Sabherwal, R., & Kumi, R. (2024). *Knowledge management: Systems and processes in the AI Era*. Taylor & Francis.

Berezina, K., Ciftci, O., & Cobanoglu, C. (2019). Robots, artificial intelligence, and service automation in restaurants. In *Robots, artificial intelligence, and service automation in travel, tourism and hospitality* (pp. 185–219). Emerald Publishing Limited.

Biancofiore, G. M., Palma, D. D., Pomo, C., Narducci, F., & Di Noia, T. (2025). Conversational user interfaces and agents. In *Human-centered AI: An illustrated scientific quest* (pp. 399–438). Springer Nature Switzerland.

Bilgihan, A., & Ricci, P. (2024). The new era of hotel marketing: Integrating cutting-edge technologies with core marketing principles. *Journal of Hospitality and Tourism Technology*, *15*(1), 123–137.

Bogue, R. (2022). The role of robots in entertainment. *Industrial Robot: The International Journal of Robotics Research and Application*, *49*(4), 667–671.

Boletsis, C., & Chasanidou, D. (2018, June). Smart tourism in cities: Exploring urban destinations with audio augmented reality. In *Proceedings of the 11th Pervasive Technologies Related to Assistive Environments Conference* (pp. 515–521). https://doi.org/10.1145/3197768.3201549

Brill, T. M., Munoz, L., & Miller, R. J. (2022). Siri, Alexa, and other digital assistants: A study of customer satisfaction with artificial intelligence applications. In *The role of smart technologies in decision making* (pp. 35–70). Routledge.

Buhalis, D., Efthymiou, L., Uzunboylu, N., & Thrassou, A. (2024). Charting the progress of technology adoption in tourism and hospitality in the era of industry 4.0. *EuroMed Journal of Business*, *19*(1), 1–20.

Buhalis, D., & Foerste, M. (2015). SoCoMo marketing for travel and tourism: Empowering co-creation of value. *Journal of Destination Marketing & Management*, *4*(3), 151–161.

Buhalis, D., Harwood, T., Bogicevic, V., Viglia, G., Beldona, S., & Hofacker, C. (2019). Technological disruptions in services: Lessons from tourism and hospitality. *Journal of Service Management*, *30*(4), 484–506.

Buhalis, D., & Jun, S. (2011). *Tourism and technology*. Goodfellow Publishers Ltd.

Buhalis, D., & Licata, M. C. (2002). The future eTourism intermediaries. *Tourism Management*, *23*(3), 207–220.

Buhalis, D., & Moldavska, I. (2022). Voice assistants in hospitality: Using artificial intelligence for customer service. *Journal of Hospitality and Tourism Technology*, *13*(3), 386–403.

Buhalis, D., O'Connor, P., & Leung, R. (2023). Smart hospitality: From smart cities and smart tourism towards agile business ecosystems in networked destinations. *International Journal of Contemporary Hospitality Management*, *35*(1), 369–393.

Bulchand-Gidumal, J. (2022). Impact of artificial intelligence in travel, tourism, and hospitality. In *Handbook of e-Tourism* (pp. 1943–1962). Springer International Publishing.

Bulchand-Gidumal, J., & William, E. (2022). Tourists and augmented and virtual reality experiences. In *Handbook of e-Tourism* (pp. 997–1016). Springer International Publishing.

Bulchand-Gidumal, J., William Secin, E., O'Connor, P., & Buhalis, D. (2023). Artificial intelligence's impact on hospitality and tourism marketing: Exploring key themes and addressing challenges. *Current Issues in Tourism*, 1–18.

Cenamor, I., de la Rosa, T., Núñez, S., & Borrajo, D. (2017). Planning for tourism routes using social networks. *Expert Systems with Applications*, *69*, 1–9.

Chen, S. X., Wang, X. K., Zhang, H. Y., Wang, J. Q., & Peng, J. J. (2021). Customer purchase forecasting for online tourism: A data-driven method with multiplex behaviour data. *Tourism Management*, *87*, 104357.

Choi, Y., Choi, M., Oh, M., & Kim, S. (2020). Service robots in hotels: Understanding the service quality perceptions of human-robot interaction. *Journal of Hospitality Marketing & Management*, *29*(6), 613–635.

Christou, P., Simillidou, A., & Stylianou, M. C. (2020). Tourists' perceptions regarding the use of anthropomorphic robots in tourism and hospitality. *International Journal of Contemporary Hospitality Management*, *32*(11), 3665–3683.

Coates, C. (2020). *Christie products power the world's first robot theme park in South Korea*. https://blooloop.com/technology/news/christie-robot-theme-park-south-korea/. Accessed on February 4, 2020.

Cohen, S. A., & Hopkins, D. (2019). Autonomous vehicles and the future of urban tourism. *Annals of Tourism Research*, *74*, 33–42.

Collins, E. C. (2017). Vulnerable users: Deceptive robotics. *Connection Science*, *29*(3), 223–229.

Cunha, M. N. (2019). The tourism journey, from inspiration to post-travel phase, and the mobile technologies. *African Journal of Hospitality, Tourism and Leisure*, *8*(5), 1–17.

De Cicco, R., Silva, S. C., & Alparone, F. R. (2020). Millennials' attitude toward chatbots: An experimental study in a social relationship perspective. *International Journal of Retail & Distribution Management*, *48*(11), 1213–1233.

Duan, Y., Edwards, J. S., & Dwivedi, Y. K. (2019). Artificial intelligence for decision making in the era of Big Data–Evolution, challenges and research agenda. *International Journal of Information Management*, *48*, 63–71.

Duncan, M., Charness, N., Chapin, T., Horner, M., Stevens, L., Richard, A., Souders, D., Crute, J., Riemondy, A., & Morgan, D. (2015). *Enhanced mobility for aging populations using automated vehicles.* https://rosap.ntl.bts.gov/view/dot/29733/dot_29733_DS1.pdf

Duvall, A., Young, S., Fish, J., Henao, A., Sperling, J., Powell, B., & Lott, S. (2022). *Roadmap to automated mobility systems: Informing the planning of a sustainable, resilient transportation ecosystem for dallas/Fort Worth International Airport (No. NREL/TP-5400-82470)*. National Renewable Energy Laboratory (NREL).

Eletxigerra, A., Barrutia, J. M., & Echebarria, C. (2021). Tourist expertise and pre-travel value co-creation: Task-related processes and beyond. *Tourism Management Perspectives*, *37*, 100772.

Fang, R., & Pan, L. (2024). Refocusing on the start and end of tourists' decision-making: Measuring thresholds and information loop limits. *Tourism Management*, *104*, 104918.

Fuentes-Moraleda, L., Muñoz-Mazón, A., Santiago-Rincón, C., & Orea-Giner, A. (2021). Defining risk reduction strategies for tourists with specific food needs: A qualitative approach. *British Food Journal*, *124*(2), 590–612.

Gajdošík, T. (2019). Big data analytics in smart tourism destinations. A new tool for destination management organizations? In *Smart tourism as a driver for culture and sustainability: Fifth International Conference IACuDiT, Athens 2018* (pp. 15–33). Springer International Publishing.

Gretzel, U., Sigala, M., Xiang, Z., & Koo, C. (2015). Smart tourism: Foundations and developments. *Electronic Markets*, *25*(3), 179–188.

Grundner, L., & Neuhofer, B. (2021). The bright and dark sides of artificial intelligence: A futures perspective on tourist destination experiences. *Journal of Destination Marketing & Management*, *19*, 100511.

Guttentag, D. A. (2010). Virtual reality: Applications and implications for tourism. *Tourism Management*, *31*(5), 637–651.

Gursoy, D. (2025). Artificial intelligence (AI) technology, its applications and the use of AI powered devices in hospitality service experience creation and delivery. *International Journal of Hospitality Management*, 104212.

Haleem, A., Javaid, M., Qadri, M. A., Singh, R. P., & Suman, R. (2022). Artificial intelligence (AI) applications for marketing: A literature-based study. *International Journal of Intelligent Networks*, *3*, 119–132.

Han, R., Lam, H. K., Zhan, Y., Wang, Y., Dwivedi, Y. K., & Tan, K. H. (2021). Artificial intelligence in business-to-business marketing: A bibliometric analysis of current research status, development and future directions. *Industrial Management & Data Systems*, *121*(12), 2467–2497.

Hsu, C. H. (2018). Tourism education on and beyond the horizon. *Tourism Management Perspectives*, *25*, 181–183.

Irawan, B. (2023). Impact of artificial intelligence on the tourism industry: A literature review. *Innovative: Journal of Social Science Research*, *3*(6), 4865–4878.

Ivanov, S., Gretzel, U., Berezina, K., Sigala, M., & Webster, C. (2019). Progress on robotics in hospitality and tourism: A review of the literature. *Journal of Hospitality and Tourism Technology*, *10*(4), 489–521.

Ivanov, S., & Webster, C. (2019). Conceptual framework of the use of robots, artificial intelligence and service automation in travel, tourism, and hospitality companies. In *Robots, artificial intelligence, and service automation in travel, tourism and hospitality* (pp. 7–37). Emerald. https://doi.org/10.1108/978-1-78756-687-320191001

Ivanov, S., Webster, C., & Berezina, K. (2022). Robotics in tourism and hospitality. *Handbook of e-Tourism*, 1873–1899.

Ivanova, M. (2019). Robots, artificial intelligence, and service automation in travel agencies and tourist information centers. In *Robots, artificial intelligence, and service automation in travel, tourism and hospitality* (pp. 221–237). Emerald Publishing Limited.

Karanam, V. S., Shukla, V. K., Khalid, M. N., & Dutta, S. (2024). Applications of robotics in the hospitality industry. In *Artificial intelligence for smart technology in the hospitality and tourism industry* (pp. 63–75). Apple Academic Press.

Katsanakis, I., Zouni, G., Spasos, S., Lykoudi, D. M., & Akriotis, N. (2025, July). Exploring the impact of artificial intelligence on the tourism industry: Opportunities and challenges. In *GMA-GAMMA Joint Symposium* (pp. 154–178). Springer Nature Switzerland.

Kaul, L. (2023). *Practical Arduino Robotics: A hands-on guide to bringing your robotics ideas to life using Arduino*. Packt Publishing Ltd.

Ketchell, S., Chinthammit, W., & Engelke, U. (2019, November). Situated storytelling with SLAM enabled augmented reality. In *Proceedings of the 17th International Conference on Virtual-Reality Continuum and Its Applications in Industry* (pp. 1–9). https://doi.org/10.1145/3359997.3365681

Köchling, A. (2021). Experiential marketing as a tool to enhance tourists' pre-travel online destination experiences? A web-based experiment. *Journal of Destination Marketing & Management*, *22*, 100669.

Leiper, N. (1979). The framework of tourism: Towards a definition of tourism, tourist, and the tourist industry. *Annals of Tourism Research*, *6*(4), 390–407.

Li, X., Pan, B., & Law, R. (2019). Exploring the value of online reviews to organizations: Implications for tourism development. *Tourism Management*, *73*, 29–40.

Lipani, A., Carterette, B., & Yilmaz, E. (2021). How am I doing?: Evaluating conversational search systems offline. *ACM Transactions on Information Systems*, *39* (4), 1–22.

Lu, L., Cai, R., & Gursoy, D. (2019). Developing and validating a service robot integration willingness scale. *International Journal of Hospitality Management*, *80*, 36–51.

Lu, V. N., Wirtz, J., Kunz, W. H., Paluch, S., Gruber, T., Martins, A., & Patterson, P. G. (2020). Service robots, customers and service employees: What can we learn from the academic literature and where are the gaps? *Journal of Service Theory and Practice*, *30*(3), 361–391.

Lukanova, G., & Ilieva, G. (2019). Robots, artificial intelligence, and service automation in hotels. In *Robots, artificial intelligence, and service automation in travel, tourism and hospitality* (pp. 157–183). Emerald Publishing Limited.

Masood, A., & Ahmad, K. (2021). A review on emerging artificial intelligence (AI) techniques for air pollution forecasting: Fundamentals, application and performance. *Journal of Cleaner Production*, *322*, 129072.

Mich, L. (2020). Artificial intelligence and machine learning. *Handbook of e-Tourism*, 1–21.

Munar, A. M., & Jacobsen, J. K. S. (2014). Motivations for sharing tourism experiences through social media. *Tourism Management*, *43*, 46–54.

Murphy, J., Gretzel, U., & Pesonen, J. (2021). Marketing robot services in hospitality and tourism: The role of anthropomorphism. In *Future of tourism marketing* (pp. 16–27). Routledge.

Nanu, L. (2025). Redefining the servicescape in hospitality through technology and artificial intelligence: A conceptual framework. *International Journal of Contemporary Hospitality Management*, *37*(9), 3042–3060.

Park, S., & Stangl, B. (2020). Augmented reality experiences and sensation seeking. *Tourism Management*, *77*, 104023.

Perrine, K. A., Kockelman, K. M., & Huang, Y. (2020). Anticipating long-distance travel shifts due to self-driving vehicles. *Journal of Transport Geography*, *82*, 102547.

Reis, J., Melão, N., Salvadorinho, J., Soares, B., & Rosete, A. (2020). Service robots in the hospitality industry: The case of Henn-na hotel, Japan. *Technology in Society*, *63*, 101423.

Rossmann, A., Zimmermann, A., & Hertweck, D. (2020). The impact of chatbots on customer service performance. In *Advances in the human side of service engineering: Proceedings of the AHFE 2020 virtual conference on the human side of service engineering, July 16–20, 2020, USA* (pp. 237–243). Springer International Publishing.

Santoso, H. B., Wang, J. C., & Windasari, N. A. (2022). Impact of multisensory extended reality on tourism experience journey. *Journal of Hospitality and Tourism Technology*, *13*(3), 356–385.

Sigala, M., Rahimi, R., & Thelwall, M. (2019). *Big data and innovation in tourism, travel, and hospitality*. Springer.

Tsaih, R. H., & Hsu, C. C. (2018). *Artificial intelligence in smart tourism: A conceptual framework*. https://api.semanticscholar.org/CorpusID:96445578

Tussyadiah, I., Li, S., & Miller, G. (2019). Privacy protection in tourism: Where we are and where we should be heading for. In *Information and communication technologies in tourism 2019: Proceedings of the international conference in Nicosia, Cyprus, January 30–February 1, 2019* (pp. 278–290). Springer International Publishing.

Tussyadiah, I., & Miller, G. (2019). Nudged by a robot: Responses to agency and feedback. *Annals of Tourism Research*, *78*, 102752.

Tussyadiah, I. P., & Park, S. (2018). Consumer evaluation of hotel service robots. In *Information and communication technologies in tourism 2018: Proceedings of the international conference in Jönköping, Sweden, January 24–26, 2018* (pp. 308–320). Springer International Publishing.

Vallabhaneni, R., Pillai, S. E. V. S., Vaddadi, S. A., Addula, S. R., & Ananthan, B. (2024). Secured web application based on Capsule Net and OWASP in the cloud. *Indonesian Journal of Electrical Engineering and Computer Science*, *35*(3), 1924–1932.

Vashishth, T. K., Sharma, V., Sharma, K. K., Kumar, B., Panwar, R., & Chaudhary, S. (2024). AI-driven learning analytics for personalized feedback and assessment in higher education. In *Using traditional design methods to enhance AI-driven decision making* (pp. 206–230). IGI Global Scientific Publishing.

Wang, D., Park, S., & Fesenmaier, D. R. (2012). The role of smartphones in mediating the touristic experience. *Journal of Travel Research*, *51*(4), 371–387.

Xiang, Z., & Gretzel, U. (2010). Role of social media in online travel information search. *Tourism Management*, *31*(2), 179–188.

Yung, R., & Khoo-Lattimore, C. (2019). New realities: A systematic literature review on virtual reality and augmented reality in tourism research. *Current Issues in Tourism*, *22*(17), 2056–2081.

Zaifri, M., Khalloufi, H., Kaghat, F. Z., Benlahbib, A., Azough, A., & Zidani, K. A. (2023). Enhancing tourist experiences in crowded destinations through mobile augmented reality: A comparative field study. *International Journal of Interactive Mobile Technologies*, *17*(20).

Zeng, Z., Chen, P. J., & Lew, A. A. (2020). From high-touch to high-tech: COVID-19 drives robotics adoption. *Tourism Geographies*, *22*(3), 724–734.

Zhou, L., Buhalis, D., Fan, D. X., Ladkin, A., & Lian, X. (2024). Attracting digital nomads: Smart destination strategies, innovation and competitiveness. *Journal of Destination Marketing & Management*, *31*, 100850.

Chapter 3

Harnessing Fintech for Visitor Economy Development: Systematic Review, Fintech Preference and Future Research Agenda

John Agyekum Addae and Sheraz Ahmed

LUT University, Finland

Abstract

The spheres of Financial Technology (Fintech) and the visitor economy have functioned in a mutually supportive manner. In this research, the authors systematically reviewed studies pertaining to the utilisation of financial technology within the visitor economy. The results reveal that crowdfunding is the most preferred Fintech offering across sectors within the visitor economy ecosystem, where central bank digital currency (CBDC), which holds the promise of being the game changer for the visitor economy, is the least explored. In order to promote progress in the discipline, the authors' analysis of theory, context, characteristics and methodology (TCCM) highlights the necessity of adopting a dual-factor theoretical approach coupled with the need for new evidence from emerging markets, cross-country and global studies. Furthermore, bridging the unexplored moderating-mediation relationship research gap is desirable.

Keywords: Fintech; tourism development; visitor economy; PRISMA; TCCM

Introduction

The visitor economy refers to those sectors of the economy that rely on tourists, such as hotels, restaurants, attractions, amusement parks, creative industries, cultural institutions and heritage sites, as well as sports and entertainment (Kim & Hall, 2020a, p. 2533). Financial Technology (Fintech) is a non-monolithic

Artificial Intelligence in Hospitality and Tourism in Africa, 39–63

doi:10.1108/978-1-80686-169-920261003

sector, leveraging digital platforms to remotely deliver various financial services to the visitor economy (WorldBank, 2020). Fintech plays an indispensable role in the visitor economy, as it fosters seamless settlement and funding into the sector.

Payment experience is a vital part of a tourist's overall satisfaction. An inefficient payment system will ruin the hospitality experience, regardless of the superiority of the hospitality service. The impact of Fintech on the visitor economy is profound. Currently, about 83%–98% of travellers are using virtual wallets and global payment systems to pay for travel-related services (Khanra et al., 2021; Ozturk et al., 2017; Radic, Quan, Ariza-Montes et al., 2022; Sun et al., 2021). According to Kim (2023), cryptocurrency was used to settle 65% of $1.7 million in travel bookings. Crowdfunding, the most preferred Fintech offering in the visitor economy, funded US$1.68 billion in projects in the tourism and leisure sectors (Kim & Hall, 2020a). Similarly, US$133 million was raised through crowdfunding to benefit tourism SMEs (M. J. Kim, Bonn, & Lee, 2020). Likewise, a crowdfunding campaign raised £1.3 million to cover a single child's medical tourism in the United Kingdom (Coutrot et al., 2020). Also, crowdfunding was a useful platform to raise $1.5 million for a hotel project (San Martín et al., 2021). Other Fintech offerings, such as smart contracts and blockchain, are transforming smart tourism and island tourism (Nam et al., 2021; Treiblmaier et al., 2021; Özgit & Adalıer, 2022). Equally, central bank digital currency (CBDC), a recent Fintech offering, also has the potential to be a game-changer for the visitor economy ecosystem (J. J. Kim et al., 2022, 2023; Radic, Quan, Koo, et al., 2022).

To date, numerous studies have analysed Fintech offerings in various industries across visitor economy ecosystems. For example, CBDC is used in travel booking (J. J. Kim et al., 2022; Radic, Quan, Koo, et al., 2022) and crowdfunding applications in medical, museum, heritage and ecotourism (Bhatia & Birchley, 2020; Coutrot et al., 2020; Riley-Huff et al., 2016). Others include the utilisation of mobile payment by restaurants, hotels, hospitality SMEs and leisure(Sun et al., 2022; Uwamariya et al., 2022); blockchain application in smart tourism and island tourism (Chang et al., 2022; Kwok & Koh, 2019); and cryptocurrencies used in religious tourism (Abdullah et al., 2023).

Although there are many scholarly works in this research field, there is a dearth of studies reviewing the interplay between Fintech and the visitor economy. Cheng et al. (2021), for example conducted a critical review of mobile payment technology in hospitality and tourism, whereas Jain et al. (2023), on the other hand, conducted a systematic review of blockchain applications in the tourism and hospitality sector. These few review scopes are scattered and tend to focus on the unitary dimension of Fintech. These studies also lack a comprehensive and holistic review of the Fintech-visitor economy interplay intellectual structure. Additionally, the introduction of CBDC and many significant events in the research domain demand a re-examination of the research field. Accordingly, the following questions drive this study to bridge the research gap:

RQ1: What is the publication trend, and in what ways is the Fintech study progressing?
RQ2: What is the most preferred Fintech type in the visitor economy ecosystem?
RQ3: In what contexts has Fintech been examined in visitors' economy ecosystem?
RQ4: What are Fintech-visitor economy interconnectedness research methodological and theoretical choices?
RQ5: What avenues are fertile for future research?

The authors utilise a systematic literature review (SLR) approach to deal with the aforementioned research questions. SLR maps out an in-depth understanding of a subject area and provides an avenue for future research. The study employed the TCCM framework to examine unexplored research themes.

Hereafter, the remaining sections describe how the review is structured. We elaborate on the study research methodology in the section Method, followed by the presentation and discussion of the findings in the section Findings and Discussion. This study concludes with directions for future studies in the section Future Research Direction.

Method

To achieve the research goals, we adopted SLR and followed research methodology protocols recommended by prior SLR studies to ensure that our findings are reliable and replicable (Goyal et al., 2021; Khatri & Duggal, 2022; Paul et al., 2023). Data for this review were sourced from Web of Science (WoS), considered as the most influential database (Goyal et al., 2021; Khatri & Duggal, 2022; Schröder et al., 2021) and the most used database for systematic reviews (Feliciano-Cestero et al., 2023). The article's search, screening and selection were guided by PRISMA and SPAR-4-SLR protocols (Khatri & Duggal, 2022; Paul et al., 2023; Sandesh et al., 2023).

We employed Boolean operators 'AND' and 'OR' to run a search query in WoS in May 2023 using a combination of keywords in the fields related to 'title', 'abstract' and 'keywords'. The search string applied was (("Financial technology" OR "fintech" OR "Mobile payment" OR "mobile money" OR "e-wallet" OR "crowdfunding" OR "robo-advis*" OR "Cryptocurrenc*" OR "intertech" OR "restech" OR "Central bank digital currenc*" OR "Digital currenc*" OR "peer-to-peer lending" OR "Cross boarder payment") AND ("tour*" OR "hospitality" OR "leisure" OR "recreation" OR "event management" OR "sustainable tourism" OR "ecotourism" OR "community-based tourism" OR "tourism employment" OR "sustainable tourism policy" OR "cultural heritage" OR "natural heritage" OR "community based conservation" OR "community-based conservation" OR "coastal ecotourism" OR "traditional ecological knowledge" OR "wildlife reserves" OR "forest conservation" OR "forest reserves" OR "United Nations World Tourism Organization" OR "UNWTO" OR "space tourism" OR "Museum*" OR "destination tourism")).

As elaborated in Fig. 1, we screen for eligibility using seven-step predefined inclusion and exclusion criteria. Most importantly, the final sample included articles published in quality journals with at least a 1.0 impact factor, as recommended by prior studies (Basu et al., 2022; Khatri & Duggal, 2022; Paul et al., 2023; Paul & Rosado-Serrano, 2019; Srivastava et al., 2022). After screening the abstract, reading the full text and excluding unsuitable articles, 69 articles were accepted as the final sample for SLR (see Appendix A). All the selected articles were coded and analysed using the TCCM framework and interpretative synthesis (Paul & Rosado-Serrano, 2019). Supported by content analysis, thematic analysis and inductive narrative, the next section captures and discusses the study findings in terms of main themes, theories, context, characteristics and methods covered in the final sample.

Findings and Discussion

Annual Publication

Our RQ1 is addressed in Table 1 and Fig. 2. As can be seen, the findings demonstrate an uptick in the annual scientific production in this research field spanning 2016 to 2022. In 2022, the annual publication reached its zenith with 29 different publications, which accounted for 42% of the whole sample. The early stage research theme was characterised by the use of crowdfunding instruments to raise funds for the tourism sector and the usage of mobile payments for tourism-related payments. Notably, three publications were devoted to CBDC use in travel booking in the year 2022. In the ecosystem of the visitor economy, CBDC holds the promise to address cross-border payment concerns within the ecosystem of the visitor economy.

Fintech Preference in Tourism Industry

Several forms of visitor economies that have utilised Fintech offerings are presented in Table 2. Providing support for RQ2, Table 2 shows that overall, crowdfunding is the most preferred form of financial technology in the tourism industry, whereas, despite its potential benefits, CBDC remains unexplored. Sectorally, crowdfunding is the most important tool for the heritage tourism industry, while mobile payment solutions provided by Fintech are heavily utilised in the restaurant industry. When it comes to booking a trip, most people prefer to use CBDC, while blockchain is being put to use to boost the growth of the island's tourism industry.

In terms of the visitor economy type, travel booking is the most studied genre of visitor economy, followed by heritage tourism, while leisure is the least studied sector.

Scholars show that about 98% of travel-related payments are concluded via virtual wallets and global payment systems (Khanra et al., 2021; Ozturk et al., 2017;

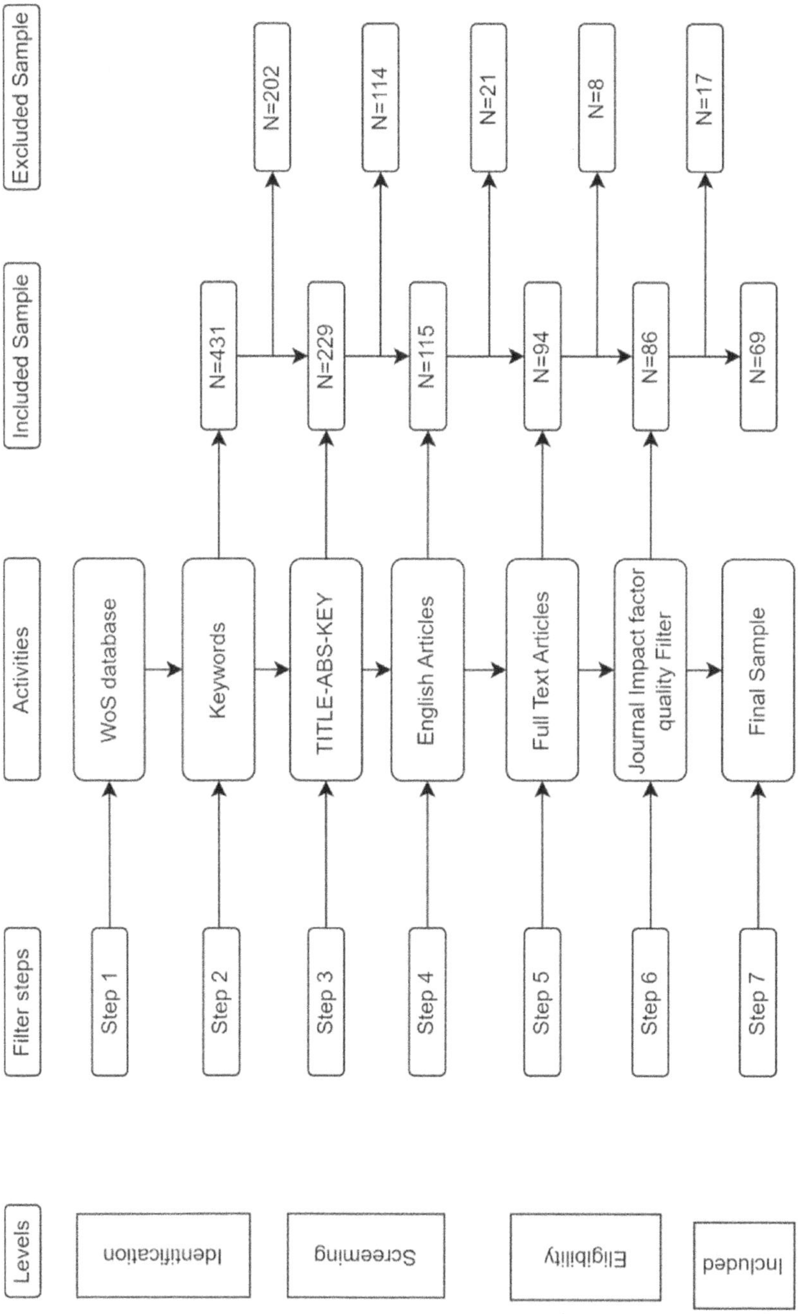

Fig. 1. PRISMA-Guided Articles Section for Systematic Review.

Table 1. Tourism-Fintech Annual Publication.

Year	Crowdfunding	Mobile Payment	Cryptocurrencies	Blockchain	CBDC	Total
2016	2	1				3
2017	1	3				4
2018	3		1			4
2019	2		1	1		4
2020	8	2	2	1		13
2021	4	4	1	3		12
2022	4	11	6	5	3	29
Total	24	21	11	10	3	69

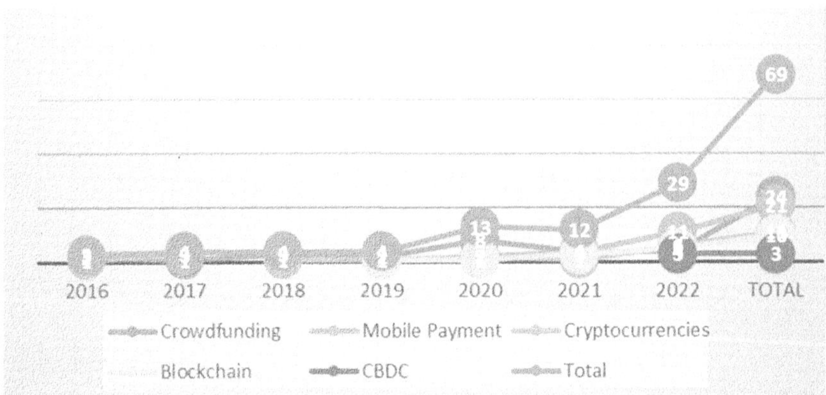

Fig. 2. Tourism Sector Annual Fintech Publication.

Radic, Quan, Ariza-Montes et al., 2022; Sun et al., 2021). The funding structure and sources for the tourism industry have witnessed significant improvement through crowdfunding schemes, including 133 million in crowdfunding investment into tourism SMEs (M. J. Kim, Bonn, & Lee, 2020); £1.3 million in crowdfunding sponsorship for a child's medical tourism (Coutrot et al., 2020); $1.5 million crowdfunded hotel project (San Martín et al., 2021). Museums have witnessed facelifts and revamping through crowdfunding fundraising campaigns (Cavalcanti Junqueira & Discua Cruz, 2019; Riley-Huff et al., 2016). Equally, blockchain is transforming ecotourism (Tham & Sigala, 2020), island tourism (Chang et al., 2022; Nam et al., 2021; Özgit & Adalıer, 2022), smart tourism (Nam et al., 2021), tourism

Table 2. Fintech Preference in Tourism Industry.

Tourism Sector	Crowdfunding	Mobile Payment	Crypto Currencies	Blockchain	CBDC	Grand Total
Travel Booking		4	2	2	3	11
Heritage Tourism	7					7
ecotourism	3	2		1		6
Hotels	2	4				6
Medical Tourism	5			1		6
Restaurant	1	5				6
Hospitality SMES	1	1	2			4
Tourism Economics		2	2			4
Island Tourism				3		3
Museums	3					3
Natural Resources Tourism	1		2			3
Outbound Tourism	1	1		1		3
Religious Tourism			2			2
Smart Tourism			1	1		2
Tourism Research		1		1		2
Leisure		1				1
Grand Total	24	21	11	10	3	69

research (Dadkhah et al., 2022) and natural resource conservation (Howson et al., 2019). In a similar vein, CBDC is utilised extensively in the booking of travel (J. J. Kim et al., 2022, 2023; Radic, Quan, Koo, et al., 2022). Abdullah et al. (2023), in their study about the connectedness between halal tourism stocks and cryptocurrencies, show that halal tourism offers significant hedging effectiveness.

Geographical Coverage

To respond to RQ3, we examine the setting in which the interplay between the visitor economy and Fintech was studied in Table 3. Only nine studies have either a global perspective or cross-country settings, which make up 13% of the reviewed studies. Global context studies focus on mobile payment in the OECD (Wu et al., 2021) and restaurant mobile payment evidence from the EU, USA, and UK (Wang & Peters, 2023). Across the United States, China and South Korea, tourists' adoption of CBDC as a payment method was explored by J. J. Kim et al. (2022). Notably, Bulut (2022) is the only study with global and cross-continent appeal focusing on initial coin offerings for hospitality SMEs. Cross-Asian economies lead the way in cross-country studies, with four studies (J. J. Kim et al., 2023; Radic, Quan, Ariza-Montes et al., 2022; Treiblmaier et al., 2021) examining cryptocurrencies used for travel booking. Mobile payment was the focus of another study that considered 44 Asian economies (Adeleye et al., 2023). The only cross-African studies focus on the MENA region hotel use of reward-based crowdfunding (Salem et al., 2022).

The United States (USA) leads with 11 publications focusing largely on crowdfunding and cryptocurrencies. Beyond the US setting, South Korea reported the second most publications with nine studies largely on crowdfunding. China, the United Kingdom and Italy followed closely. Conspicuously, the North American and Caribbean continents are missing, while Africa is under-represented with only two studies from Rwanda (Uwamariya et al., 2022) and South Africa. The geographical setting of most studies is centred on advanced economies rather than emerging and developing nations. These results present an opportunity for further research in Africa, North America, the Caribbean and across the globe. Even the developed economy context studies lack depth because limited countries such as the United States, South Korea, China, the United Kingdom and Italy have received traction.

Theoretical Focus

The authors have advanced a great deal of theories in an effort to explain the research field. There were 36 theories used in 60% of the studies published in both tourism and non-tourism journals, as shown in Table 4.

The first category of theories employs technology acceptance theories to back up their research. The Unified Theory of Acceptance and Use of Technology (UTAUT) and the Theory of Planned Behaviour (TPB) are the most widely used theories, with six articles each. Through the lens of UTAUT, performance expectancy, effort expectancy, social influence and facilitating condition constructs influence Fintech use in the visitor economy ecosystem (Hameed et al., 2022; M. J. Kim & Hall, 2020b; Xu et al., 2023). Similarly, using TPB theoretical

Table 3. Geographical Coverage.

Continent	Countries	Crowd Funding	Mobile Payment	Crypto Currency	Block Chain	CBDC	Total	Exemplary Articles Codes
Global	OECD		1				1	[34]
	The EU, the USA, the UK		1				1	[66]
	The USA, China, South Korea					1	1	[60]
	Cross Continent			1			1	[48]
America	The USA	4	2	4	1		11	[4],[43],[59],[63]
	Canada	2					2	[32],[36]
Europe	The UK	3		1			4	[8],[12],[15],[28]
	Italy	4					4	[5],[10],[11],[62]
	Spain	1			1		2	[38],[39]
	Portugal		1				1	[54]
	Austria				1		1	[29]
	Turkey				1		1	[46]
Asia	South Korea	7			1	1	9	[17],[23],[41],[49]
	China		5				5	[31],[37],[50],[52]
	Malaysia		2		1		3	[13],[26],[27]
	India		3				3	[6],[7],[30]
	Iran	1			1		2	[16],[45]

(Continued)

Table 3. *(Continued)*

Continent	Countries	Crowd Funding	Mobile Payment	Crypto Currency	Block Chain	CBDC	Total	Exemplary Articles Codes
	Australia	1			1		2	[18],[19]
	Dubai, UAE				2		2	[33],[61]
	Bangladesh		1				1	[55]
	New Zealand		1				1	[67]
	Taiwan			1			1	[21]
	Thailand		1				1	[44]
	Pakistan		1				1	[58]
	Qatar			1			1	[24]
	Cross Asia		1	2		1	4	[35],[47],[57],[69]
Africa	South Africa			1			1	[9]
	Rwanda		1				1	[53]
	MENA	1					1	[42]
	Grand Total	24	21	11	10	3	69	

Table 4. Theoretical Focus.

Theories Applied	Tourism Journal	Non-tourism Journal	Total	Exemplary Articles Codes
UTAUT	4	2	6	[2],[17],[41],[57],[67]
Theory of Planned Behaviour	4	2	6	[16],[39],[42],[51],[60]
Diffusion of Innovation Theory	2	2	4	[33],[45],[47],[54]
Technology Acceptance Model (TAM)	2	1	3	[21],[31],[57]
Risk Theory	3	0	3	[23],[42]
Trust Theory	3	0	3	[23],[25],[42]
Theory of Reasoned Action	1	1	2	[39],[55]
Innovation Resistance Theory	1	1	2	[30],[58]
Attitude Formation Theory	1	0	1	[39]
Attribution Theory	1	0	1	[25]
Contingency Theory	1	0	1	[35]
Finance-Growth Nexus Theory	1	0	1	[34]
Game-Theory	1	0	1	[59]
Herding Behaviour Theory	1	0	1	[40]
Motivation Theory	1	0	1	[23]
Prospect Theory	1	0	1	[37]
Push-Pull-Mooring	1	0	1	[66]
Self Determination Theory	1	0	1	[50]
Signalling Theory	1	0	1	[48]
Social Cognition Theory	1	0	1	[2]
Social Exchange Theory	1	0	1	[43]
Transaction Costs Theory	1	0	1	[29]
Uncertainty Theory	1	0	1	[20]
Valence Theory	1	0	1	[4]

(Continued)

Table 4. *(Continued)*

Theories Applied	Tourism Journal	Non-tourism Journal	Total	Exemplary Articles Codes
Venture Quality Theory	1	0	1	[20]
Connectivism Learning Theory	0	1	1	[41]
Coping Theory	0	1	1	[58]
Critical Mass Theory	0	1	1	[26]
Flow Theory	0	1	1	[26]
Gratifications Theory	0	1	1	[56]
Market Integration Theory	0	1	1	[63]
Norm Activation Theory	0	1	1	[14]
Random Utility Theory	0	1	1	[1]
Self-Efficacy Theory	0	1	1	[26]
Theory Of Internationalisation	0	1	1	[27]
Value Theory	0	1	1	[22]
No Theoretical Application	12	16	28	[44],[49],[62],[68]

support, Fintech adoption and repurchase intention in the visitor economy are influenced by visitors' attitudes and subjective norms (Radic, Quan, Koo, et al., 2022; Sun et al., 2022). Other technology acceptance models employed are Diffusion of Innovation Theory (DIT), Technology Acceptance Model (TAM) and Theory of Reasoned Action (TRA).

The second category of theories focuses on innovation resistance-related theories. Explaining barriers to Fintech adoptions, risk theory, trust theory and innovation resistance theory (IRT) were all beneficial and essential theories utilised in this field for explaining the reasons behind people's natural hesitation to adopt Fintech. Using risk theory, J. J. Kim et al. (2023) show that perceived risks and time risk have an adverse effect on attitudes towards CBDC payment, which, in turn, affects the intention to adopt. On the contrary, funders' perceived risk about tourism crowdfunding is not associated with their crowdfunding participation (M. J. Kim, Bonn, & Lee, 2020). Based on trust theory, M. J. Kim, Hall and Kim (2020) contend that willingness to crowdfund is more influenced by trust in the platform than trust in the fundraiser. IRT provides a framework that delineates the functional and psychological barriers to Fintech adoption.

Their IRT study shows that usage barriers and image barriers influence mobile payment postponement (Khanra et al., 2021).

Curiously, 28 papers representing hopping 40% make no use of any theoretical framework to ground their research (see De Crescenzo et al., 2022; Kakinuma, 2022; Kim, 2023; Uwamariya et al., 2022; Wakefield et al., 2022; Yousaf et al., 2023). Our analysis also shows that scholars merely mention theories rather than delving into them in greater detail or drawing on them when hypothesising (see Sun et al., 2021; Treiblmaier, 2021; Wu et al., 2021). Table 4 lists the remaining theoretical frameworks used in this study area. These results answer research question 4 (RQ4) concerning the theoretical perspectives for studying the interplay of Fintech and the visitor economy.

Statistical Techniques and Methods

In this section, we categorised the articles according to the statistical methods and tools that were used in order to establish which method is the most widely utilised for analysis. Table 5 provides an overview of many different quantitative

Table 5. Data Analysis Techniques.

Analysis Technique	Tourism Journal	Non-Tourism Journal	Total	Exemplary Articles Codes
Part A: Quantitative				
SEM	19	9	28	[2],[4],[17],[20],[26],[30],[35][39],[49],[50],[52],[57],[60],[69]
Regression: Logistic	2	0	2	[43],[48]
Regression: GMM	1	1	2	[47], [68]
Regression: PSR-VAR	1	0	1	[34]
Regression: OLS	0	1	1	[64]
T-Test	1	2	3	[3],[36],[37]
Factor Analysis	1	0	1	[5]
Chi-Square	0	1	1	[1]
Cross-Correlation Analysis	0	1	1	[63]
FSQCA Analysis	0	1	1	[62]
Mann–Whitney Tests	0	1	1	[65]

(Continued)

Table 5. *(Continued)*

Analysis Technique	Tourism Journal	Non-Tourism Journal	Total	Exemplary Articles Codes
Part B: Qualitative				
Thematic Analysis	6	6	12	[16],[31],[33],[45],[53],[56],[61]
Conceptual	6	4	10	[7],[13],[27],[29],[38]
Descriptive	0	3	3	[15],[18],[46]
Document Content Analysis	2	0	2	[8],[19]
Total	39	30	69	

and qualitative techniques that were used, together with their relative frequency of usage. Structural equation modelling (SEM) is the most commonly employed quantitative analytical tool in 28 papers, accounting for 40% of studies (see Lew et al., 2020; Makki et al., 2016). Multiple regression techniques were also used, such as PSR-VAR estimation (see Wu et al., 2021); IV-GMM (see Adeleye et al., 2023) and logistic (see Bulut, 2022; Yang & Koh, 2022). Current studies are combining SEM and FSQCA for multiple group comparative analysis (Salem et al., 2022).

Thematic analysis predominates among qualitative analysis methods. Ten studies were conducted, leading to conceptualisation. Seven studies have also used descriptive analysis, whereas documentary content analysis was also the choice of two studies.

Methodological Design

In Table 6 (Part A), the methodological research design is presented. Approximately 62% of the study designs used were quantitative, whereas 38% of the research utilised a qualitative approach.

Table 6 in Part B displays the research field's chosen method of data collection. The most popular data collection tools were online questionnaires supplemented by self-administered questionnaires. Our analysis also shows that 26 articles relied on secondary data. The use of interviews and archival data was relatively minimal.

Table 6 Part C shows the type of study. The majority of the studies are empirical in nature. We observed that 16 articles opted for the case study approach. Our analysis also reveals that 10 studies were conducted, leading to conceptualisation.

Table 6. Research Design and Methodological Choices (N = 69).

Research Design	Tourism Journal	Non-Tourism Journal	Total	Exemplary Articles Codes
Part A: Research Design				
Quantitative	25	18	43	[34],[43],[62],[69]
Qualitative	14	12	26	[19],[38],[46],[61]
Part B: Data Collection Methods				
Online Questionnaire	18	9	27	[2],[4],[34],[60],[67]
Secondary data	14	12	26	[34],[43],[47],[48],[68]
Interviews	2	5	7	[16],[37],[46],[53],[62]
Self-administered questionnaire	3	3	6	[26],[36],[39],[42],[50]
Archival	2	1	3	[8],[10],[28],
Part C: Type of Study				
Empirical	25	18	43	[17],[34],[39],[62],[68]
Case study	10	6	16	[31],[45],[51],[53]
Conceptual	6	4	10	[7],[13],[27],[29],[38]
Part D: Moderating-Mediation Relationship				
Moderating Relationship	8	1	9	[30],[35],[60],[66],[67],[69]
Mediation Relation	2	2	4	[17],[22],[25],[55]
Moderating-Mediation Relationship	5	4	9	[20],[23],[41],[49]
Unexplored Moderating-Mediation Relationship	24	23	47	[2],[4],[26],[39],[50],[58]

Table 6 Part D was devoted to studies on moderating and mediating relationships. We found that around 68% of the papers that were analysed did not test moderating and mediating relationships. Few scholars have attempted to bridge this research gap (see Kakinuma, 2022).

Future Research Direction

In light of the growing interest in the research field, we answer RQ-5 in this section by offering more avenues for future research. This study makes use of a theory–context–characteristics–methodology (TCCM) framework to provide a comprehensive agenda for future research (Mandler et al., 2021, p. 429). Our recommendations for the direction of future research have been divided into four distinct categories: new theoretical views (theory), alternative research environments (context), different constructs and new relationships (characteristics) and methodological improvement (Method). Table 7 offers future research directions and exemplary enquiries for each category max 3.

Table 7. Direction for Future Research.

Dimension	**Issue**	**Example**
New Theory	Dual Factor theory	i. Application of dual-factor models to examine enablers and barriers influencing Fintech adoption and resistance.
		ii. Examination of cost-benefit analysis of BTC use in tourism Comparative analysis of users and non-Fintech users.
Alternative research environments (Context)		Examine the Fintech use by small- to medium-sized hospitality businesses.
Different constructs and New relationship (Characteristics)		i. Examining CBDC Adoption in the Visitor's Economy.
		ii. What are the factors affecting the success of tourism ICOs?
		iii. An examination of Fintech service failure and recovery.

Table 7. *(Continued)*

Dimension	Issue	Example
		iv. What are the factors influencing mobile payment switching intention in the visitor's economy ecosystem?
		v. An examination of the use of blockchain to improve medical tourism providers' competitiveness and reputation, and enhance medical tourists' experience.
Methodological improvement (Method)	Longitudinal study design	Implementation of a longitudinal study to test the impact of Fintech on both inbound and outbound tourism and economic development.
	QCA methodology	Application of fsQCA methodology and SEM to deepen the mixed-methods approach in the research field.
	Moderating-mediation relationship	New evidence testing the moderating-mediation relationship is encouraged.

Conclusion

This paper conducted an SLR using the WoS database, considered the most influential database and the most used database for systematic reviews. Our article search, screening and selection were guided by a seven-step protocol as shown in Fig. 1. Our analysis shows a significant increase over time in Fintech studies in the visitor economy ecosystem. Our research shows that among the sectors of the visitor's economy, crowdfunding is the most researched Fintech solution, while CBDC is the least explored. The research field commonly employs SEM data analysis methodologies and technology acceptance theories. Most studies also conducted quantitative studies using questionnaires. In terms of study context, cross-country studies are seldom. Further, few studies test moderation and mediation relationships. We also offered avenues for future research.

References

Abdullah, M., Chowdhury, M. A. F., & Sulong, Z. (2023). Asymmetric efficiency and connectedness among green stocks, halal tourism stocks, cryptocurrencies, and commodities: Portfolio hedging implications. *Resources Policy*, *81*(October 2022), 103419. https://doi.org/10.1016/j.resourpol.2023.103419

Adeleye, B. N., Aderounmu, B., Owolabi, O., Okafor, V., & Ohonba, A. (2023). Examining the influence of ICT innovation in the finance-tourism nexus in Asia. *Transnational Corporations Review*, *15*(3), 43–59. https://doi.org/10.1080/19186444.2022.2107331

Bagheri, A., Chitsazan, H., & Koolaji, S. (2020). Deterrents of tourism business crowdfunding: Aversion decision and aversion behavior. *International Journal of Hospitality Management*, *88*(October 2019), 102517. https://doi.org/10.1016/j.ijhm.2020.102517

Baig, M. A., & Ali, S. N. (2020). The expanding scope and scale of Ḥalāl market. *Journal of King Abdulaziz University - Islamic Economics*, *33*(2), 159–172. https://doi.org/10.4197/Islec.33-2.12

Balasubramanian, S., Sethi, J. S., Ajayan, S., & Paris, C. M. (2022). An enabling framework for blockchain in tourism. *Information Technology & Tourism*, *24*(2), 165–179. https://doi.org/10.1007/s40558-022-00229-6

Basu, R., Paul, J., & Singh, K. (2022). Visual merchandising and store atmospherics: An integrated review and future research directions. *Journal of Business Research*, *151*(June 2021), 397–408. https://doi.org/10.1016/j.jbusres.2022.07.019

Bhatia, N., & Birchley, G. (2020). Medical tourism and the best interests of the critically ill child in the era of healthcare globalisation. *Medical Law Review*, *28*(4), 696–730. https://doi.org/10.1093/medlaw/fwaa029

Bulut, E. (2022). Blockchain-based entrepreneurial finance: Success determinants of tourism initial coin offerings. *Current Issues in Tourism*, *25*(11), 1767–1781. https://doi.org/10.1080/13683500.2021.1980505

Camilleri, M. A. (2018). Nurturing travel and tourism enterprises for economic growth and competitiveness. *Tourism and Hospitality Research*, *18*(1), 123–127. https://doi.org/10.1177/1467358415621947

Cavalcanti Junqueira, M. I., & Discua Cruz, A. (2019). Crowdfunding and museums: A field trip exemplar in the United Kingdom. *Entrepreneurship Education and Pedagogy*, *2*(2), 151–170. https://doi.org/10.1177/2515127418801728

Chang, M., Walimuni, A. C. S. M., Kim, M., & Lim, H. (2022). Acceptance of tourism blockchain based on UTAUT and connectivism theory. *Technology in Society*, *71*(May), 102027. https://doi.org/10.1016/j.techsoc.2022.102027

Cheng, N. T. Y., Fong, L. H. N., & Law, R. (2021). Mobile payment technology in hospitality and tourism: A critical review through the lens of demand, supply and policy. *International Journal of Contemporary Hospitality Management*, *33*(10), 3636–3660. https://doi.org/10.1108/IJCHM-02-2021-0261

Cheung, C., Fang, C. C., & Wang, Y. C. (2022). Consumer behavior and mobile payment: An empirical study of the restaurant industry. *Journal of China Tourism Research*, *18*(4), 735–755. https://doi.org/10.1080/19388160.2021.1972072

Chew, B. C., Shen, X., & Ansell, J. (2020). Alipay entered Malaysia: A closer look at the new market entry strategy driven by Chinese tourists. *Qualitative Research in Financial Markets*, *12*(4), 561–577. https://doi.org/10.1108/QRFM-06-2019-0069

Coutrot, I. P., Smith, R., & Cornelsen, L. (2020). Is the rise of crowdfunding for medical expenses in the United Kingdom symptomatic of systemic gaps in health and social care?. *Journal of Health Services Research and Policy*, *25*(3), 181–186. https://doi.org/10.1177/1355819619897949

Dadkhah, M., Rahimnia, F., & Filimonau, V. (2022). Evaluating the opportunities, challenges and risks of applying the blockchain technology in tourism: A Delphi study approach. *Journal of Hospitality and Tourism Technology*, *13*(5), 922–954. https://doi.org/10.1108/JHTT-04-2021-0115

De Crescenzo, V., Simeoni, F., Ulrich, K., & Ribeiro Navarrete, S. (2022). Searching for the crowd in sustainable tourism and leisure projects. *European Journal of Innovation Management*, *26*(7), 110–126. https://doi.org/10.1108/EJIM-02-2022-0095

Di Carlo, A., Leveridge, M., & McGregor, T. B. (2021). Crowdfunding in urology: Canadian perspective. *Canadian Urological Association Journal*, *15*(3), 139–143. https://doi.org/10.5489/CUAJ.6572

Di Pietro, L., Guglielmetti Mugion, R., & Renzi, M. F. (2018). Heritage and identity: Technology, values and visitor experiences. *Journal of Heritage Tourism*, *13*(2), 97–103. https://doi.org/10.1080/1743873X.2017.1384478

Feliciano-Cestero, M. M., Ameen, N., Kotabe, M., Paul, J., & Signoret, M. (2023). Is digital transformation threatened? A systematic literature review of the factors influencing firms' digital transformation and internationalization. *Journal of Business Research*, *157*(January 2022), 113546. https://doi.org/10.1016/j.jbusres.2022.113546

Ferreira, M. C., Oliveira, M., & Dias, T. G. (2022). To use or not to use? Investigating what drives tourists to use mobile ticketing services in tourism. *Sustainability (Switzerland)*, *14*(11). https://doi.org/10.3390/su14116622

Gamage, T. C., Tajeddini, K., & Tajeddini, O. (2022). Why Chinese travelers use WeChat to make hotel choice decisions: A uses and gratifications theory perspective. *Journal of Global Scholars of Marketing Science: Bridging Asia and the World*, *32*(2), 285–312. https://doi.org/10.1080/21639159.2021.1961599

Goyal, K., Kumar, S., & Xiao, J. J. (2021). Antecedents and consequences of personal financial management behavior: A systematic literature review and future research agenda. *International Journal of Bank Marketing*, *39*(7), 1166–1207. https://doi.org/10.1108/IJBM-12-2020-0612

Hameed, I., Mubarik, M. S., Khan, K., & Waris, I. (2022). Can your smartphone make you a tourist? Mine does: Understanding the consumer's adoption mechanism for mobile payment system. *Human Behavior and Emerging Technologies*, *2022*. https://doi.org/10.1155/2022/4904686

Howson, P., Oakes, S., Baynham-Herd, Z., & Swords, J. (2019). Cryptocarbon: The promises and pitfalls of forest protection on a blockchain. *Geoforum*, *100*(August 2018), 1–9. https://doi.org/10.1016/j.geoforum.2019.02.011

Jain, P., Singh, R. K., Mishra, R., & Rana, N. P. (2023). Emerging dimensions of blockchain application in tourism and hospitality sector: A systematic literature review. *Journal of Hospitality Marketing & Management*, *32*(4), 454–476. https://doi.org/10.1080/19368623.2023.2184440

Kakinuma, Y. (2022). Financial literacy and quality of life: A moderated mediation approach of Fintech adoption and leisure. *International Journal of Social Economics*, *49*(12), 1713–1726. https://doi.org/10.1108/IJSE-10-2021-0633

Karim, R. A., Sobhani, F. A., Rabiul, M. K., Lepee, N. J., Kabir, M. R., & Chowdhury, M. A. M. (2022). Linking Fintech payment services and customer loyalty intention in the hospitality industry: The mediating role of customer experience and attitude. *Sustainability (Switzerland)*, *14*(24). https://doi.org/10.3390/su142416481

Khanra, S., Dhir, A., Kaur, P., & Joseph, R. P. (2021). Factors influencing the adoption postponement of mobile payment services in the hospitality sector during a pandemic. *Journal of Hospitality and Tourism Management*, *46*(March 2020), 26–39. https://doi.org/10.1016/j.jhtm.2020.11.004

Khatri, P., & Duggal, H. K. (2022). Well-being of higher education consumers: A review and research agenda. *International Journal of Consumer Studies*, *46*(5), 1564–1593. https://doi.org/10.1111/ijcs.12783

Kim, H. (2023). The impact of the COVID-19 pandemic on travel cryptocurrency and stock market performances: An event-study approach. *Journal of Hospitality and Tourism Technology*, *14*(2), 172–187. https://doi.org/10.1108/JHTT-02-2022-0053

Kim, M. J., Bonn, M., & Lee, C. K. (2020). The effects of motivation, deterrents, trust, and risk on tourism crowdfunding behavior. *Asia Pacific Journal of Tourism Research*, *25*(3), 244–260. https://doi.org/10.1080/10941665.2019.1687533

Kim, H., & Chang, B. (2020). A study on the effects of crowdfunding values on the intention to visit local festivals: Focusing on mediating effects of perceived risk and e-WOM. *Sustainability (Switzerland)*, *12*(8). https://doi.org/10.3390/SU12083264

Kim, M. J., & Hall, C. M. (2019). Can co-creation and crowdfunding types predict funder behavior? An extended model of goal-directed behavior. *Sustainability (Switzerland)*, *11*(24). https://doi.org/10.3390/su11247061

Kim, M. J., & Hall, C. M. (2020a). Investment crowdfunding in the visitor economy: The roles of venture quality, uncertainty, and funding amount. *Current Issues in Tourism*, *23*(20), 2533–2554. https://doi.org/10.1080/13683500.2019.1656178

Kim, M. J., & Hall, C. M. (2020b). What drives visitor economy crowdfunding? The effect of digital storytelling on unified theory of acceptance and use of technology. *Tourism Management Perspectives*, *34*(June 2019), 100638. https://doi.org/10.1016/j.tmp.2020.100638

Kim, M. J., Hall, C. M., & Kim, D. K. (2020). Why do investors participate in tourism incentive crowdfunding? The effects of attribution and trust on willingness to fund. *Journal of Travel & Tourism Marketing*, *37*(2), 141–154. https://doi.org/10.1080/10548408.2020.1722784

Kim, J. J., Kim (Sam), S., Hailu, T. B., Ryu, H. B., & Han, H. (2023). Does Central Bank Digital Currency (CBDC) payment create the opportunity for the tourism industry?. *Journal of Hospitality & Tourism Research*, 109634802311587. https://doi.org/10.1177/10963480231158773

Kim, M. J., & Petrick, J. F. (2021). The effect of herding behaviors on dual-route processing of communications aimed at tourism crowdfunding ventures. *Journal of Travel Research*, *60*(5), 947–964. https://doi.org/10.1177/0047287520919515

Kim, J. J., Radic, A., Chua, B. L., Koo, B., & Han, H. (2022). Digital currency and payment innovation in the hospitality and tourism industry. *International Journal of Hospitality Management*, *107*(August), 103314. https://doi.org/10.1016/j.ijhm.2022.103314

Kwok, A. O. J., & Koh, S. G. M. (2019). Is blockchain technology a watershed for tourism development?. *Current Issues in Tourism*, *22*(20), 2447–2452. https://doi.org/10.1080/13683500.2018.1513460

Lew, S., Tan, G. W. H., Loh, X. M., Hew, J. J., & Ooi, K. B. (2020). The disruptive mobile wallet in the hospitality industry: An extended mobile technology acceptance model. *Technology in Society*, *63*(March), 101430. https://doi.org/10.1016/j.techsoc.2020.101430

Makki, A. M., Ozturk, A. B., & Singh, D. (2016). Role of risk, self-efficacy, and innovativeness on behavioral intentions for mobile payment systems in the restaurant industry. *Journal of Foodservice Business Research*, *19*(5), 454–473. https://doi.org/10.1080/15378020.2016.1188646

Mandler, T., Sezen, B., Chen, J., & Özsomer, A. (2021). Performance consequences of marketing standardization/adaptation: A systematic literature review and future research agenda. *Journal of Business Research*, *125*(January), 416–435. https://doi.org/10.1016/j.jbusres.2020.12.023

Marchegiani, L. (2017). From Mecenatism to crowdfunding: Engagement and identification in cultural-creative projects. *Journal of Heritage Tourism*, *13*(2), 143–151. https://doi.org/10.1080/1743873X.2017.1337777

Mofokeng, N. E. M., & Matima, T. K. (2018). Future tourism trends: Utilizing non-fungible tokens to aid wildlife conservation. *African Journal of Hospitality, Tourism and Leisure*, *7*(4), 1–20.

Nam, K., Dutt, C. S., Chathoth, P., & Khan, M. S. (2021). Blockchain technology for smart city and smart tourism: Latest trends and challenges. *Asia Pacific Journal of Tourism Research*, *26*(4), 454–468. https://doi.org/10.1080/10941665.2019.1585376

Nuryyev, G., Wang, Y. P., Achyldurdyyeva, J., Jaw, B. S., Yeh, Y. S., Lin, H. T., & Wu, L. F. (2020). Blockchain technology adoption behavior and sustainability of the business in tourism and hospitality SMEs: An empirical study. *Sustainability (Switzerland)*, *12*(3). https://doi.org/10.3390/su12031256

Önder, I., & Gunter, U. (2022). Blockchain: Is it the future for the tourism and hospitality industry?. *Tourism Economics*, *28*(2), 291–299. https://doi.org/10.1177/1354816620961707

Özgit, H., & Adalıer, A. (2022). Can blockchain technology help small islands achieve sustainable tourism? A perspective on North Cyprus. *Worldwide Hospitality and Tourism Themes*, *14*(4), 374–383. https://doi.org/10.1108/WHATT-03-2022-0037

Ozturk, A. B., Bilgihan, A., Salehi-Esfahani, S., & Hua, N. (2017). Understanding the mobile payment technology acceptance based on valence theory: A case of restaurant transactions. *International Journal of Contemporary Hospitality Management*, *29*(8), 2027–2049. https://doi.org/10.1108/IJCHM-04-2016-0192

Paul, J., Khatri, P., & Duggal, H. K. (2023). Frameworks for developing impactful systematic literature reviews and theory building : What, Why and How ?. *Journal of Decision Systems*. https://doi.org/10.1080/12460125.2023.2197700

Paul, J., & Rosado-Serrano, A. (2019). Gradual internationalization vs born-global/International new venture models: A review and research agenda. *International Marketing Review*, *36*(6), 830–858. https://doi.org/10.1108/IMR-10-2018-0280

Peterson, J., Wilson, T. F., Watt, M. H., Gruhl, J., Davis, S., Olsen, J., Parsons, M. W., Kann, B. H., Swire-Thompson, B., Fagerlin, A., Warner, E. L., King, A. J., Chino, F., & Johnson, S. B. (2023, January). International medical tourism of US cancer patients for alternative cancer treatments: Financial, demographic, and clinical profiles of online crowdfunding campaigns. *Cancer Medicine*, 8871–8879. https://doi.org/10.1002/cam4.5636

Radic, A., Quan, W., Ariza-Montes, A., Lee, J. S., & Han, H. (2022a). You can't hold the tide with a broom: Cryptocurrency payments and tourism in South Korea and China. *Tourism Management Perspectives*, *43*(August), 101000. https://doi.org/10.1016/j.tmp.2022.101000

Radic, A., Quan, W., Koo, B., Chua, B. L., Kim, J. J., & Han, H. (2022b). Central bank digital currency as a payment method for tourists: Application of the theory of planned behavior to digital Yuan/Won/Dollar choice. *Journal of Travel & Tourism Marketing*, *39*(2), 152–172. https://doi.org/10.1080/10548408.2022.2061677

Riley-Huff, D. A., Herrera, K., Ivey, S., & Harry, T. (2016). Crowdfunding in libraries, archives and museums. *Bottom Line*, *29*(2), 67–85. https://doi.org/10.1108/BL-03-2016-0014

Roesch-McNally, G. E., & Rabotyagov, S. S. (2016). Paying for forest ecosystem services: Voluntary versus mandatory payments. *Environmental Management*, *57*(3), 585–600. https://doi.org/10.1007/s00267-015-0641-7

Salem, I. E., Elkhwesky, Z., Baber, H., & Radwan, M. (2022). Hotel resuscitation by reward-based crowdfunding: A critical review and moderated mediation model. *Tourism Management Perspectives*, *43*(May), 100986. https://doi.org/10.1016/j.tmp.2022.100986

San Martín, H., Hernández, B., & Herrero, Á. (2021). Social consciousness and perceived risk as drivers of crowdfunding as a socially responsible investment in tourism. *Journal of Travel Research*, *60*(1), 16–30. https://doi.org/10.1177/0047287519896017

Sandesh, S. P., Sreejesh, S., & Paul, J. (2023). Key account management in B2B marketing: A systematic literature review and research agenda. *Journal of Business Research*, *156*(November 2022), 113541. https://doi.org/10.1016/j.jbusres.2022.113541

Schröder, K., Tiberius, V., Bouncken, R. B., & Kraus, S. (2021). Strategic entrepreneurship: Mapping a research field. *International Journal of Entrepreneurial Behaviour & Research*, *27*(3), 753–776. https://doi.org/10.1108/IJEBR-11-2020-0798

Simeoni, F., & De Crescenzo, V. (2018). Ecomuseums (on clean energy), cycle tourism and civic crowdfunding: A new match for sustainability?. *Sustainability (Switzerland)*, *10*(3). https://doi.org/10.3390/su10030817

Singh, S. (2017a). Car sharing for sustainable tourism. *Tourism Recreation Research*, *42*(4), 540–545. https://doi.org/10.1080/02508281.2017.1367897

Singh, S. (2017b). Mobile money for promoting conservation and community-based tourism and ecotourism in underdeveloped regions. *Tourism Recreation Research*, *42*(1), 108–112. https://doi.org/10.1080/02508281.2016.1251011

Srivastava, E., Sivakumaran, B., Maheswarappa, S. S., & Paul, J. (2022). Nostalgia: A review, propositions, and future research agenda. *Journal of Advertising*, *52*(4), 1–20. https://doi.org/10.1080/00913367.2022.2101036

Sun, S., Law, R., Schuckert, M., & Hyun, S. S. (2022). Impacts of mobile payment-related attributes on consumers' repurchase intention. *International Journal of Tourism Research*, *24*(1), 44–57. https://doi.org/10.1002/jtr.2481

Sun, S., Law, R., & Zhong, L. (2021). Mobile payment failure during travel. *Journal of China Tourism Research*, *17*(1), 73–89. https://doi.org/10.1080/19388160.2019.1702605

Tham, A., & Sigala, M. (2020). Road block(chain): Bit(coin)s for tourism sustainable development goals?. *Journal of Hospitality and Tourism Technology*, *11*(2), 203–222. https://doi.org/10.1108/JHTT-05-2019-0069

Treiblmaier, H. (2021). The token economy as a key driver for tourism: Entering the next phase of blockchain research. *Annals of Tourism Research*, *91*, 103177. https://doi.org/10.1016/j.annals.2021.103177

Treiblmaier, H., Leung, D., Kwok, A. O. J., & Tham, A. (2021). Cryptocurrency adoption in travel and tourism–an exploratory study of Asia Pacific travellers. *Current Issues in Tourism*, *24*(22), 3165–3181. https://doi.org/10.1080/13683500.2020.1863928

Tyan, I., Guevara-Plaza, A., & Yagüe, M. I. (2021). The benefits of blockchain technology for medical tourism. *Sustainability (Switzerland)*, *13*(22). https://doi.org/10.3390/su132212448

Uwamariya, M., Cremer, S., & Loebbecke, C. (2022). Mobile payment enhancing tourism in emerging markets: A qualitative study among small and medium-sized enterprises (SMEs) in Rwanda's tourism sector. *Journal of African Business*, *23*(2), 480–496. https://doi.org/10.1080/15228916.2021.1874782

Vassell, A., Crooks, V. A., & Snyder, J. (2021). What was lost, missing, sought and hoped for: Qualitatively exploring medical crowdfunding campaign narratives for Lyme disease. *Health (United Kingdom)*, *25*(6), 707–721. https://doi.org/10.1177/1363459320912808

Wakefield, S., Molinari, S., & Grove, K. (2022). Crypto-urban statecraft: Post-pandemic urban governance experiments in Miami. *Urban Geography*, *44*(8), 1–9. https://doi.org/10.1080/02723638.2022.2125664

Wang, R., & Peters, M. (2023). Consumer intention to switch from cash to mobile payment in restaurants during and after pandemic. *Journal of Quality Assurance in Hospitality & Tourism*, *26*(1), 1–34. https://doi.org/10.1080/1528008X.2023.2201696

WorldBank. (2020). *The global covid-19 FinTech market rapid assessment study* (pp. 28–32). World Economic Forum. http://www3.weforum.org/docs/WEF_The_Global_Covid19_FinTech_Market_Rapid_Assessment_Study_2020.pdf

Wu, P. C., Liu, H. Y., Liu, S. Y., & Hsiao, J. M. (2021). Can financial technology development change the causality between tourism and economic growth?. *Current Issues in Tourism*, *24*(11), 1613–1630. https://doi.org/10.1080/13683500.2020.1828307

Xu, P., Kim, C. S., Bai, B., & Kim, P. B. (2023). Determinants of Chinese travellers' use of mobile payment applications when staying at an overseas hotel. *Journal of Quality Assurance in Hospitality & Tourism*, *26*(1), 1–21. https://doi.org/10.1080/1528008X.2023.2196036

Yang, Y., & Koh, Y. (2022). Is restaurant crowdfunding immune to the COVID-19 pandemic?. *International Journal of Contemporary Hospitality Management*, *34*(4), 1353–1373. https://doi.org/10.1108/IJCHM-06-2021-0817

Yousaf, I., Abrar, A., & Goodell, J. W. (2023). Connectedness between travel & tourism tokens, tourism equity, and other assets. *Finance Research Letters*, *53* (October 2022), 103595. https://doi.org/10.1016/j.frl.2022.103595

Appendix A: Code Numbers for Selected Articles According to Year of Publication

Code and Article Details	Code and Article Details	Code and Article Details	Code and Article Details
[1] Roesch-McNally and Rabotyagov (2016)	[19] Bhatia and Birchley (2020)	[37] Sun et al. (2021)	[55] Karim et al. (2022)
[2] Makki et al. (2016)	[20] M. J. Kim and Hall (2020a)	[38] Tyan et al. (2021)	[56] Gamage et al. (2022)
[3] Riley-Huff et al. (2016)	[21] Nuryyev et al. (2020)	[39] San Martín et al. (2021)	[57] Radic, Quan, Ariza-Montes, et al. (2022)
[4] Ozturk et al. (2017)	[22] Kim and Chang (2020)	[40] M. J. Kim and Petrick (2021)	[58] Hameed et al. (2022)
[5] Marchegiani (2017)	[23] M. J. Kim, Bonn, and Lee (2020)	[41] Chang et al., (2022)	[59] Önder and Gunter (2022)
[6] Singh (2017a)	[24] (Baig & Ali, 2020)	[42] Salem et al. (2022)	[60] Radic, Quan, Koo, et al. (2022)
[7] Singh (2017b)	[25] M. J. Kim, Hall, and Kim (2020)	[43] Yang and Koh (2022)	[61] Balasubramanian et al. (2022)
[8] Camilleri (2018)	[26] Lew et al. (2020)	[44] Kakinuma (2022)	[62] De Crescenzo et al. (2022)
[9] Mofokeng and Matima (2018)	[27] Chew et al. (2020)	[45] Dadkhah et al. (2022)	[63] Abdullah et al. (2023)
[10] Di Pietro et al. (2018)	[28] Coutrot et al. (2020)	[46] Özgit and Adalıer (2022)	[64] Yousaf et al. (2023)

(Continued)

Code and Article Details	Code and Article Details	Code and Article Details	Code and Article Details
[11] Simeoni and De Crescenzo (2018)	[29] Treiblmaier (2021)	[47] Adeleye et al. (2023)	[65] Peterson et al. (2023)
[12] Howson et al. (2019)	[30] Khanra et al. (2021)	[48] Bulut (2022)	[66] Wang and Peters (2023)
[13] Kwok and Koh (2019)	[31] Cheng et al. (2021)	[49] J. J. Kim et al. (2022)	[67] Xu et al. (2023)
[14] M. J. Kim and Hall (2019)	[32] Vassell et al. (2021)	[50] Cheung et al. (2022)	[68] Kim (2023)
[15] Cavalcanti Junqueira and Discua Cruz (2019)	[33] Nam et al. (2021)	[51] Wakefield et al. (2022)	[69] J. J. Kim et al. (2023)
[16] Bagheri et al. (2020)	[34] Wu et al. (2021)	[52] Sun et al. (2022)	
[17] M. J. Kim and Hall (2020b)	[35] Treiblmaier et al. (2021)	[53] Uwamariya et al. (2022)	
[18] Tham and Sigala (2020)	[36] (Di Carlo et al., 2021)	[54] Ferreira et al. (2022)	

Chapter 4

The Impact of AI on Customer Experience in the Tourism and Hospitality Industry: Perspectives from Developing Market Destinations

Desmond Tutu Ayentimi[a], *Ricky Yao Nutsugbodo*[b] *and Anna Arthur-Amissah*

[a]University of Tasmania, Australia
[b]University of Energy And Natural Resources, Ghana

Abstract

Artificial Intelligence (AI) is transforming the tourism and hospitality industry's value chain. Its contribution to the industry is evidenced in innovative tools and robots – tech-based applications and services used for improving customer service quality and customer service experience. Generally, the acceptance and adoption of AI in developing hospitality and tourism market destinations mostly found in Africa have been progressively slow, owing to underlying constraints impacting the deployment of AI–powered capabilities. Even though the awareness of AI adoption is widespread and increasing, little attention is paid to AI utilisation in the industry, particularly in developing market destinations. This chapter highlights the impact of AI-powered technologies on customer service experience. It provides an important lens and new insight into how tourism and hospitality practitioners can embrace AI-powered technologies in customer service delivery.

Keywords: Artificial Intelligence; hospitality and tourism; customer experience; technology; robots

Artificial Intelligence in Hospitality and Tourism in Africa, 65–79

doi:10.1108/978-1-80686-169-920261004

Introduction

The notion of the global economic divide, which is advanced economies on the one hand and developing economies on the other, can be extended to the hospitality and tourism industry. Primarily, destinations in developed countries are more advanced in technology adoption to deliver outstanding customer service than markets that are less developed and characterised by several customer service challenges combined with low technology utilisation in customer service delivery (Limna, 2023). Generally, destinations in developing countries are characterised mainly by poor communication and information dissemination, prolonged lead time and transaction errors (Ayentimi, 2020). Poor customer service can be attributed to several reasons, including inadequate training of workers, long hours of work with no corresponding remuneration, inadequate employee motivation initiatives and inadequate infrastructure to support technology adoption in customer service delivery (Ayentimi, 2020). However, it is important to note that much is expected within the hospitality and tourism industry, as a single service encounter can have severe consequences. The effort it takes to orchestrate a customer experience can very easily be tainted due to service providers' actions and inactions. Indeed, Artificial Intelligence (AI)-powered technologies may offer new opportunities to address many customer service challenges in developing hospitality and tourism destinations.

There is a surge in digital transformation across every sector and industry, with AI-powered technologies transforming business processes and helping to deliver better customer service experiences. Over the last decade, different economic sectors, including the hospitality and tourism sectors, have come to recognise and adopt AI-powered technologies in various aspects of the value chain (Buhalis et al., 2024; Huang & Rust, 2018). In the hospitality and tourism sector, digital transformation has benefited various aspects of the value chain. Notable among them are smart technologies such as chatbots and content generators to assist in product personalisation for a better customer experience, as well as the introduction of humanoid robots to provide guests with information about hotel services and robotic virtual agents to offer information and assistance to tourists (Ben Saad, 2024; Tussyadiah & Miller, 2019).

There is also the ambient intelligence system, where hotel rooms are designed to adapt automatically to things like temperature and light based on the user's feelings, motions or activities without specific requirements by users. Interestingly, the tourist can also be directed through ambient intelligence or recommender systems based on acquired data from the tourist's internet activity and user profile, from which patterns are recognised to suggest interest for the tourist (Basiri et al., 2018; Song & He, 2023). In addition, the recommender systems are equipped to give best-fit options to tourists with the dense available options to customers (Ricci et al., 2015). Essentially, AI-powered technologies support and foster personalisation and customisation while eliminating prolonged service processes and possible human errors due to the advantage of less effort required to communicate with these systems. Most importantly, there is ease in decision-making, an experience akin to human interaction, which ultimately provides a better customer experience (Tussyadiah & Miller, 2019).

Over the last decade, AI-powered technology applications in the hospitality industry have highlighted its strategic role in digital transformation, from manual operations to digitalisation and automation for enhanced operational efficiency while delivering a better customer experience. The benefits of AI adoption range from cost reduction, improved customer experience and achieving and sustaining competitive advantage (Belanche et al., 2019). Given that the hospitality industry essentially provides services and experiences for people away from the comfort of familiar environments, the strategy for meeting such customer expectations requires some level of efficiency and accuracy. AI adoption is therefore supporting service automation to enhance visitors' experiences. For example, smart tools and robot-based applications such as chatbots allow customer interactions in booking and reception roles. Global distribution systems for booking and reservation allow guests to choose services they require from a service provider (Bulchand-Gidumal, 2022). Likewise, service robots communicate with humans in rendering service akin to human labour by mimicking behavioural norms expected by humans. For tourists, personal travel assistants' applications, language translation applications, voice recognition and recommender systems support travelling convenience and enhance their travel experiences (Bulchand-Gidumal, 2022).

AI adoption holds several advantages over human labour, with interesting predictions suggesting that 25% of labour-intensive tasks in the hospitality industry will be replaced and performed by AI-powered technologies in the next decade (Nam et al., 2021). Indeed, there are already increasing levels of anxiety and uneasiness among critics and the public that AI is fast overtaking the roles of humans in almost every area of the economy and society. For example, service robots have been projected to take over the hotel workforce soon, considering the successes in AI development and adoption in the industry (Nam et al., 2021; Zalama et al., 2014). This shift towards digital transformation is evident and beneficial from the perspective of both the service provider and the consumer. AI adoption in the hospitality industry is timely given the surge in service personalisation, which is becoming necessary and not business as usual. Customers can co-construct their service experience (Lei et al., 2022; McColl-Kennedy et al., 2015). For example, the client journey with a hotel will be more interactive, personalised and memorable (Nam et al., 2021).

Although the adoption of AI in hospitality and tourism operations has received considerable attention in developed hospitality and tourism market destinations, little recognition has been given to developing market destinations, particularly those located in sub-Saharan Africa (SSA), and how they can benefit from AI-powered technologies to address the many customer service challenges. Evidence suggests that hospitality firms, especially hotels that have incorporated emerging high-tech systems into their operations, have, on average, 70% of their guests' requests handled without human involvement (He, 2018). This chapter offers an important lens and new insight by exploring AI adoption and how AI-powered technologies can help enhance the customer service experience in developing hospitality and tourism market destinations. This resonates with the assertion put forward by Wixom and Todd (2005) that, though appreciating AI acceptability, it delivers reliable projections of technology utilisation; it is fundamental to concentrate on the influence of the technology on customer experience. The ability to use AI-powered technologies to enhance customer experience underscores the value of technology in delivering customer service. It is important to acknowledge that even though AI adoption offers a wide range of prospects for developing market destinations, the challenge of finding the ideal balance between technology and human interaction remains.

The Notion of Customer Experience

Customer experience represents an individual's overall impression of a service provider based on his/her encounter with and opinions about the service provider's brand (Bolton et al., 2014). Customer experience reflects every stage of the customer's interaction with a service provider, ranging from pre-consumption to consumption and post-consumption (Kandampully & Solnet, 2015). This implies that the outcome of a service encounter is greatly influenced by this exchange between a customer and a service provider. Limna (2023) asserts that incorporating AI gives a positive view of customer experience while eliminating the majority of human interaction. According to Hoyer et al. (2020), every service exchange results in a customer experience, regardless of the form or condition of the transaction. Prior literature provides an interesting outline and categories of the multidimensional nature of the total customer experience (McColl-Kennedy et al., 2015; Tung & Au, 2018). These include the sensory element representing what people experience through their senses, encompassing lighting, layout, signage and technology. It further incorporates related features such as a friendly user interface. The emotional dimension of the customer service experience deals with how people feel about a service. This element can be pleasant or negative, such as joy, surprise, regret, wrath or indignation, because of the complicated nature of people's emotions (Bolton et al., 2014). The cognitive dimension emphasises what people think about the service – perception, memory and abstract thinking (Bolton et al., 2014). The physical dimension recognises how people interact, socialise and share. Remarkably, customer service experience can also be influenced by other people, such as family, friends and a customer's more expansive social network (Ameen et al., 2021). AI makes it possible for people to operate more intelligently, which improves corporate outcomes. It also develops new skills and talents of service providers, making services memorable for customers (Ivanov & Webster, 2019; Ruel & Njoku, 2021). Importantly, a customer is more likely to become engrossed with a company's service if they have a memorable, valuable and participatory experience with that company (Hayes & MacLeod, 2016).

The idea of customer experience has become a key strategic tool for achieving competitive advantage and sustaining a firm's long-term competitiveness. This is why businesses strongly build capabilities such as adopting AI to generate and deliver authentic customer experiences through every episode and touchpoint of their customer interaction (Kandampully et al., 2018). Continuous delivery of exceptional client value is essential to survive the competition in the hotel industry, requiring service providers to be precise and accurate in service delivery (Chao et al., 2021).

Indeed, the judgement a customer will pass about the quality of a service is dependent on what measurement and value they attach to the service delivered. Several factors represent the basis for measuring the value of quality for the ultimate customer experience – atmospherics such as the aesthetics, lighting, ambience and servicescape (Ryu & Jang, 2008). Servicescapes underscore the effect of the physical environment, such as the layout of the service area, coupled with the service processes (Vaisanen et al., 2023). Servicescapes contribute both negatively and positively to the formation of customers' impressions and directly have a positive influence on customers' perceptions (Lugosi et al., 2023). According to Ritchie and Hudson (2009), atmospheric stimuli, which include the physical environment and human interaction elements, are often at the heart of consumer experience. For example, during a hotel visit, guests are emotionally and personally engaged in memorable experiences that affect their decision to make a future purchase and spread the word to others (Cetin & Dincer, 2014). Even though for customers to have pleasant service experiences, there should be a balance between service quality and price, the quality of staff, procedures and tangible evidence, and how they are utilised also play a role in creating diners' eating experiences (Chao et al., 2021).

Conceptually, customer experience can be delivered via many interactions and relationships throughout the customer's purchase and consumption journey. Since services are intangible, the physical environment and social interactions have a greater role in hospitality than product-based sectors (Lugosi et al., 2023). Of particular importance is the fact that in the hospitality and tourism business, customers buy not only products but also experiences. For a tourist, experience is the primary outcome after a leisure trip, and for the hotel guest, a clean, secure and comfortable bed or the attractive hotel environment remains important. Therefore, if the quality of service with all its measurement scales is not up to the customer's expectations, then the experience will not be up to par. Importantly, if firms can meet customers' service quality measurement and provide them with a superior customer experience, it opens a door to gaining customer loyalty (Klaus & Maklan, 2011; Singh et al., 2023).

In summary, customer experience involves more than just what customers get from their primary food, beverage, accommodation and transportation requests. To provide a quality service experience to customers, other features that augment the primary desires that make up the totality of quality needs must be present. For example, websites and their design, online and offline technological features for guests and firm interactions, facility designs and interactions with service personnel and other customers are essential to enhance the customer experience (Kandampully et al., 2018; Singh et al., 2023). Within this context, this chapter seeks to examine how developing market destinations can leverage AI-powered technologies to improve customer service experience. The next section outlines how AI-powered technologies are deployed to improve customer experience in the hospitality and tourism industry.

The Deployment of AI-Powered Technologies to Enhance Customer Experience

AI is powered to act as a human would in performing tasks, communication and learning (Hasan et al., 2021). AI-powered technologies deployed in the hospitality and tourism industry can be categorised into intelligent devices, self-service technologies, chatbots and service robots, and each has a different impact on customer experience.

Intelligent Devices

The hospitality industry, just like any service-based industry, attaches importance to the interaction between guests and employees so that guests' feelings may be directed based on the behaviour of employees (Cetin & Walls, 2016; Han & Back, 2007). The tourist or the hotel guest must be involved emotionally and functionally in the experience-creating process (Harkison, 2017). This draws attention to the fact that this service industry has inseparability as a characteristic, where service production and consumption happen in situ and require that the customer and the service provider be present for the service to happen (Vaisanen et al., 2023). Within the experience-creating process, one cannot downplay the critical role of employees as a component of a guest experience (Harkison, 2017). Interestingly, the visibility of AI-powered technologies' adoption and engagement in the industry can be seen in voice-activated assistants and AI-powered E-travel agents that manage travel plans, car rentals and hotel bookings (Nguyen et al., 2021). Other AI-powered service systems include online check-in, self-check-in kiosks in hotels and airports, automated border control gates with biometric passport/ID card readers and mobile boarding passes for airports. Restaurants also feature conveyor belts for food delivery and food and beverage vending machines (Kiliçhan & Yilmaz, 2020). What this means for customer experience is that customers benefit from a high level of service accuracy, consistent quality and service performance that may not be guaranteed by only human engagement in the service delivery. This implies that deploying AI-powered technologies in service delivery potentially guarantees consistent performance and service quality (Prentice & Nguyen, 2020).

A typical characteristic of hospitality service delivery is that customer experiences are created at the point of interaction between the customer and the service provider. Also, during this point of encounter, emotional connections are made between the two communicating parties. This implies that experiences are co-constructed between the customer and the service provider (Harkison, 2017). Morgan (2006) acknowledges the importance of training hospitality professionals to visualise customers' requests and better cater to them, but there are limitations associated with human visualisation of customers' requests. However, services offered by AI-powered technologies are made possible through learning from available data and pattern identification, by which decisions are made through interaction with the guest who requires the service (Nguyen et al., 2021).

The information the customer feeds to the service system is likely high quality, unlike human interaction, where employees may have to be trained to predict customers' behaviour (Morgan, 2006). Users perceive the quality of AI-powered technologies by the quality of response or information the customer requires and the service system provides (Singh & Singh, 2024; Wixom & Todd, 2005). For instance, to satisfy client needs, AI-powered e-travel agents that assist with managing trip arrangements, renting vehicles and booking hotels present up-to-date and accurate information compared to human-managed record systems. Essentially, AI-powered tools and systems are purposefully designed to create a seamless experience for guests with a non-interruptive and easy flow of interaction for the experience to be attained and appreciated (Nguyen et al., 2021). The use of AI service systems in service delivery can generate enjoyment and attachment because when a business offers a worthwhile, interactive and memorable experience to the customer, it generates a state of immersion and attachment towards the business (Hayes & MacLeod, 2016). Indeed, customer flow is influenced by service system design, which, in turn, impacts positive emotions, user satisfaction and purchase intention (Wu & Liang, 2011).

Chatbots

A chatbot is an AI-powered technology designed to provide self-service to customers and serve as a virtual assistant or virtual agent (Melián-González et al., 2019). An important characteristic of service is variability, which concerns the difficulty in standardising service production and performance because of factors such as the service provider's knowledge, mood, time, the customer and the environment (Moeller, 2010). Given that the quality of service will depend on who is providing it and when and where it is delivered, it may be challenging to rely on humans to provide consistency in the service delivered. For example, with the seasonal nature of the hospitality industry, when there is a smaller number of customers during off-peak seasons, the person delivering the service may be more specific and polite. However, delivering services to many customers during peak seasons means service providers will likely be busy and might lose some service to customers or may be inconsistent with their service. In addition, while human labour may be required to work within a particular number of hours per week, AI-powered applications can operate 24/7. In the area of multitasking, human beings can only do so much. However, AI-powered systems such as chatbots can handle giving service to a large customer base all at once over web pages and mobile applications of customers and featuring self-service functions to assist customers (Melián-González et al., 2019).

Service Robots/Robotic Technologies

Robots and robot-based technologies have seen a rise in usage and are becoming the most common applications in the hospitality industry (Kiliçhan & Yilmaz, 2020). Notable among them are robot concierges, robot bellboys, delivery robots, robot receptionists, drones and robot guides (Davis, 2016; Kiliçhan & Yilmaz, 2020). AI-powered technologies are more efficient in providing accurate, flexible, personalised and reliable service that will engage and elevate all the elements of customer experience: cognitive, emotional, physical, social and extraordinary experiences (West et al., 2018). Customer experiences with robots may differ from those of other AI-powered technologies because of how robots may be designed to appear and how customers can relate to them. Robots may need to be designed to have human features, enabling customers to see robots as active physical players in the service encounter (Bulchand-Gidumal, 2022). Where customers can equate the service, they are likely to get from humans to humanoid robots, the emotional connection obtained from human-to-human interaction is also obtained in human-to-humanoid robot interaction. This potentially affects the emotional and sensory dimensions of customer experience. Moreover, Tung and Au (2018) contend that humans have strong sensory abilities that enable them to see and understand events as they happen and react to them appropriately. Interestingly, robotics being used in hospitality and tourism service delivery has the potential to offer maximum customer experience as some robots are designed to possess human qualities such as the ability to detect and understand a customer's gestures and discern social cues in order to connect emotionally to customers (Weiss et al., 2009).

Key Concerns of AI-Powered Technologies in the Hospitality and Tourism Industry

Interestingly, AI-powered technologies are helping the hospitality and tourism industry to redefine the customer service experience. Although advancing AI adoption in the hospitality industry has proven valuable in enhancing customer service experience, specific macro (general business environment) and micro (firm-level) challenges remain, including poor ICT infrastructure, inadequate technological skill and know-how, and inadequate financial resources for the development and use of AI-powered technologies. These macro-level and micro-level challenges affect user acceptability, AI usefulness and user experience. In this section, we highlight three key considerations likely to undermine the leveraging of AI-powered technologies in enhancing customer experience in the hospitality and tourism industry in developing market destinations. These are (i) user acceptability, (ii) AI usefulness and (iii) user experience.

User Acceptability

Consumer behaviour theorists have found that willingness or individual behavioural intention precedes actual behaviour to act (Cronan et al., 2018). Studies show that challenges are found in the predictors of AI technology acceptance behaviour (Gursoy et al., 2019). For instance, technology ease, individual attitudes and user self-efficacy are important variables in correlating customers' acceptance of technology (Lin et al., 2019). Other studies have found perceived usefulness, appearance, quality features, capabilities and customers' expectations (Taherdoost, 2018; Weiss et al., 2009) as important predictors of technology and AI acceptability. Where a customer perceives an AI device to help fulfil his/her needs and wants, it is easier for them to accommodate its use to meet those needs. Customers are comfortable with familiarity and would mostly turn towards services that are familiar to meet their needs. Additionally, customers exhibit considerable levels of hedonic benefit expectancies in terms of memorable experiences (Lin et al., 2019). Due to the traditional notion of human touch required for optimum service experience in the hospitality industry, customers will evaluate AI by comparing performances between AI and humans (Osei et al., 2020). By this assertion, customers are likely to place importance on evaluating AI and associated technologies compared to the services that human employees are expected to offer (Chi et al., 2020). Users' negative attitudes and perceptions towards AI devices, systems and technologies may be attributed to their novelty and unfamiliarity with such technology (Tussyadiah & Miller, 2019), potentially undermining user acceptability.

AI Usefulness

According to Bowen and Morosan (2018), the main drivers of AI adoption are perceived usefulness and performance. For technology to be considered useable, it must be effective, efficient, easy to learn and use, flexible and robust (Dautenhan, 1998). AI technology influence can, however, trigger loss of customers, a notion attributed to the fact that human employees are usually at the core of hospitality services. Therefore, human-to-human encounters create emotional connections and further create some unique experiences (Harkison, 2017). Moreover, Morgan (2006) and Sarrab et al. (2016) asserted that employees can be trained to predict customers' behaviour. If a customer's behaviour is predicted to offer better service flexibility, it triggers a feeling of contentment and uplifts the customer's experience. Further to the above assertion, emotions have been found to play a significant role in predicting human technology use (Nafees & Sujood, 2024; Weiss et al., 2009). For the customer to have good experiences, AI service systems such as robots should have human features that can read and predict human emotions and characteristics to actively respond to people's affection in interaction to give service to the customer (Stock & Merkle, 2017). The absence of such characteristics will potentially undermine its effectiveness in delivering a superior customer experience.

Significantly, the judgement of AI adoption would be based on user-friendliness or ease of use, fulfilling the guest's request with accurate information, and flexibility in adjusting where necessary (Weiss et al., 2009). Users tend to experience satisfaction when their encounter with technology meets their expectations. However, discomfort from complicated systems with too much navigation creates a sense of insecurity and anxiety in the customer, thereby marring the experience for the customer. Gursoy et al. (2019) noted that anxiety from the use of unfamiliar technologies reduces customers' trust and acceptance. For example, when customer judges an AI service system to be reliable and supportive, their sense of emotions, cognition, social, physical and sensory elements are mobilised and create a good experience for them (Gursoy et al., 2019).

User Experience

Alben (1996) described user experience as how users engage with interactive products and how well such products fulfil their needs across an experiential context. User experiences differ across various types of technology. Individual experiences with advanced technologies such as robots may differ from their experiences with daily technological systems, gadgets and applications due to the operating characteristics of each technology (Bulchand-Gidumal, 2022). For example, a tourist may be conversant with navigation systems such as GPS on their phones but may find it difficult and uncomfortable to use the self-check-in kiosk at the hotel or to interact with a robot that is going to take their order. Systems and innovations that are new to the customer tend to create anxiety in the customer and further discourage them from using them (Gursoy et al., 2019). Knowing the technology's navigation adds to the service's seamlessness and enhances customer experience. For instance, tourists can find their way through new environments with the aid of technologies they can use, thereby reducing the sense of anxiety and fear of the unknown (Bulchand-Gidumal, 2022).

AI innovations must come with design guidance to improve human interaction with that technology to enhance customer experience. Apart from the design guideline, considerations of human-oriented perception and embodiment to evaluate user experience are also essential. Embodiment describes the lifelike design and characteristics of AI innovations such as robots (Weiss et al., 2009). This helps users to relate to and interact with robots as active participants in the service process (Bulchand-Gidumal, 2022). Robots with human-oriented perception may recognise and comprehend events as they happen, as well as react to user commands (Tung & Au, 2018). This encourages meaningful interactions through familiarity and reduces anxiety borne by novelty, and the user's feelings are turned into delightful ones that create satisfaction in the customer experience.

Conclusion

The benefits of AI adoption span from reducing work tasks, simplifying work tasks, providing accurate information and making service processes easier for both the consumer and the service provider. Customers can make bookings and hotel reservations, choose destinations accurately and check in and check out without necessarily having face-to-face interaction with the service provider, all with the help of intelligent systems, robots and chatbots (Prentice & Nguyen, 2020). The hospitality industry is embracing these technologies to give the ultimate service to its clientele and stay ahead of the competition. However, how businesses will leverage AI to enhance the customer experience in the industry now and in the future remains a challenge in the case of developing market destinations. Interestingly, multinational hotel chains are increasingly entering into developing markets through franchises and chains. Evidence shows that developed hospitality and tourism destination markets use more advanced technologies than developing market destinations in the hotel sector (Ezzaouia & Bulchand-Gidumal, 2020). Most of these hotel chains come from developed economies, so their entry into developing market destinations can offer high-level technological capabilities primarily associated with such multinational hotels' operations.

Customers like to identify with a brand because of what it stands for, and businesses that incorporate technology into their operations can benefit from brand attractiveness (Buhalis, 2020). For the customer, using technology could make a brand attractive, which, in turn, drives them to identify with the brand. Brand identification is developed when the customer has a good experience with that brand (Rahman, 2014). While visitors become more technology savvy daily, hotels must likewise modernise through novel service delivery methods. AI service systems integrated and embedded into existing applications, such as personalisation systems, language translation applications and voice assistants, will help create convenience for the customer and allow interactions with customers for a better customer experience.

References

Alben, L. (1996). Defining the criteria for effective interaction design. *Interactions, 3* (3), 11–15.

Ameen, N., Tarhini, A., Reppel, A., & Anand, A. (2021). Customer experiences in the age of artificial intelligence. *Computers in Human Behavior, 114*, 106548.

Ayentimi, D. T. (2020). Who is a customer? In R. E. Hinson, O. Adeola, T. Lituchy, & A. F. O. Amartey (Eds.), *Customer service management: A strategic and operational perspective* (pp. 11–22). Routledge.

Basiri, A., Amirian, P., Winstanley, A., & Moore, T. (2018). Making tourist guidance systems more intelligent, adaptive and personalised using crowd-sourced movement data. *Journal of Ambient Intelligence and Humanized Computing, 9*(2), 413–427.

Belanche, D., Casalo, L. V., Flavian, C., & Schepers, J. (2019). Service robot implementation: A theoretical framework and research agenda. *Service Industries Journal, 40*(3–4), 203–225.

Ben Saad, S. (2024). The digital revolution in the tourism industry: Role of anthropomorphic virtual agent in digitalized hotel service. *International Journal of Contemporary Hospitality Management, 36*(11), 3751–3773.

Bolton, R. N., Gustafsson, A., McColl-Kennedy, J. R., Sirianni, N. J., & Tse, D. K. (2014). Small details that make big differences: A radical approach to consumption experience as a firm's differentiating strategy. *Journal of Service Management, 25*(2), 253–274.

Bowen, J., & Morosan, C. (2018). Beware, hospitality industry: The robots are coming. *Worldwide Hospitality and Tourism Themes, 10*(6), 726–733.

Buhalis, D. (2020). Technology in tourism-from information communication technologies to e-tourism and smart tourism towards ambient intelligence tourism: A perspective article. *Tourism Review*, *75*(1), 267–272.

Buhalis, D., Efthymiou, L., Uzunboylu, N., & Thrassou, A. (2024). Charting the progress of technology adoption in tourism and hospitality in the era of industry 4.0. *EuroMed Journal of Business*, *19*(1), 1–20.

Bulchand-Gidumal, J. (2022). Impact of artificial intelligence in travel, tourism, and hospitality. In *Handbook of e-Tourism* (pp. 1943–1962). Springer International Publishing.

Cetin, G., & Dincer, F. I. (2014). Influence of customer experience on loyalty and word-of-mouth in hospitality operations. *Anatolia*, *25*(2), 181–194.

Cetin, G., & Walls, A. (2016). Understanding the customer experiences from the perspective of guests and hotel managers: Empirical findings from luxury hotels in Istanbul, Turkey. *Journal of Hospitality Marketing & Management*, *25*(4), 395–424.

Chao, R.-F., Fu, Y., & Liang, C.-H. (2021). Influence of servicescape stimuli on word-of-mouth intentions: An integrated model to indigenous restaurants. *International Journal of Hospitality Management*, *96*, 102978.

Chi, O. H., Denton, G., & Gursoy, D. (2020). Artificially intelligent device use in service delivery: A systematic review, synthesis and research agenda. *Journal of Hospitality Marketing & Management*, *29*(7), 757–786.

Cronan, T. P., Mullins, J. K., & Douglas, D. E. (2018). Further understanding factors that explain freshman business students' academic integrity intention and behaviour: Plagiarism and sharing homework. *Journal of Business Ethics*, *147*(1), 197–220.

Dautenhan, K. (1998). The art of designing socially intelligent agents: Science, fiction, and the human in the loop. *Applied Artificial Intelligence*, *12*(7), 573–617.

Davis, L. K. (2016). *Hilton and IBM pilot "Connie," the world's first Watson-enabled hotel concierge robot*. https://www.prnewswire.com/news-releases/hilton-and-ibm-pilot-connie-the-worlds-first-watson-enabled-hotel-concierge-300233140.html

Ezzaouia, I., & Bulchand-Gidumal, J. (2020). Factors influencing the adoption of information technology in the hotel industry. an analysis in a developing country. *Tourism Management Perspectives*, *34*, 100675.

Gursoy, D., Chi, O. H., Lu, L., & Nunkoo, R. (2019). Consumers' acceptance of artificially intelligent (AI) device use in service delivery. *International Journal of Information Management*, *49*, 157–169.

Han, H., & Back, K. J. (2007). Assessing customers' emotional experiences influencing their satisfaction in the lodging industry. *Journal of Travel & Tourism Marketing*, *23*(1), 43–56.

Harkison, T. (2017). The importance of the human touch in the luxury accommodation sector. *Research in Hospitality Management*, *7*(1), 59–64.

Hasan, R., Weaven, S., & Thaichon, P. (2021). Blurring the Line between physical and digital environment: The Impact of artificial intelligence on customers' relationship and customer experience. In P. Thaichon & V. Ratten (Eds.), *Developing digital marketing* (pp. 135–153). Emerald Publishing Limited.

Hayes, D., & MacLeod, N. (2016). Packaging places: Designing heritage trails using an experience economy perspective to maximize visitor engagement. *Journal of Vacation Marketing*, *13*(1), 45–58.

He, E. (2018). Can artificial intelligence make work more human?. *Strategic HR Review*, *17*(5), 263–264.

Hoyer, W. D., Kroschke, M., Schmitt, B., Kraume, K., & Shankar, V. (2020). Transforming the customer experience through new technologies. *Journal of Interactive Marketing*, *51*(1), 57–71.

Huang, M. H., & Rust, R. T. (2018). Artificial intelligence in service. *Journal of Service Research*, *21*(2), 155–172.

Ivanov, S., & Webster, C. (2019). Conceptual framework of the use of robots, artificial intelligence and service automation in travel, tourism, and hospitality companies. In *Robots, artificial intelligence, and service automation in travel, tourism and hospitality* (pp. 7–37). Emerald. https://doi.org/10.1108/978-1-78756-687-320191001

Kandampully, J., & Solnet, D. (2015). *Service management principles for hospitality and tourism* (3rd ed.). Goodfellow Publishers Limited.

Kandampully, J., Zhang, T. C., & Jaakkola, E. (2018). Customer experience management in hospitality: A literature synthesis, new understanding and research agenda. *International Journal of Contemporary Hospitality Management*, *30*(1), 21–56.

Kiliçhan, R., & Yilmaz, M. (2020). Artificial intelligence and robotic technologies in the tourism and hospitality industry. *Erciyes Üniversitesi Sosyal Bilimler Enstitüsü Dergisi*, *50*, 353–380.

Klaus, P., & Maklan, S. (2011). Bridging the gap for destination extreme sports: A model of sports tourism customer experience. *Journal of Marketing Management*, *27*(13/14), 1341–1365.

Lei, S. I., Wang, D., & Law, R. (2022). Mobile-based value co-creation: Contextual factors towards customer experiences. *Tourism Review*, *77*(4), 1153–1165.

Limna, P. (2023). Artificial intelligence (AI) in the hospitality industry: A review article. *International Journal of Computing Sciences Research*, *7*, 1306–1317.

Lin, H., Chi, O. H., & Gursoy, D. (2019). Antecedents of customers' acceptance of artificially intelligent robotic device use in hospitality services. *Journal of Hospitality Marketing & Management*, *29*(5), 1–20.

Lugosi, P., O'Brien, C., Olya, H., Pink, R. C., & Lavender, V. (2023). Evaluating impacts of the physical servicescape on satisfaction in cancer care waiting experiences. *International Journal of Hospitality Management*, *112*, 103386.

McColl-Kennedy, J. R., Cheung, L., & Ferrier, E. (2015). Co-creating service experience practices. *Journal of Service Management*, *26*(2), 249–275.

Melián-González, S., Gutiérrez-Taño, D., & Bulchand-Gidumal, J. (2019). Predicting the intentions to use chatbots for travel and tourism. *Current Issues in Tourism*, *24* (1), 1–19.

Moeller, S. (2010). Characteristics of services – A new approach uncovers their value. *Journal of Services Marketing*, *24*(5), 359–368.

Morgan, M. (2006). Making space for experiences. *Journal of Retail and Leisure Property*, *5*(4), 305–313.

Nafees, S., & Sujood. (2024). The power of emotions: Combining emotional attachment theory (EAT) and the technology acceptance model (TAM) to predict consumers' intention to use interactive technologies (ITs) at tourism destinations. In *Tourism Recreation Research* (pp. 1–18). Taylor & Francis.

Nam, K., Dutt, C. S., Chathoth, P., Daghfous, A., & Khan, M. S. (2021). The adoption of artificial intelligence and robotics in the hotel industry: Prospects and challenges. *Electronic Markets*, *31*, 553–574.
Nguyen, T.-M., Quach, S., & Thaichon, P. (2021). The effect of AI quality on customer experience and brand relationship. *Journal of Consumer Behaviour*, *21*(3), 481–493.
Osei, B. A., Ragavan, N. A., & Mensah, H. K. (2020). Prospects of the fourth industrial revolution for the hospitality industry: A literature review. *Journal of Hospitality and Tourism Technology*, *11*(3), 479–494.
Prentice, C., & Nguyen, M. (2020). Engaging and retaining customers with AI and employee service. *Journal of Retailing and Consumer Services*, *56*, 102186.
Rahman, M. (2014). Differentiated brand experience in brand parity through branded branding strategy. *Journal of Strategic Marketing*, *22*(7), 603–615.
Ricci, F., Rokach, L., & Shapira, B. (2015). Recommender systems: Introduction and challenges. In *Recommender systems handbook* (pp. 1–34). Springer.
Ritchie, J. B., & Hudson, S. (2009). Understanding and meeting the challenges of consumer/tourist experience research. *International Journal of Tourism Research*, *11*(2), 111–126.
Ruel, H., & Njoku, E. (2021). AI redefining the hospitality industry. *Journal of Tourism Futures*, *7*(1), 53–66.
Ryu, K., & Jang, S. (2008). Dinescape: A scale for customers' perception of dining environments. *Journal of Foodservice Business Research*, *11*(1), 2–22.
Sarrab, M., Elbasir, M., & Alnaeli, S. (2016). Towards a quality model of technical aspects for mobile learning services: An empirical investigation. *Computers in Human Behavior*, *55*, 100–112.
Singh, V., Sharma, M. P., Jayapriya, K., Kumar, B. K., Chander, M. A. R. N., & Kumar, B. R. (2023). Service quality, customer satisfaction and customer loyalty: A comprehensive literature review. *Journal of Survey in Fisheries Sciences*, *10*(4S), 3457–3464.
Singh, P., & Singh, V. (2024). The power of AI: Enhancing customer loyalty through satisfaction and efficiency. *Cogent Business & Management*, *11*(1), 2326107.
Song, Y., & He, Y. (2023). Toward an intelligent tourism recommendation system based on artificial intelligence and IoT using Apriori algorithm. *Soft Computing*, *27*(24), 19159–19177.
Stock, R., & Merkle, M. (2017). A service robot acceptance model: User acceptance of humanoid robots during service encounters. In *IEEE International Conference on Pervasive Computing and Communications Workshops* (pp. 339–344). https://doi.org/10.1109/PERCOMW.2017.7917585
Taherdoost, H. (2018). A review of technology acceptance and adoption models and theories. *Procedia Manufacturing*, *22*, 960–967.
Tung, V. W. S., & Au, N. (2018). Exploring customer experiences with robotics in hospitality. *International Journal of Contemporary Hospitality Management*, *30*(7), 2680–2697.
Tussyadiah, I., & Miller, G. (2019). Perceived impacts of artificial intelligence and responses to positive behaviour change intervention. In *Information and communication technologies in tourism* (pp. 359–370). Springer.

Vaisanen, H.-M., Uusitalo, O., & Ryynanen, T. (2023). Towards sustainable servicescape – Tourists' perspectives of accommodation service attributes. *International Journal of Hospitality Management*, *110*, 103449.

Weiss, A., Bernhaupt, R., Lankes, M., & Tscheligi, M. (2009). The USUS evaluation framework for human-robot interaction. In *AISB2009: Proceedings of the symposium on new Frontiers in human-robot interaction* (Vol. 4, No. 1, pp. 11–26). https://www.bing.com/search?pglt=163&q=Weiss%2C+A.%2C+Bernhaupt%2C+R.%2C+Lankes%2C+M.%2C+%26+Tscheligi%2C+M.+(2009).+The+USUS+evaluation+framework+for+human-robot+interaction.+I&cvid=210c494b158f4ba599a85c6c15a4cdf0&gs_lcrp=EgRlZGdlKgYIABBFGDkyBggAEEUYOTIICAEQ6QcY_FUyBwgCEOsHGEDSAQc4NzNqMGoxqAIAsAIA&FORM=ANNAB1&PC=U531&ntref=1

West, A., Clifford, J., & Atkinson, D. (2018). "Alexa, build me a brand" – An investigation into the impact of artificial intelligence on branding. *Business and Management Review*, *9*(3), 321–330.

Wixom, B. H., & Todd, P. A. (2005). A theoretical integration of user satisfaction and technology acceptance. *Information Systems Research*, *16*(1), 85–102.

Wu, C. H.-J., & Liang, R.-D. (2011). The relationship between white-water rafting experience formation and customer reaction: A flow theory perspective. *Tourism Management*, *32*(2), 317–325.

Zalama, E., García-Bermejo, J. G., Marcos, S., Domínguez, S., Feliz, R., Pinillos, R., & López, J. (2014). Sacarino, a service robot in a hotel environment. In M. Armada, A. Sanfeliu, & M. Ferre (Eds.), *Robot 2013: First Iberian robotics conference (Vol. 2) - Advances in intelligent systems and computing* (pp. 3–14). Springer.

Chapter 5

Challenges and Opportunities Presented by AI in the Tourism and Hospitality Sector in Emerging Economies

Sarah Blankson-Stiles-Ocran[a], *Cornelius Tengan*[b], *Richmond Sakyi*[c] *and Reginald Olympas Akua Awusiedu*[c]

[a]The Hong Kong Polytechnic University, Hong Kong
[b]Bolgatanga Technical University, Ghana
[c]Ho Technical University, Ghana

Abstract

The adoption of Artificial Intelligence (AI) has become very significant in the contemporary hospitality and tourism economies worldwide. This is because of the numerous opportunities it presents to the industry, such as decreased costs, improved customer satisfaction, increased profits, improved quality, enhanced customer service, segmentation, personalisation and revenue management for better marketing activities. However, the application of AI to positions requiring customer interactions is hampered by issues, including clients' mistrust, fear, bad experiences, loss of control brought on by autonomous robots and worries about privacy, safety and security. This chapter aims to provide an overview of the adoption of AI in the contemporary hospitality and tourism industries by helping readers appreciate the concept, opportunities, challenges and future trends associated with the adoption of AI in the hospitality and tourism industries. The plausible strategies and way forward for a successful implementation are also recommended in this chapter. This review article may help readers better grasp how AI is being adopted in the hospitality and tourism sectors and the best ways to utilise it amid its challenges. Additionally, it provides support for managers, marketers and other businesses in the hospitality and tourism industries to achieve and improve high

Artificial Intelligence in Hospitality and Tourism in Africa, 81–96

Published under exclusive licence by Emerald Publishing Limited
doi:10.1108/978-1-80686-169-920261005

business performance by putting the right plans in place to use AI to satisfy the demands and expectations of both customers and staff.

Keywords: Customer service; personalisation; AI adoption; revenue management; challenges

Introduction

The tourism and hospitality sectors are changing due to Artificial Intelligence (AI). Companies are experimenting with and using chatbots, robots and other automated procedures (Pillai & Sivathanu, 2020). The use of AI in this industry can be broadly separated into two categories: efficiency and service provision enhancement techniques that use AI to enhance back-of-house functionality, and customer-facing areas like the installation of information points and customer service representatives (Khanh & Khang, 2021). Although there is currently a limited amount of AI being used in the travel and hospitality sectors, it is anticipated that as competition grows and the advantages become more obvious, an increasing number of businesses will employ AI (Ivanov & Webster, 2019). Despite expensive initial installation costs, automated service agents and different types of robots can drastically reduce expenses over time (Ivanov & Webster, 2017). Considering the current state of the world economy and the numerous problems that the tourism and hospitality sectors are facing, this argument is extremely important. It is anticipated that AI will become increasingly alluring due to its potential cost-saving advantages. In addition to producing findings faster and more accurately than humans, intelligent systems can also display information in a way that is easier for users to comprehend (Chatterjee et al., 2022; Flavián et al., 2022; Limna, 2023).

AI today comes in many forms and plays a big part in our daily lives. From highly intelligent robots used in the auto industry to sophisticated personal assistants on our smartphones, such as Microsoft's Cortana and Apple's Siri (Girasa & Girasa, 2020). With pattern matching or large data, it facilitates data analysis and visualisation. AI is now a widely accepted field that has advanced significantly. John McCarthy originally used the term 'artificial intelligence' (AI) in 1956 at the Dartmouth Conference. AI refers to the ability of a computer-based system to carry out tasks that often call for human intelligence. Artificial General Intelligence (Strong AI) and Narrow AI (Weak AI) are the two main categories into which AI systems fall (Fjelland, 2020; Drexler, 2019). Narrow AI refers to systems created to solve particular problems or perform particular jobs. Watson and other virtual personal assistants from IBM are examples of limited AI. In addition to using machine learning to give in-depth question answers, Watson can undertake specialised tasks like playing chess or Jeopardy.

Research indicates that more than 80% of consumers like chatbots over human communication due to the rapidity at which they respond (Adam et al., 2021). This increases client happiness and loyalty by enabling businesses to provide 24/7 customer assistance at a relatively cheap cost. Additionally, chatbots can pick up knowledge from interactions and grow 'smarter' (Ahmad et al., 2018). As demonstrated by businesses like Amazon and Netflix, companies can hone in on their expertise in a good or service and eventually forecast consumer behavior and even offer recommendations. When it comes to cost, AI can be incredibly effective at solving problems. One instance from the hospitality sector would be the labour cost-saving automatic reshuffling of employee schedules based on employee preferences and peak sales periods (Lester, 2020). Thus, the overview of AI, implementation challenges, opportunities and case studies of AI integration in emerging economies and strategies for overcoming obstacles and optimising opportunities for AI integration in hospitality and tourism are the main topics of this chapter.

Literature Review

Overview of AI Applications in Tourism and Hospitality

The use of AI in our daily lives is growing (Elliott, 2019; Stahl, 2021). Intelligent systems are distinguished from non-intelligent ones by their capacity to comprehend the circumstances, gather and retain information, conclude past experiences and react swiftly and effectively to novel situations (Chowdhary, 2020; Khanh & Khang, 2021). According to Mousavinasab et al. (2021), intelligent systems are characterised by two primary attributes: their capacity to perceive their surroundings and their capacity to conclude their activities to optimise the achievement of specific goals. AI, robotics and service automation are extensively employed across diverse industries (Flavián & Casaló, 2021). It should be mentioned that, during the past two years, there appears to have been a rise in the number of scholarly publications on the topic. It can be related to the fact that in 2017 AI was recognised as a megatrend in the tourist and hospitality industries by the largest industry intelligence platform, which offers media, insights and marketing to important travel-related sectors (Doorly, 2020).

AI in Customer Service and Experience Enhancement

AI has been incorporated into customer service and experience enhancement for the hotel and tourism industry, which is a notable development that has fundamentally changed how businesses engage with their customers and offer services (Gaur et al., 2021; Nam et al., 2021). Doborjeh et al. (2022) claim that hospitality businesses may gather and analyse massive amounts of customer data using AI to personalise experiences depending on preferences. Therefore, Filieri et al. (2021) propose that AI enhances the overall customer experience by making it more relevant and personalised, from generating restaurant and activity recommendations based on past behaviour to providing personalised travel plans.

AI-powered chatbots, according to Gupta et al. (2022), can handle repetitive tasks like booking reservations, providing facility information and overseeing check-ins and check-outs. They can also reply to customer enquiries instantaneously. These virtual assistants might provide client support that is more accessible and effective by working around the clock (Adam et al., 2021). According to Zohdi et al. (2022), hospitality and tourism companies can use AI algorithms to foresee future patterns in customer behaviour and analyse historical data to anticipate changes in demand and optimise their pricing strategies. By managing inventory, more efficiently allocating resources and utilising predictive analytics to deploy targeted promotions, hotels and tour operators can boost revenue and customer satisfaction (Anubala, 2023; Samara, 2018). Furthermore, Zeng (2020) attested to the fact that voice-activated assistants – like Google Assistant and Amazon's Alexa – are becoming more and more common in hotel rooms and travel experiences. These assistants allow guests to interact with them to request services, control amenities and obtain information. Thus, this hands-free interaction improves accessibility and convenience for visitors, particularly for those who are disabled or have language barriers (Stangl et al., 2018).

According to Bin Ahmed (2022), sentiment analysis systems powered by AI monitor social media mentions, online reviews and customer feedback to ascertain customer satisfaction levels and identify problem areas. According to Ghosh (2024), by analysing sentiment trends and identifying recurring issues, companies may proactively handle complaints, enhance the quality of their services and maintain a strong brand reputation. The use of AI in customer service and experience enhancement within the hotel and tourism sector is driven by the need to boost productivity, personalise interactions and deliver remarkable experiences that surpass consumers' expectations. Therefore, as technology develops, AI's impact on the future of travel and hospitality will only increase (Pillai & Sivathanu, 2020).

AI in Marketing and Personalisation

Research indicates that the field of tourism and hospitality marketing covers a broad range of activities, many of which hold great promise for the application of AI. These tasks include reputation management, segmentation, value proposition, product and experience design, distribution, pricing and customer relationship management (Bulchand-Gidumal et al., 2023; Thakur, 2022). AI systems can examine vast amounts of consumer data, including browsing habits, past reservations, social media activity and demographic information, claim (Inanc–Demir & Kozak, 2019). As a result, Lv et al. (2022) point out that companies in the hotel and tourism industries can modify their marketing strategies by examining these data to gain valuable insight into the tastes, patterns and actions of their clientele.

Furthermore, Inanc–Demir and Kozak (2019) state that AI assists hospitality and tourism enterprises in creating highly focused and customised email marketing campaigns by evaluating consumer data and behaviour. AI-powered recommendation engines can provide personalised travel itineraries, hotel choices and activity ideas based on past traveller behaviour and user preferences (Aljizawi, 2024; Doborjeh et al., 2022).

According to a study by Tomczyk et al. (2022), companies in the hospitality and tourism industries can utilise AI to create dynamic pricing strategies that take real-time demand, competitor pricing and other market factors into account. This allows for the implementation of dynamic pricing optimisation, which enables hotels, airlines and tour operators to provide clients with competitive prices while also increasing revenue and occupancy rates.

AI in Operations and Efficiency Improvement

The usage of AI has drastically changed the operations and efficiency of the tourism and hospitality industries. In light of this, Samara et al. (2020) point out that AI can significantly affect the hotel and tourism sectors by boosting customer satisfaction and operational effectiveness, both of which will ultimately lead to higher profitability. For example, research indicates that AI-powered chatbots can be used to provide easy booking requests, personalised offers and support, as well as interactive 24/7 customer service (Melián-González et al., 2021; Yun & Park, 2022). Pereira et al. (2024) claim that enhancing customer service and reducing response times can raise guest engagement, loyalty and happiness.

According to Kim et al. (2024), AI will play a major role in the growth of space tourism. Furthermore, Ahmed et al. (2023) state that AI-powered systems can assess data from sensors and Internet of Things (IoTs) devices to foresee equipment failures and maintenance requirements in hotels, aircraft and other hospitality enterprises. Foreseeing issues before they happen may help the business save maintenance costs, reduce downtime and ensure a faultless guest experience.

AI algorithms can enhance supply chain operations, according to Dash et al. (2019), by forecasting demand, optimising inventory levels and identifying opportunities for cost savings. The authors claim that since tour operators and other travel agencies in the tourism industry are responsible for making the necessary arrangements for housing, transportation and other services, this is particularly crucial.

According to Akilandeeswari et al. (2024), AI-driven revenue management systems can optimise pricing strategies in real time by analysing competitor pricing, market trends and historical data. Thus, by constantly altering prices in response to shifts in demand and other factors, hotels, airlines and other hospitality businesses can use AI to maximise income (Zaki, 2022; Ilo, 2018; Vives et al., 2018; William et al., 2023).

According to Casteleiro-Roca et al. (2018), AI systems can evaluate building data, occupancy trends and weather predictions to improve energy use in lodging facilities such as hotels and resorts. Li (2021) claims that real-time system modifications for heating, cooling and lighting assist these establishments in reducing energy waste and utility costs without compromising the comfort of their customers.

Challenges of AI Implementation

Inadequate infrastructure is a major barrier to the deployment of AI in the hotel and tourism industries in developing countries. Reliable high-speed internet connections are essential because AI systems usually require real-time data processing and a connection to cloud servers, according to Habeeb et al. (2019). Japutra and Situmorang (2021) draw attention to the fact that many rising economies, especially those in rural areas, may lack adequate or unstable internet infrastructure. Therefore, a slow internet connection may make it difficult to use AI-powered apps like online booking platforms, virtual concierge services and personalised recommendation engines. Bui et al. (2022) pointed out that in many developing countries, the infrastructure for data collection and storage may be complex, which makes it hard to get and compile relevant data.

According to Bulchand-Gidumal (2022), if the hospitality and tourism industries lack access to comprehensive and reliable data sets, they may find it difficult to develop effective AI solutions for client segmentation, demand forecasting and targeted marketing. Baus and Krešić (2024) point out that voltage fluctuations and power outages are common occurrences in many developing economies, particularly in remote and rural areas. However, Alnahari and Ariaratnam (2022) point out that it would be challenging to get and maintain such hardware in emerging nations due to financial limitations, high import taxes and a lack of technology providers. Because of this, the authors speculate that businesses would have trouble obtaining the equipment needed to put AI solutions into practice, which would limit their ability to exploit cutting-edge technology. According to Sarker (2022), to design and manage AI systems, one needs specific skills in domains like data science, machine learning and software development. However, Peter et al. (2023) point out that in many developing countries, there is a shortage of professionals with the necessary technological know-how. Restricted access to educational resources and training programmes exacerbates the skills gap and makes it more challenging to develop and execute AI efforts in the hotel and tourism sectors (Adeyinka-Ojo et al., 2020; Rodríguez-Abitia et al., 2020).

It is important to remember that the legal environment in developing countries, with outdated or unclear regulations governing data protection, technological deployment and intellectual property rights, may pose problems for the use of AI (Zekos, 2021). Uncertainty regarding regulatory compliance may deter businesses from investing in AI efforts, which can also slow down the rate of innovation in the hospitality and tourism sector (Webster & Cain, 2024; Zhao & Gómez Fariñas, 2023). Concerns about data security and privacy may arise in developing countries with less stringent data protection legislation, according to Fabrègue and Bogoni (2023). Therefore, Sarma et al. (2023) reveal that guests may be reluctant to provide private information with AI-powered platforms, especially if they believe there is a potential for data misuse or unlawful activity. The tourist and hospitality industries welcome visitors from a variety of backgrounds and profit from cultural diversity, as demonstrated by Walters et al. (2021). Therefore, miscommunications, erroneous interpretations and inadvertent violations may occur when AI systems are implemented without taking cultural sensitivity or awareness into account (Badawy, 2023).

Poor visitor communication could result from AI-driven language translation systems' inability to accurately explain cultural idiosyncrasies and conditions, for example (Karakas, 2023). According to Lembani et al. (2020), problems with digital literacy and technology access may contribute to a digital divide between residents of emerging nations' urban and rural areas (King & Petty, 2021; Rydzik & Kissoon, 2022).

Opportunities Presented by AI

Tirkkonen (2021) asserts that AI technology can expedite operations through the automation of repetitive tasks such as customer enquiries, inventory optimisation and booking administration. As a result, less manual intervention is required. Thus, according to Kannan (2024), AI-driven automation can lead to significant cost reductions and operational improvements, allowing businesses to use resources more wisely, particularly in developing countries where labour costs may be high relative to revenues. Furthermore, Lv et al. (2022) said that AI allows the hotel and tourism industries to gather and analyse massive amounts of customer data, allowing the industries to personalise interactions, modify services and forecast customer needs. According to Rane (2023), organisations in the hotel and tourism industries can use AI to boost consumer pleasure and loyalty by offering customised experiences, niche incentives and individualised suggestions. As a result, this will promote customer loyalty and positive word-of-mouth recommendations (Nguyen & Malik, 2022).

For travel agencies, the most well-known digital systems are the Global Distribution Systems (GDSs), which are an advancement of Computer Reservation Systems (CRS) and the legacy of information technology-based systems covering a range of services (Mich, 2020). When consumers gained access to digital services via the Internet and the Web, middlemen and other operators in the tourism industry in developing countries were either eliminated or had their roles altered. This was a significant upheaval in those systems. AI algorithms enable GDSs to automate new analytics processes, gathering insights to assist operational, management and decision activities. This is made possible by the vast volume of data related to a range of online interactions and transactions (Benckendorff et al., 2019). Businesses that use AI technologies include Amadeus, Sabre and Travelport. These companies do things like estimate demand, identify tourist profiles, detect fraud, monitor internal systems, automate agency duties and support e-commerce and e-marketing (Sorrells, 2018).

AI approaches are employed to forecast ticket prices or identify the most efficient detour in the event of a disruption (e.g. extracting information for travellers from rail operators' tweets). Travel agencies and other businesses can provide new services that are accessible to mobile apps by exchanging data. Robot concierges are a useful tool for automating face-to-face client care in the hospitality industry. Businesses could increase overall efficiency and reduce lines at information or reception desks in this way. A robot uses speech recognition and natural language processing (NLP) to communicate with users; Hilton has implemented Connie for this purpose. It also uses robotics features to assist users with more manual tasks, including moving bags (Mich, 2020; Reis et al., 2020). Through franchising, these services can be expanded to include multinational chain hotels in developing nations.

Claire is an example of an artificial concierge in the form of a holographic, life-size persona that is accessible via foot (Mich, 2020). Using Wikipedia as a knowledge base, it has been trained to respond to enquiries regarding the weather, travel, lodging, restaurants, cars for rent and flights, in addition to general enquiries. Modern 3D animation and visuals are employed in Claire, along with voice recognition, text-to-speech voice synthesis, dialogue and an NL classifier as AI technology. By using AI tools to automate asset management, businesses in emerging nations can use these technologies to improve smart tourism (Buhalis et al., 2023).

Review of Key Findings

The advantages/disadvantages that one tourism/hospitality business faces might not apply to another. For instance, a five-star hotel with thousands of rooms in Las Vegas can easily afford to use tens of robots for informational, cleaning, entertainment and promotional purposes in restaurants and casinos, as well as for room service delivery. However, for a small, family-run hotel with only 20 rooms, most of which are located in developing countries, investing in robots is a needless waste of money. This supports the Bui et al. (2022) study, which highlights that certain rising economies may struggle with infrastructure for data collection and storage, making it harder to gather and compile relevant data.

There will be a wide range of activities offered by both the front and back of houses at hotels and restaurants. A large portion of front-of-house functions in hotels will be provided by robots. Nowadays, it is feasible to automate the hotel check-in and check-out procedures. To obtain a key, make a payment or check out of the hotel, guests are not required to speak with a live employee. Therefore, a large number of front-of-house tasks are currently available in an automated style and don't necessitate significant involvement from staff members. For instance, Pizza Hut (Ivanov et al., 2017) and Tanuki restaurant in Dubai, United Arab Emirates (Berezina et al., 2019), have employed robotic hosts to welcome patrons.

Pepper (a semi-humanoid robot) may perform the duties of both a host and a waiter by helping clients place their orders and make payments. Furthermore, many visitors already have cell phones and Internet connections that can provide some services that improve efficiency and personalised services, which buttress

Samara et al. (2020) and customer services (Melián-González et al., 2021; Yun & Park, 2022). As a result, some services, like concierge services and other support services (like wake-up calls), are already made largely redundant.

Future back-of-house operations have a lot of potential since they will ensure that many tedious, hazardous, repetitive and dangerous duties are completed by robots rather than by people. Even while there have been debates about various extremely complex jobs that can be delegated to robots, like food preparation (Sun & Wang, 2022), many back-of-house hospitality operation duties are fairly complex and are now beyond the capabilities of robots. Examples of fairly complex tasks that call for a lot of dexterity, physical strength and judgement are cleaning a bathroom and changing a bed's linens. Later, these robots extended to other hotel chains, including Holiday Inn Express and Residence Inn by Marriott. Relay robots let hotel employees deliver goods to visiting guests. They are capable of carrying everything from a pillow to a toothbrush. The robots are autonomous in navigating the hotel floors. The robots can phone the hotel rooms to let them know that a delivery is on its way, navigate the hotel levels on their own and utilise the elevators. Robots aid cooks in the back of the house by flipping burgers, preparing sushi, chopping noodles and even baking pizzas (Berezina et al., 2019; Collins & Šabanović, 2021). For instance, Flippy the robot might be assigned to fry. Additionally, some restaurants – like the Spyce robotic kitchen and the Creator burger robot – have completely automated their kitchen operations (Berezina et al., 2019).

The study conducted by Peter et al. (2023) on the cost of hiring experts and their availability in developing countries is confirmed by the financial costs associated with the acquisition of robots, their installation, maintenance, electricity consumption and software updates; the robot-friendliness of the facilities; the hiring of specialists to operate and maintain the robots; staff training; and insurance costs (for damages caused by and to the robots).

Conclusion

AI in marketing and personalisation is being adopted by the tourism and hospitality sectors to increase customer interaction, optimise marketing budgets and deliver unique, traveller-focused experiences. Therefore, as the hotel and tourism sectors increase, so too will the impact of AI technology on marketing in these sectors in the future. Customers' willingness to utilise robots, their cost-effectiveness and the necessity to substitute human labour for activities all emerge in the dynamic environment that propels technological growth.

Since many industrialised countries have ageing populations and something needs to be done to replace human work, it is anticipated that technology that can replace labour will continue to advance. In terms of their immediate impact and political acceptability, robots are the answer to the labour shortage (Ivanov & Webster, 2019). Therefore, it makes sense that technology would advance to benefit the hospitality and tourism sectors in growing nations that struggle to find skilled workers and provide knowledgeable customer service.

How the industry will use the new technologies is a key factor to take into account, and this is dependent on assessing the potential and difficulties associated with their adoption. The obstacles encompass both direct financial (new technology purchases and facility redesigns) and non-financial (consumer opposition, data security and lack of access to AI experts) aspects. The choice to implement robots in front-of-house and back-of-house operations will need to be carefully considered because each unique commercial facility will have different target markets and products/services that they wish to offer to their clients. A hasty and impulsive adoption of robots could prove to be catastrophic. Although such a quick and thoughtless adoption of technology may offer first-movers a competitive edge, it will necessitate significant financial outlays.

One can hold an optimistic perspective. According to this perspective, society can deal with AI's primary issues. Worker and AI system collaboration will be possible, privacy concerns will be resolved and connectivity will be established to enable the deployment of AI systems. Ultimately, the most important factor to take into account is how consumers will react to robotic technologies in the travel and hospitality industry. Customers might not adopt AI technologies quickly unless these issues are resolved, which will require significant investment by relevant government policies. A better understanding of how robotic technologies will be implemented in hospitality and economies where data and access to technologies are high.

Companies will have a deeper understanding of their clientele, enabling them to create experiences, services and goods that are more precisely suited to their requirements. Additionally, companies will be able to dynamically develop customised bundles. Certain tasks will be replaced by technologies, which will complement them and lower total operating expenses. These savings can then be partially passed on to customers. Additionally, it implies that companies would be able to charge a reasonable price for services that were previously unaffordable (Bowen & Morosan, 2018). In other instances, technology can improve specific jobs or relieve employees of certain duties, resulting in better customer service and assistance.

From the standpoint of the consumer, AI will enable them to arrange their trip more rapidly, with much cheaper transaction fees and with a completely customised package that meets their requirements and preferences. Predictive offers that meet their needs will be sent to them. Technologies will make it easier for travellers to navigate unfamiliar areas while travelling, which will lessen their dread and anxiety. Cultural and linguistic disparities won't be obstacles to travel but rather an added draw. Technology will enable consumers to get the greatest service while maintaining the highest level of privacy protection (Bowen & Morosan, 2018). Comprehension of the use of AI in the hospitality sector. Furthermore, employing suitable tactics to satisfy the requirements and expectations of both clients and staff through the use of AI may help entrepreneurs, managers and marketers in the hospitality sector – or any other sector – achieve and improve high company performance.

Future Outlook and Trends in AI Adoption in Developing Countries

For those who are interested in learning more about how robots may soon be used in the tourism and hospitality sectors, there are plenty of options. It is reasonable to assume that advances in robotics and AI will lead to increased profitability, provided that the technological foundation and advancements originate from sources other than the hotel and tourism sector. However, the integration of these technologies into the service industry work environment raises research questions that need to be answered to guarantee the development of more AI-friendly, user-friendly technologies that can function offline with less effort to operate effectively, efficiently and economically in developing countries. The largest and most sensible area of study to focus on is client segmentation and how each group of clients interacts with the new technologies. This line of enquiry ought to be able to identify the obstacles that stand in the way of the service industries' consumers' desire and expectation to use the new technology. Finding out more about how facilities need to adapt to the new technology is another important area of research that needs to be done. Even while new technologies might eliminate the need for human labour, they might need to reconsider surfaces on which they can be used, as well as other more fundamental concerns, such as where robots will be fixed and recharged so they can operate offline.

References

Adam, M., Wessel, M., & Benlian, A. (2021). AI-based chatbots in customer service and their effects on user compliance. *Electronic Markets*, *31*(2), 427–445.

Adeyinka-Ojo, S., Lee, S., Abdullah, S. K., & Teo, J. (2020). Hospitality and tourism education in an emerging digital economy. *Worldwide Hospitality and Tourism Themes*, *12*(2), 113–125.

Ahmad, N. A., Che, M. H., Zainal, A., Abd Rauf, M. F., & Adnan, Z. (2018). Review of chatbots design techniques. *International Journal of Computer Applications*, *181*(8), 7–10.

Ahmed, S., Yong, J., & Shrestha, A. (2023). The integral role of intelligent IoT systems, cloud computing, artificial intelligence, and 5G in the user-level self-monitoring of COVID-19. *Electronics*, *12*(8), 1912.

Akilandeeswari, S. V., Nagpal, P., Vinotha, C., Jain, K., Chatterjee, R., & Gundavarapu, M. R. (2024). Transforming E-commerce: Unleashing the potential of dynamic pricing optimization through artificial intelligence for strategic management. *Migration Letters*, *21*(S3), 1250–1260.

Aljizawi, J. (2024). *Personalized travel recommendations and marketing automation for Saudi Arabia: Harnessing AI for enhanced user experience and business growth.* http://hdl.handle.net/20.500.14131/1502

Alnahari, M. S., & Ariaratnam, S. T. (2022). The application of blockchain technology to smart city infrastructure. *Smart Cities*, *5*(3), 979–993.

Anubala, R. (2023). The future of hospitality: Predictive analytics in hotel management. *International Journal for Multidimensional Research Perspectives*, *1*(3), 38–58.

Badawy, W. (2023). Data-driven framework for evaluating digitization and artificial intelligence risk: A comprehensive analysis. *AI and Ethics*, *5*, 1–26.

Baus, D., & Krešić, D. (2024). Solar energy for tourism in Croatia. In *Managing destinations* (Vol. 14, pp. 161–175). Emerald Publishing Limited.

Benckendorff, P. J., Xiang, Z., & Sheldon, P. J. (2019). *Tourism information technology*. Cabi.

Berezina, K., Ciftci, O., & Cobanoglu, C. (2019). Robots, artificial intelligence, and service automation in restaurants. In *Robots, artificial intelligence, and service automation in travel, tourism and hospitality* (pp. 185–219). Emerald Publishing Limited.

Bin Ahmed, O. (2022). *Implementing AI based solutions to understand & predict consumer sentiment*. https://dspace.bracu.ac.bd/xmlui/bitstream/handle/10361/18836/17104126_BBA.pdf?sequence=1&isAllowed=y

Bowen, J., & Morosan, C. (2018). Beware hospitality industry: The robots are coming. *Worldwide Hospitality and Tourism Themes*, *10*(6), 726–733.

Buhalis, D., O'Connor, P., & Leung, R. (2023). Smart hospitality: From smart cities and smart tourism towards agile business ecosystems in networked destinations. *International Journal of Contemporary Hospitality Management*, *35*(1), 369–393.

Bui, T. D., Tseng, J. W., Tseng, M. L., & Lim, M. K. (2022). Opportunities and challenges for solid waste reuse and recycling in emerging economies: A hybrid analysis. *Resources, Conservation and Recycling*, *177*, 105968.

Bulchand-Gidumal, J. (2022). Impact of artificial intelligence in travel, tourism, and hospitality. In *Handbook of e-Tourism* (pp. 1943–1962). Springer International Publishing.

Bulchand-Gidumal, J., William Secin, E., O'Connor, P., & Buhalis, D. (2023). Artificial intelligence's impact on hospitality and tourism marketing: Exploring key themes and addressing challenges. *Current Issues in Tourism*, *27*(14), 1–18.

Casteleiro-Roca, J. L., Calvo-Rolle, J. L., Jove, E., Quintián, H., Calero-Garcia, F., Jove, E., Calero-Garcia, F., Méndez-Perez, J. A., Gómez-González, J. F., Acosta Martín, J. F., Gonzalez Perez, S., Gonzalez Diaz, B., & Calero-Garcia, F. (2018). Prediction of the energy demand of a hotel using an artificial intelligence-based model. In F. de Cos Juez et al. (Eds.), *Hybrid artificial intelligent systems (HAIS 2018)* (Lecture Notes in Computer Science, Vol. 10870). Springer. https://doi.org/10.1007/978-3-319-92639-1_49

Chatterjee, S., Chaudhuri, R., Vrontis, D., & Jabeen, F. (2022). Digital transformation of organization using AI-CRM: From microfoundational perspective with leadership support. *Journal of Business Research*, *153*, 46–58.

Chowdhary, K. R. (2020). *Fundamentals of artificial intelligence* (pp. 603–649). Springer India.

Collins, S., & Šabanović, S. (2021, August). "What does your robot do?" A tabletop role-playing game to support robot design. In *2021 30th IEEE International Conference on Robot & Human Interactive Communication (RO-MAN)* (pp. 1097–1102). IEEE.

Dash, R., McMurtrey, M., Rebman, C., & Kar, U. K. (2019). Application of artificial intelligence in automation of supply chain management. *Journal of Strategic Innovation and Sustainability*, *14*(3), 43–53.

Doborjeh, Z., Hemmington, N., Doborjeh, M., & Kasabov, N. (2022). Artificial intelligence: A systematic review of methods and applications in hospitality and tourism. *International Journal of Contemporary Hospitality Management*, *34*(3), 1154–1176.

Doorly, V. B. (2020). *Megatrends defining the future of tourism: A journey within the journey in 12 universal truths* (Vol. 6). Springer Nature.

Drexler, K. E. (2019). *Reframing superintelligence: Comprehensive AI services as general intelligence.* https://ora.ox.ac.uk/objects/uuid:9c05427a-6390-4b42-9c55-ee45f73a26ad/files/sf4752j50k

Elliott, A. (2019). *The culture of AI: Everyday life and the digital revolution.* Routledge. https://doi.org/10.4324/9781315387185

Fabrègue, B. F., & Bogoni, A. (2023). Privacy and security concerns in the smart city. *Smart Cities*, *6*(1), 586–613.

Filieri, R., D'Amico, E., Destefanis, A., Paolucci, E., & Raguseo, E. (2021). Artificial intelligence (AI) for tourism: An European-based study on successful AI tourism start-ups. *International Journal of Contemporary Hospitality Management*, *33*(11), 4099–4125.

Fjelland, R. (2020). Why general artificial intelligence will not be realized. *Humanities and Social Sciences Communications*, *7*(1), 1–9.

Flavián, C., & Casaló, L. V. (2021). Artificial intelligence in services: Current trends, benefits and challenges. *Service Industries Journal*, *41*(13–14), 853–859.

Flavián, C., Pérez-Rueda, A., Belanche, D., & Casaló, L. V. (2022). Intention to use analytical artificial intelligence (AI) in services–the effect of technology readiness and awareness. *Journal of Service Management*, *33*(2), 293–320.

Gaur, L., Afaq, A., Singh, G., & Dwivedi, Y. K. (2021). Role of artificial intelligence and robotics to foster the touchless travel during a pandemic: A review and research agenda. *International Journal of Contemporary Hospitality Management*, *33*(11), 4079–4098.

Ghosh, D. (2024). Unleashing customer insights: Harnessing machine learning approaches for sentiment analyzing and leveraging customer feedback. In *Human-centered approaches in industry 5.0: Human-machine interaction, virtual reality training, and customer sentiment analysis* (pp. 265–280). IGI Global.

Girasa, R. (2020). Applications of AI and projections of AI impact. In *Artificial intelligence as a disruptive technology: Economic transformation and government regulation* (pp. 23–67).

Gupta, S., Modgil, S., Lee, C. K., Cho, M., & Park, Y. (2022). Artificial intelligence enabled robots for stay experience in the hospitality industry in a smart city. *Industrial Management & Data Systems*, *122*(10), 2331–2350.

Habeeb, R. A. A., Nasaruddin, F., Gani, A., Hashem, I. A. T., Ahmed, E., & Imran, M. (2019). Real-time big data processing for anomaly detection: A survey. *International Journal of Information Management*, *45*, 289–307.

Ilo, N. (2018). *Robotic Process Automation implementation in record-to-report process.* https://www.theseus.fi/bitstream/handle/10024/158271/Ilo_Nina.pdf?sequence=1

Inanc-Demir, M., & Kozak, M. (2019). Big data and its supporting elements: Implications for tourism and hospitality marketing. In *Big data and innovation in tourism, travel, and hospitality: Managerial approaches, techniques, and applications* (pp. 213–223).

Ivanov, S. H., & Webster, C. (2017). Adoption of robots, artificial intelligence and service automation by travel, tourism and hospitality companies–a cost-benefit analysis. In *Artificial intelligence and service automation by travel, tourism and hospitality companies–a cost-benefit analysis*.
Ivanov, S., & Webster, C. (2019). Conceptual framework of the use of robots, artificial intelligence and service automation in travel, tourism, and hospitality companies. In *Robots, artificial intelligence, and service automation in travel, tourism and hospitality* (pp. 7–37).
Ivanov, S. H., Webster, C., & Berezina, K. (2017). Adoption of robots and service automation by tourism and hospitality companies. *Revista Turismo & Desenvolvimento*, *27*(28), 1501–1517.
Japutra, A., & Situmorang, R. (2021). The repercussions and challenges of COVID-19 in the hotel industry: Potential strategies from a case study of Indonesia. *International Journal of Hospitality Management*, *95*, 102890.
Kannan, R. (2024). Revolutionizing the tourism industry through artificial intelligence: A comprehensive review of AI integration, impact on customer experience, operational efficiency, and future trends. *International Journal for Multidimensional Research Perspectives*, *2*(2), 01–14.
Karakas, A. (2023). Breaking down barriers with artificial intelligence (AI): Cross-cultural communication in foreign language education. In *Transforming the language teaching experience in the age of AI* (pp. 215–233). IGI Global.
Khanh, H. H., & Khang, A. (2021). The role of artificial intelligence in blockchain applications. In *Reinventing manufacturing and business processes through artificial intelligence* (pp. 19–38). CRC Press.
Kim, M. J., Hall, C. M., Kwon, O., & Sohn, K. (2024). Space tourism: Value-attitude-behavior theory, artificial intelligence, and sustainability. *Journal of Retailing and Consumer Services*, *77*, 103654.
King, B., & Petty, R. (2021). *The rise of technosocialism: How inequality, AI and climate will usher in a new world*. Marshall Cavendish International Asia Pte Ltd.
Lembani, R., Gunter, A., Breines, M., & Dalu, M. T. B. (2020). The same course, different access: The digital divide between urban and rural distance education students in South Africa. *Journal of Geography in Higher Education*, *44*(1), 70–84.
Lester, T. W. (2020). Restructuring restaurant work: Employer responses to local labor standards in the full-service restaurant industry. *Urban Affairs Review*, *56* (2), 605–639.
Li, Q. Y. (2021). *A novel real-time monitoring, notification, analytics system, and personal thermal sensations model for indoor air quality and energy efficiency in commercial buildings*. https://theses.lib.polyu.edu.hk/handle/200/11153
Limna, P. (2023). Artificial intelligence (AI) in the hospitality industry: A review article. *International Journal of Computing Sciences Research*, *7*, 1306–1317.
Lv, H., Shi, S., & Gursoy, D. (2022). A look back and a leap forward: A review and synthesis of big data and artificial intelligence literature in hospitality and tourism. *Journal of Hospitality Marketing & Management*, *31*(2), 145–175.
Melián-González, S., Gutiérrez-Taño, D., & Bulchand-Gidumal, J. (2021). Predicting the intentions to use chatbots for travel and tourism. *Current Issues in Tourism*, *24* (2), 192–210.
Mich, L. (2020). Artificial intelligence and machine learning. In *Handbook of e-Tourism* (pp. 1–21).

Mousavinasab, E., Zarifsanaiey, N., R. Niakan Kalhori, S., Rakhshan, M., Keikha, L., & Ghazi Saeedi, M. (2021). Intelligent tutoring systems: A systematic review of characteristics, applications, and evaluation methods. *Interactive Learning Environments*, *29*(1), 142–163.

Nam, K., Dutt, C. S., Chathoth, P., Daghfous, A., & Khan, M. S. (2021). The adoption of artificial intelligence and robotics in the hotel industry: Prospects and challenges. *Electronic Markets*, *31*, 553–574.

Nguyen, T. M., & Malik, A. (2022). Impact of knowledge sharing on employees' service quality: The moderating role of artificial intelligence. *International Marketing Review*, *39*(3), 482–508.

Pereira, T., Limberger, P. F., Minasi, S. M., & Buhalis, D. (2024). New insights into consumers' intention to continue using chatbots in the tourism context. *Journal of Quality Assurance in Hospitality & Tourism*, *25*(4), 754–780.

Peter, O., Pradhan, A., & Mbohwa, C. (2023). Industrial internet of things (IIoT): Opportunities, challenges, and requirements in manufacturing businesses in emerging economies. *Procedia Computer Science*, *217*, 856–865.

Pillai, R., & Sivathanu, B. (2020). Adoption of AI-based chatbots for hospitality and tourism. *International Journal of Contemporary Hospitality Management*, *32*(10), 3199–3226.

Rane, N. (2023). Enhancing customer loyalty through artificial intelligence (AI), internet of things (IoT), and big data technologies: Improving customer satisfaction, engagement, relationship, and experience. In *Internet of Things (IoT), and big data technologies: Improving customer satisfaction, engagement, relationship, and experience* (October 13, 2023).

Reis, J., Melão, N., Salvadorinho, J., Soares, B., & Rosete, A. (2020). Service robots in the hospitality industry: The case of Henn-na hotel, Japan. *Technology in Society*, *63*, 101423.

Rodríguez-Abitia, G., Martínez-Pérez, S., Ramirez-Montoya, M. S., & Lopez-Caudana, E. (2020). Digital gap in universities and challenges for quality education: A diagnostic study in Mexico and Spain. *Sustainability*, *12*(21), 9069.

Rydzik, A., & Kissoon, C. S. (2022). Decent work and tourism workers in the age of intelligent automation and digital surveillance. *Journal of Sustainable Tourism*, *30* (12), 2860–2877.

Samara, D. (2018). *The impact of artificial intelligence in tourism industry: A systematic literature review*. https://api.semanticscholar.org/CorpusID:115444714

Samara, D., Magnisalis, I., & Peristeras, V. (2020). Artificial intelligence and big data in tourism: A systematic literature review. *Journal of Hospitality and Tourism Technology*, *11*(2), 343–367.

Sarker, I. H. (2022). AI-Based modeling: Techniques, applications and research issues towards automation, intelligent and smart systems. *SN Computer Science*, *3*(2), 158.

Sarma, M., Senaratne, C., & Matheus, T. (2023).Challenges and opportunities of ethical AI and digital technology use in emerging economies. In *Elgar companion to regulating AI and big data in emerging economies* (pp. 42–58).

Sorrells, M. (2018). What travel marketers need to know for digital engagement. https://www.phocuswire.com/Bing-Phocuswright-digital-travel-marketing-study

Stahl, B. C. (2021). *Artificial intelligence for a better future: An ecosystem perspective on the ethics of AI and emerging digital technologies* (p. 124). Springer Nature.

Stangl, A. J., Kothari, E., Jain, S. D., Yeh, T., Grauman, K., & Gurari, D. (2018, October). Browsewithme: An online clothes shopping assistant for people with visual impairments. In *Proceedings of the 20th International ACM SIGACCESS Conference on Computers and Accessibility* (pp. 107–118).

Sun, Y., & Wang, R. (2022). The research framework and evolution of service robots. *Journal of Computer Information Systems*, *62*(3), 598–608.

Thakur, A. (2022). Technological innovations in the hospitality and tourism industry. In *Mobile computing and technology applications in tourism and hospitality* (pp. 72–97). IGI Global.

Tirkkonen, T. (2021). *Improving customer experience with artificial intelligence, Data analysis, and automation in Azets.*

Tomczyk, A. T., Buhalis, D., Fan, D. X., & Williams, N. L. (2022). Price-personalization: Customer typology based on hospitality business. *Journal of Business Research*, *147*, 462–476.

Vives, A., Jacob, M., & Payeras, M. (2018). Revenue management and price optimization techniques in the hotel sector: A critical literature review. *Tourism Economics*, *24*(6), 720–752.

Walters, G., Huck, L., Robinson, R. N., & Stettler, J. (2021). Commercial hospitality in tourism: A global comparison of what culturally matters. *International Journal of Hospitality Management*, *95*, 102939.

Webster, C., & Cain, L. (2024). Regulation, automated technologies, and competitiveness in the hospitality industry. *Journal of Hospitality & Tourism Research*, *49*(2), 10963480241229233.

William, P., Tidake, V. M., Thorat, S. R., & Verma, A. (2023). Future of digital work force in robotic process automation. In *Robotic process automation* (pp. 297–314).

Yun, J., & Park, J. (2022). The effects of chatbot service recovery with emotion words on customer satisfaction, repurchase intention, and positive word-of-mouth. *Frontiers in Psychology*, *13*, 922503.

Zaki, K. (2022). Implementing dynamic revenue management in hotels during Covid-19: Value stream and wavelet coherence perspectives. *International Journal of Contemporary Hospitality Management*, *34*(5), 1768–1795.

Zekos, G. I. (2021). *Economics and law of artificial intelligence*. Springer Books.

Zeng, D. (2020). *An investigation of mature travelers' usage intention of intelligent voice assistants in hotels (doctoral dissertation*. Purdue University.

Zhao, J., & Gómez Fariñas, B. (2023). Artificial intelligence and sustainable decisions. *European Business Organization Law Review*, *24*(1), 1–39.

Zohdi, M., Rafiee, M., Kayvanfar, V., & Salamiraad, A. (2022). Demand forecasting based machine learning algorithms on customer information: An applied approach. *International Journal of Information Technology*, *14*(4), 1937–1947.

Chapter 6

AI and Robotics: Exploring the Opportunities and Challenges for the Tourism and Hospitality Industry in Emerging Markets

Ricky Yao Nutsugbodo[a], *Anna Arthur-Amissah*[a] *and Desmond Tutu Ayentimi*[b]

[a]University of Energy and Natural Resources, Ghana
[b]University of Tasmania, Australia

Abstract

Artificial Intelligence (AI), robotics and related technologies are changing how customers engage with service providers, and they are also helping to improve service quality, delivery and customer experience in the tourism and hospitality industry. Given that the industry is largely service-oriented and relies heavily on human services, AI adoption is increasing, especially during the COVID-19 pandemic, when businesses need to provide contactless services to customers. Even though introducing AI technologies in the industry has been a huge success, there is limited uptake and adoption in emerging markets. This chapter examines the varied AI and robotic technologies available and applicable in the industry to highlight their prospects and challenges. This chapter highlights several implications around the technological divide in emerging markets that affect the industry's capacity to respond and cope with COVID-19 disruptions and technological changes to enhance customer service delivery and remain competitive in a dynamic and ever-changing market.

Keywords: Technology; Artificial Intelligence; robotics; emerging markets; tourism and hospitality

Artificial Intelligence in Hospitality and Tourism in Africa, 97–112

Published under exclusive licence by Emerald Publishing Limited
doi:10.1108/978-1-80686-169-920261006

Introduction

Technological advancement is at the heart of every industry and sector, including the tourism and hospitality (T&H) industry, and directly underpins the growth of industrialisation on a global scale since the first industrial revolution (Abdelfattah et al., 2023; Belvedere et al., 2013; Osei et al., 2020). This extends to the Fourth Industrial Revolution (4IR), which redefines all aspects of human and industrial activities, driven by emergent disruptive trends such as the rise of analytics, advances in robotics, human–machine interaction and data and connectivity. The 4IR and its associated technological advancements have prompted paradigm shifts across all industries and economies, irrespective of the stage of development – poor, emerging or advanced (Ayentimi, 2020). This wave of technological development holds significant potential for the current and future of the T&H industry, similar to other industries and sectors. The T&H industry is broad, with several categories, including lodging, food and beverage, entertainment, recreation and travel. Technology adoption makes customer service accessible and more easily transmissible along the industry's value chain. For example, the automation of services such as bookings and reservations, and the development of the central reservation and global distribution systems, as well as the integration of web-based technologies which resulted in the shift from traditional tourism to e-tourism, are a few highlights of the potential for technology adoption in T&H service delivery (Gretzel et al., 2015). On the one hand, scaling technology adoption in the T&H value chain has immeasurable benefits for consumers, employees and other stakeholders. These benefits are also far-reaching and extend to the Sustainable Development Goals (SDGs) in developing and developed countries. Leveraging technology to harness the benefits of the T&H industry towards the SDGs has been well documented by the World Tourism Organisation, an umbrella body of the United Nations.

The T&H industry is considered the largest industry in the world in terms of market size. Despite the effects of the global COVID-19 pandemic, the industry anticipates continuous growth. In 2024, the T&H industry contributed about US $10.9 trillion to the global GDP, about 10% of the global gross domestic product (GDP) (The World Travel and Tourism Council, 2023). Within the global T&H industry, emerging destinations have overtaken developed markets with the largest market share. Since the evolution of the 4IR and the increasing impact of 4IR technologies, including cyber-physical systems, the Internet of Things (IoT), big data, Artificial Intelligence (AI) and robotics, some areas of the industry have witnessed exponential growth (Huang et al., 2021). The industry will continue to expand and change dramatically in the future as smart technologies are used more frequently and broadly and become more accessible in emerging and developing markets (Wang et al., 2016).

More specifically, AI, one of the key technologies of the 4IR, has witnessed significant growth and proliferation among T&H businesses, ranging from airlines to hotels and restaurants (Loureiro, 2018; Ndhlovu et al., 2024a, 2024b). AI refers to computer programs, algorithms and machines that exhibit intelligence (Knani et al., 2022). AI also includes artificial neural networks, machine learning, the IoT and other intelligent technologies and tools for building smart robots and other virtual and augmented reality applications using big data and algorithms (Pereira et al., 2021). An AI system senses external information, understands it, acts accordingly to accomplish predetermined goals and learns from its experiences (Ferras et al., 2020). AI uses intelligent machines to think, learn, draw conclusions and make decisions comparable to that of the human brain (Knani et al., 2022). The adoption and use of technology, particularly AI, represents a shift from overdependence on humans to help improve service quality, delivery and customer experience. It has also led to fundamental changes in how the industry operates and functions, particularly in developed destinations like Europe, the United States and some parts of Asia.

The T&H industry has historically been concerned with making financial gains, with a common practice of poaching experienced employees from competitor businesses to deliver better customer service. Today, T&H businesses are focusing on how to deploy technology to ensure customer satisfaction by delivering excellent customer service and improving the customer service experience. This shift in the T&H management orientation necessitates leveraging emerging cutting-edge technologies to deliver an excellent customer service experience (Buhalis, 2020). Technology adoption and, by extension, AI represent the future of the T&H industry. The debate on adopting and using AI and robotics in the industry has been ongoing even before the global COVID-19 pandemic. However, there is a vast technological divide among countries and across T&H businesses. This technological divide is shown in the low uptake of AI and robotics in emerging markets. Indeed, the impact of the global COVID-19 pandemic on the T&H industry was dire, and technology adoption could have alleviated some of the impacts in terms of employee layoffs as a result of plummeting revenue and the fear of employees getting infected with the disease (Parvez et al., 2022). The adoption and use of AI could be a seamless transition from a human-dependent industry to a technology-driven industry, particularly during the pandemic. However, the technological divide among T&H businesses in emerging markets affects their capacity to respond and cope with COVID-19 disruptions, considering that the least technologically advanced T&H firms are also less capable and less resilient (UNCTAD, 2022).

Therefore, addressing the technological divide in emerging markets is a necessity that will demand technology uptake and upgrading of T&H businesses. Even though many T&H businesses in emerging markets are lagging in the cutting-edge technology space, it directly implies that there are potential prospects for T&H businesses' adoption of AI and robotics to improve efficiency and deliver high-quality customer service. This chapter explores the prospects and challenges of the adoption of AI and robotics technology in the T&H industry in emerging markets. The chapter further highlights important lessons for emerging markets. By highlighting the prospects and challenges of T&H businesses' adoption of AI and robotics technologies, practitioners and policymakers can better develop firm-level strategic interventions and an appropriate policy fit to help T&H businesses adopt high-tech technologies. Their use in T&H businesses can deliver considerable gains and value in service quality and competitiveness.

AI in the T&H Industry

AI-powered technologies are the foundation of many smart devices, which have been developed and used in the T&H industry and have impacted interactions between service providers and customers, as well as helping to personalise customer experience (Pillai & Sivathanu, 2020). For instance, AI has expanded the use of robotics applications to enhance customer engagement in hotels, restaurants and airlines (Doborjeh et al., 2021). AI also helps customers find more relevant information to improve their decision-making and provide a better experience (Bulchand-Gidumal, 2020). These technologies have implications for service, operations, management and marketing in the T&H industry (Buhalis et al., 2019). For example, smart technologies like automation and AI-based solutions, such as chat robots (chatbots) and robotics, have changed the way the industry presently operates in most countries (Tussyadiah, 2020). Although the T&H industry is service-oriented and strongly emphasises having people provide services, interact with customers and undertake marketing activities, these sophisticated technologies are rapidly replacing the 'human faces' in the industry. In effect, AI-based systems are not just triggering the automation of service(s) and process(es); they are also being used for direct interaction with customers at the expense of humans (Pillai & Sivathanu, 2020).

Notably, the 4IR has ushered in AI in several industries, including agriculture, manufacturing, logistics, transportation, medical and education; this also extends to the T&H industry with new AI-based technologies (Khaliq et al., 2022). These technologies offer various benefits to service providers, such as enhancing productivity and operational efficiency and creating convenient and personalised customer service experiences (Huang et al., 2021). The T&H industry is adopting and using many AI applications to deliver services. These notably include biometric identification applications, virtual and augmented reality applications, chat robots (chatbots), robots and autonomous vehicles, voice-activated technologies, kiosks and self-service screens, search and booking engines, Google Maps and language translators.

Biometric Identification

The development and application of biometric identification systems support the use of physical and behavioural traits to identify and authenticate personnel and customers (Abdulrahman & Alhayani, 2023; De Keyser et al., 2021). AI is used to develop user profiles, improve recognition, execute financial transactions and increase security. In the travel business, facial recognition enhances seamless travel and tourist traffic flow at airports. For example, the ShoCard Organisation actively implements this technology for airlines (Saulat, 2018). Biometric technologies are also employed in hotels and restaurants, incorporating self-service technologies (e.g. kiosks and self-service displays). Customers registered using biometric information (typically face details) are easily recognised and receive personalised services. Biometric technologies are also used internally for Point of Sale (POS) authorisation and employee time management, preventing employees from clocking in for each other, combating fraud and boosting staff responsibility and human resource record accuracy (Berezina et al., 2019). Hotels (e.g. the Marriott International hotel) use the facial recognition check-in application to handle guest check-ins. Also, fast-food restaurants (e.g. KFC in China) use the smile-to-pay facial recognition system to validate clients' personal information and complete transactions they have ordered (Huang et al., 2021).

Virtual Reality (VR) Applications

VR technology is helping T&H businesses deliver virtual tours of facilities, tourist destinations, hotel locations and restaurants to consumers via 3D videos. In addition, VR apps such as virtual hotel tours, virtual travel experiences and virtual booking interfaces give clients virtual experiences (Ben Saad, 2024; McLean & Barhorst, 2022). Hotels such as Marriott and Atlantis Dubai have collaborated to provide virtual experiences to their clients. On the one hand, airlines also provide VR technology to passengers who use the virtual booking interface to stroll inside a plane and choose their desired seats. ETIPS Augmented Reality (ETIPS AR) travel software, in-room augmented reality maps, VR travel booking services, VR honeymoon headsets and teleporters, augmented reality (AR) in-room athlete encounters and AR fine arts windows are some demonstrable examples of VR applications in the T&H industry offering enhanced customer experiences.

Chatbots

Chatbots are internet programs that can have human-like chat discussions via voice or text. They use machine learning and natural language processing to learn from the conversational data provided and reply in the same way as humans (Berezina et al., 2019; Dongbo et al., 2023). Chatbots have been used in the T&H industry to improve customer experience, provide convenient and personalised service experiences and give high-profile personalised services to clients (Huang et al., 2021). By 2025, 85% of customers will connect to T&H businesses without human interaction or involvement (Goasduff, 2019). For example, Google Assistant, Amazon Alexa, Chatbot Edward, Macy's on Call, Tacobot, My Starbucks Barista and Subway Order Bot are examples of chatbots being utilised. In addition, chatbots can also be assigned a range of tasks based on the service provider's objectives and customer needs, supporting the capability to offer personalised services to clients (Huang et al., 2021).

Robots and Autonomous Vehicles

Robots are a sort of AI technology that is gaining traction among T&H businesses. These technology-driven assistants use the IoTs technology to do simple tasks such as receiving guests, taking orders from guests, handling guest luggage and complaints and serving as concierges. Robot receptionists have grown in popularity in the T&H industry, taking care of the room service components so that visitors do not encounter any problems while checking in and checking out of a hotel room. Similarly, robots are being utilised in airports as guides and assistants. Some of the key benefits of robots in the T&H industry are improved client experience, simplified labour processes, enabling humans to focus on other activities and helping to improve the efficiency of operations (Huang et al., 2021). For instance, Knightscope robots, Travelmate autonomous bags, Hilton concierge robots (Connie), Domino's Pizza autonomous delivery and Flippy robots benefit from industrial robots and autonomous vehicles in the T&H industry.

Voice-Activated Technologies

Voice-activated technologies expanded the chatbot concept by combining voice recognition and speech synthesis (Balamurugan et al., 2024; Chung et al., 2017). Voice-activated assistants such as Google Assistant, Amazon's Alexa, Apple's Siri and Microsoft's Cortana are available on smartphones, desktops and smart speakers, which allows consumers and staff to engage (Chung et al., 2017). Employees can use voice-activated assistants to communicate effectively and efficiently among themselves. For instance, by using smart speakers or hands-free devices, chefs can communicate seamlessly with waiters about any happenings in the kitchen (Berezina et al., 2019). It allows waiters to swiftly respond to customer requests and orders. On the one hand, customers can use voice-activated assistants or technologies to search for restaurants, find contact information, initiate a phone call to the restaurant, study their menu and place an order.

Search and Booking Engines

Hotels, restaurants and tourism services are largely booked through search and booking engines. Machine learning, computer vision and natural language processing create these search and booking engines (Huang et al., 2021). Allora hotel search and booking engine, Resy restaurant search and booking engine, Allset restaurant search and booking engine, Airbnb home search and booking engine and Wayblazer search and booking engine are demonstrable examples of the application of search and booking engines in creating accessibility and customer service experience. For example, Allora is a background system that has been implemented into the official websites of over 600 hotels or resort groups worldwide, allowing company owners to achieve optimal website configuration (Anup et al., 2017).

Google Maps

Google Maps' AI technology uses Global Positioning Systems (GPS) to deliver information about roads and public and private transportation. It also gives information on traffic incidents, congestion and the shortest or alternate route.

The app currently uses Virtual Positioning Systems (VPS) to give information on surrounding T&H facilities such as hotels and lodging, restaurants, bars, discotheques, recreational places and malls (Xiao et al., 2018). Google Maps assists travellers in gaining access to ordinary infrastructure as well as tourism infrastructure facilities with ease, without the need to engage a tourist guide.

Language Translators

Language translators are AI apps used by travellers or customers to assist visitors in communicating with residents in their language when visiting a place with an unfamiliar language. Google Translate offers text and audio voice translation services, allowing users and travellers to input or record their language and have it translated by AI (Tatwany & Ouertani, 2017). Language translators play an important role in destination tourist infrastructure, replacing local guides, eliminating language barriers and making tourism more accessible, less expensive and less stressful.

The Prospects of AI and Robotics in the T&H Industry

Generally, during earlier technological revolutions, the T&H industry was at the centre of the adoption of the available technologies. However, this was mostly confined to T&H operators in developed markets in Europe, the United States and some parts of Asia. Information communication technology (ICT) and the internet, for example enabled the automation of hospitality services, such as the emergence of the central reservation system and global distribution systems and the integration of web-based technologies supporting e-tourism (Gretzel et al., 2015). Since the arrival of the 4IR, the industry has seen an exponential increase in the uptake of innovative technology such as AI in several operational areas. The primary goal of these advanced systems for the T&H industry is their application in improving the value chain and enhancing the guest experience to maximise the organisation's competitiveness and consumer satisfaction (Buhalis & Amaranggana, 2015). This further extends to leveraging AI to build resilience and business agility for the long-term sustainability of their operations. These 4IR technologies have a significant impact not only on the competitiveness of businesses but also on visitors and their experiences (Huang et al., 2017). Although 4IR technologies are already known in the industry and offer great benefits, adoption of these technologies, especially in emerging markets, is still minimal.

The financial gains connected with the adoption and use of AI are substantial for the T&H industry, despite the initial cost concerns. These financial gains stem from improvements in operational efficiencies, cost reductions and increased productivity (Lin et al., 2021). Ivanov and Webster (2017) emphasised that reducing labour expenses does not always imply replacing personnel with technologies but improving operational efficiencies. For example, self-service kiosks, service robots and chatbots run all day and exceed human employees' typical 40-hour work week. These automated services can serve many clients and deliver a consistent customer service experience. As a result, if these AI technologies can do specific activities efficiently and effectively, there will be clear financial and productivity benefits for T&H businesses. Furthermore, these systems may directly lead to increased sales as they are virtually available 24/7.

AI-based technological systems can help hospitality businesses handle seasonal employment and labour utilisation (Kuo et al., 2017; Yilmazdogan, 2024). By offering new employee-based technology interfaces, self-service technologies augment human services. Unlike human employees, who become tired of monotonous, repetitive and cognitively unchallenging duties (Ivanov & Webster, 2017), AI systems can complete tasks multiple times. Furthermore, as the hotel business is generally struggling with high staff turnover, AI-based technologies can help moderate the increasing demand for employees in hotel service delivery. For example, when an employee resigns, the firm's inventive potential and intellectual capital suffer due to knowledge loss. According to Shamim et al. (2017), having structures for knowledge retention in a T&H business is very logical. AI adoption is one of the surest ways to achieve knowledge retention.

Technologies of the 4IR have provided opportunities for T&H businesses to improve their operations and enhance the performance of their staff (Gretzel et al., 2015; Ndhlovu et al., 2024a, 2024b; Osei et al., 2020). Adopting these technologies, in particular, saves employees time from completing laborious and repetitive duties, which they may utilise for more creative and revenue-generating activities (Osei et al., 2020). Enhanced productivity and the ability of AI-based technologies to serve more visitors with the same or fewer personnel are advantages. Since AI-based technologies do not shirk from work as humans regularly do, they help boost service capacity and simplify operational scheduling and planning (Avula & Sithole, 2024; Xu et al., 2018). These technologies also enable employees to be more efficient by making more informed and intelligent judgements. The availability of data or information allows these technologies to make informed judgements and respond swiftly to customer needs (Vecchio et al., 2018).

AI-based technologies boost customer service quality by introducing a novel and appealing mode of customer engagement, information systems and service delivery (Li et al., 2017; Sharma et al., 2024). This may be accomplished through client communication and involvement with these advanced automated systems. Staff are usually challenged in terms of the number of languages they can communicate with customers, unlike self-service kiosks and chatbots that are programmed to communicate in various languages, which helps improve customer satisfaction (Kuo et al., 2017). Thus, these technologies add value to guests by making service delivery more enjoyable, interesting and engaging (Osei et al., 2020). In a nutshell, T&H businesses that use these AI-based systems stand to benefit from a favourable perceived image and word of mouth, which most high-tech businesses benefit from regarding AI adoption.

The ability to ensure supply chain efficiency can be achieved when the appropriate AI-based technology is used. Technology has considerably changed the way and manner in which T&H businesses provide services to customers (Shamim et al., 2017). The adoption and use of AI-based systems have fast-tracked the way businesses access information about their suppliers and vice versa. The IoT has made the supply chain processes of businesses more innovative and efficient (Huang et al., 2017). T&H businesses now have their smart device applications for booking and other services. Also, businesses, through the use of AI technologies, are linked with third-party booking agencies that provide intermediary services for them and sell packages to clients on their behalf. This has brought about more collaboration, made the supply chain process smoother and more efficient and increased the impact of disintermediation (Shamim et al., 2017). Most customers are now technologically savvy and feel at ease with the innovative self-service technologies that hotels, restaurants and airlines provide. AI-based technologies also ensure that T&H activities do not harm the environment, as automation of services helps in the reduction of waste and eliminates needless procedures, thereby reducing resource usage and wastage (Loureiro, 2018) and directly contributing to the protection of the environment, a key element of sustainability and the SDGs.

AI-based systems can guarantee full-service automation and new employment development in the T&H industry (Gupta et al., 2022; Ivanov et al., 2017). These technologies aid in the redesign of service delivery processes to improve operations. For example, AI has made it possible to integrate self-service kiosks, chatbots and robots into service delivery processes to enhance customer service delivery and the experience of guests (Osei et al., 2020). Even though the digitisation of T&H services has led to labour turnovers, it also creates alternative ICT-related jobs such as data analysts, cyber security, programming, systems analysts, software developers and many others. Using technological systems requires professionals who can manage and program these systems to deliver quality service to their clients. Despite the fear of AI adoption causing job losses, new business models grounded in ICT are potentially emerging to generate new employment opportunities. This may require individuals to develop high-skill digital capabilities and qualifications to benefit from such job opportunities.

The Challenges of AI and Robotics in the T&H Industry in Emerging Markets

While we acknowledge the enormous prospects of AI technologies ranging from customer service experience to employees and business owners and the wider society, their uptake and adoption, especially in emerging markets, have been sluggish due to firm- and institutional-level challenges. First, there are the impending financial constraints with the application of AI-based technologies. The financial costs associated with the automation of AI-based technologies require significant financial investment for their purchase, installation, maintenance, software updates and space creation to allow for robot mobility (Ivanov & Webster, 2017). Additionally, the cost of hiring experts and developing staff capacity to operationalise and sustain these technologies makes the adoption of AI-based technologies expensive, particularly for small and medium-sized T&H businesses. Interestingly, outsourcing robots instead of building or purchasing, for instance, will help reduce the cost associated with the adoption and use of AI-based technologies. This may offer a lean window for medium-sized T&H businesses to leverage AI technologies to support their growth and competitiveness in an increasingly competitive market.

Second, job losses and employees' resistance concerns remain key issues. Practitioners, academic scholars and policy analysts have opined about the dark side of AI-based technologies: job losses as existing roles in the industry become obsolete. This position has further been exacerbated by the increasing requirement of redesigning existing jobs and operating procedures to meet the skill set and competencies needed in AI-based work design (Lee et al., 2018). As noted by Fu et al. (2022), employees may be resistant to embracing new technologies if they perceive the shift as a danger to their jobs. Employee resistance is an important concern that needs to be addressed when deciding on technology adoption, since employees might refuse to utilise it effectively and destroy the technology. This transition also needs to be managed, as it is likely to give a negative perception of the T&H business involved, as they might be perceived as prioritising financial gains over employee welfare.

Third, employees are not the only key actors who resist technology adoption; this may extend to customers. There are instances where some customers may not be technologically savvy enough to be able to use the technology being deployed. Technology-phobic or technology-resistant customers can hinder the implementation of new technologies by insisting on services to be delivered by humans rather than technology. For example, customers may reject the use of technology since they might feel intimidated by some of the technologies (robots) or may not have had enough exposure to ICT to be able to navigate their way out (Ivanov et al., 2018). According to Huang et al. (2017), some customers may see services delivered by technology as inferior to those delivered by humans. Also, customers may feel that the adopted technologies (especially robots) cannot think on their feet to meet their needs compared to humans. Such customers may not be willing to pay or even pay less for services rendered by technology other than humans. This kind of customer attitude will lead to the failure of newly adopted technologies.

Harnessing AI for Improved Service Delivery: Implications for Emerging Markets

Despite the challenges of adopting AI technologies to enhance service delivery, there is no uncertainty across the divide regarding the unlimited prospects these technologies can offer the T&H industry in emerging markets. Historical records of new technologies are mostly reassuring, even with the initial resistance from their end-users. They have spurred the creation of many more jobs than they have destroyed. However, many economic, institutional and social challenges that weaken and compromise their adoption in emerging markets must be fine-tuned to generate their full potential in the T&H industry. This is where T&H businesses need to develop better firm-level strategic capabilities and appropriate policy fit to adopt high-tech technologies to deliver considerable gains and value in service quality and competitiveness.

Second, there is also the opportunity for T&H businesses in emerging markets to leverage the partnership of their multinational or franchise affiliates or form a consortium to share the cost of navigating the resource and capacity constraints to technology adoption. Multinational or franchise-owned facilities such as Marriott, Hilton, InterContinental Hotels Group (IHG) and Wyndham can, as part of their franchising agreements, provide some AI-based technologies for their franchisees to use in their operations. For instance, chatbots, voice-assisted technologies, biometric technologies and service robots can be part of the franchising package for franchisees. Also, small and medium-sized T&H establishments in emerging markets can form a consortium to outsource their AI technological needs. This will reduce the financial requirements for acquiring, installing and maintaining such technologies. As proposed by Ivanov and Webster (2017), renting or leasing AI technologies, especially service robots, will partially mitigate the costs of adopting AI-based technologies, which will help T&H businesses in emerging markets use these technologies to enhance their operations and service delivery.

In addition, notwithstanding the efforts of T&H businesses in emerging markets to adopt AI-based technologies, investment in ICT infrastructure, such as high-speed internet, remains a challenge. High-speed internet connectivity remains the backbone for businesses to generate the needed impact from adopting AI technologies. High-speed internet availability will enable customers to communicate using chatbots, voice-assisted technologies and other AI technologies and receive real-time feedback, just as it would have been if humans delivered the service. This requires governments in emerging markets to invest in ICT infrastructure. Once this is achieved, rolling out AI technologies in the T&H industry will be worthwhile.

Furthermore, there are implications for human capital development with the adoption of AI-based technologies in emerging markets. The recurring skilled labour shortage and skills mismatch (Singh & Jaykumar, 2019) in emerging markets call for a proactive human capital development strategy at both the business and national levels. The T&H industry will primarily benefit from the availability of a skilled workforce, not only for the installation and maintenance of such technologies but also for their application in the service delivery process. There is therefore a requirement for upskilling and reskilling of existing staff to acquire these skills and capabilities. Interestingly, the high labour turnover rate in the industry raises an important concern about whether it will be prudent for businesses to invest in the upskilling and reskilling of existing staff. Important lessons and implications exist around investment in employee training, development and talent retention.

Finally, there are privacy concerns about the vulnerability of compromised robot security systems, affecting the confidentiality of the data generated (Tussyadiah, 2020). These technologies necessitate the development of other technologies that will guarantee user data security. Technology users may encounter unfavourable institutional and regulatory constraints in many emerging destinations. For instance, the absence of transparency, weak regulatory systems and corruption can intensify data security risks with the possibility of discouraging potential investors and may weaken the prospects of exploiting AI-based technologies in emerging markets (Ayentimi, 2020; Kshetri, 2012). Indeed, developing markets are generally characterised by weak institutional and regulatory constraints and may lack the capacity and resources to adequately guarantee the privacy of users and the security of their data (Ayentimi, 2020). There is a need to put in place the necessary structures and regulatory framework to address data protection and security concerns. This will enable customers to feel confident in the use of such technologies.

Conclusion

AI and its associated technologies are transforming not only the T&H industry but all sectors and industries. Implementing AI technologies in T&H services should consider the multiple actors that underpin AI technology adoption, such as employees, customers, regulatory agencies and investors. The T&H industry was impacted mainly by the global COVID-19 pandemic disruptions, owing to its dependence on human-delivered services and mandatory lockdowns to curb the spread of the virus. Interestingly, the pandemic has facilitated the industry's swift transition to technology adoption to reduce the intensity of human-delivered services, eliminate operational inefficiencies towards recovery from the losses during the pandemic and respond to future crises. It is important to acknowledge that the industry's swift transition to technology adoption is still confined to most developed markets in the United States, Europe and some parts of Asia, as many emerging markets are still lagging due to financial, infrastructural and human capability constraints. To harness the potential of AI, emerging markets need to address the key challenges around infrastructure, particularly ICT and human capital development, and establish the appropriate regulatory framework for data protection and security. Aside from changing customer expectations and preferences, the T&H industry and all its sub-sectors will continue to be impacted by technological changes post-COVID-19. Therefore, businesses in the T&H industry that can win in this dynamic and ever-changing market are agile, resilient and able to adapt.

References

Abdelfattah, F., Al-Alawi, A., Abdullahi, M. S., & Salah, M. (2023). Embracing the industrial revolution: The impact of technological advancements and government policies on tourism development in Oman. *Journal of Policy Research in Tourism, Leisure and Events*, 1–25.

Abdulrahman, S. A., & Alhayani, B. (2023). A comprehensive survey on the biometric systems based on physiological and behavioural characteristics. *Materials Today: Proceedings*, *80*, 2642–2646.

Anup, S., Goel, A., & Padmanabhan, S. (2017). Visual positioning system for automated indoor/outdoor navigation. *TENCON 2017-2017 IEEE Region 10 Conference* (pp. 1027–1031).

Avula, M., & Sithole, T. (2024). Artificial intelligence's potential to improve operational efficiency and customer experience in the hospitality and tourism sectors. In *Impact of AI and tech-driven solutions in hospitality and tourism* (pp. 351–382). IGI Global.

Ayentimi, D. T. (2020). The 4IR and the challenges for developing economies. In K. Dayaram, L. Lambey, J. Burgess, & T. W. Afrianty (eds), *Developing the workforce in an emerging economy: The case of Indonesia*. Routledge.

Balamurugan, A., Thiruppathi, D., Santhoshkumar, S. P., & Susithra, K. (2024, March). Artificial intelligence-based chatbot with voice assistance. *2024 International Conference on Trends in Quantum Computing and Emerging Business Technologies* (pp. 1–6). IEEE.

Belvedere, V., Grando, A., & Bielli, P. (2013). A quantitative investigation of the role of information and communication technologies in the implementation of a product-service system. *International Journal of Production Research*, *51*(2), 410–426.

Ben Saad, S. (2024). The digital revolution in the tourism industry: Role of anthropomorphic virtual agent in digitalized hotel service. *International Journal of Contemporary Hospitality Management*, *36*(11), 3751–3773.

Berezina, K., Ciftci, O., & Cobanoglu, C. (2019). Robots, artificial intelligence, and service automation in restaurants. In S. Ivanov & C. Webster (eds), *Robots, artificial intelligence, and service automation in travel, tourism and hospitality* (pp. 185–219). Emerald Publishing Limited.

Buhalis, D. (2020). Technology in tourism-from information communication technologies to eTourism and smart tourism towards ambient intelligence tourism: A perspective article. *Tourism Review*, *75*(1), 267–272.

Buhalis, D., & Amaranggana, A. (2015). Smart tourism destinations: Enhancing tourism experience through personalization of services. In I. Tussyadiah & A. Inversini (eds), *Information and communication technologies in tourism* (pp. 377–389). Springer.

Buhalis, D., Harwood, T., Bogicevic, V., Viglia, G., Beldona, S., & Hofacker, C. (2019). Technological disruptions in services: Lessons from tourism and hospitality. *Journal of Service Management*, *30*(4), 484–506.

Bulchand-Gidumal, J. (2020). Impact of artificial intelligence in travel, tourism and hospitality. In: *Handbook on e-tourism* (pp. 1–20).

Chung, H., Iorga, M., Voas, J., & Lee, S. (2017). Alexa, can I trust you?. *Computer*, *50*(9), 100–104.

De Keyser, A., Bart, Y., Gu, X., Liu, S. Q., Robinson, S. G., & Kannan, P. K. (2021). Opportunities and challenges of using biometrics for business: Developing a research agenda. *Journal of Business Research*, *136*, 52–62.

Doborjeh, Z., Hemmington, N., Doborjeh, M., & Kasabov, N. (2021). Artificial intelligence: A systematic review of methods and applications in hospitality and tourism. *International Journal of Contemporary Hospitality Management*, *34*(3), 1154–1176.

Dongbo, M., Miniaoui, S., Fen, L., Althubiti, S. A., & Alsenani, T. R. (2023). Intelligent chatbot interaction system capable for sentimental analysis using hybrid machine learning algorithms. *Information Processing & Management, 60* (5), 103440.

Ferras, X., Hitchen, E. L., Tarrats-Pons, E., & Arimany-Serrat, N. (2020). Smart tourism empowered by artificial intelligence: The case of Lanzarote. *Journal of Cases on Information Technology*, *22*(1), 1–13.

Fu, S., Zheng, X., & Wong, I. A. (2022). The perils of hotel technology: The robot usage resistance model. *International Journal of Hospitality Management*, *102*, 103174.

Goasduff, L. (2019). Chatbots will appeal to modern workers. *Gartner*. 20/12/2021. www.gartner.com/smarterwithgartner/chatbots-will-appeal-to-modern-workers. Retrieved on April 29, 2023.

Gretzel, U., Sigala, M., Xiang, Z., & Koo, C. (2015). Smart tourism: Foundations and developments. *Electronic Markets*, *25*(3), 179–188.

Gupta, S., Modgil, S., Lee, C. K., Cho, M., & Park, Y. (2022). Artificial intelligence enabled robots for stay experience in the hospitality industry in a smart city. *Industrial Management & Data Systems*, *122*(10), 2331–2350.

Huang, A., Chao, Y., de la Mora Velasco, E., Bilgihan, A., & Wei, W. (2021). When artificial intelligence meets the hospitality and tourism industry: An assessment framework to inform theory and management. *Journal of Hospitality and Tourism Insights*, *5*(5), 1080–1100.

Huang, C. D., Goo, J., Nam, K., & Yoo, C. W. (2017). Smart tourism technologies in travel planning: The role of exploration and exploitation. *Information and Management*, *54*(6), 757–770.

Ivanov, S., & Webster, C. (2017). Adoption of robots, artificial intelligence and service automation by travel, tourism and hospitality companies – a cost benefit analysis. *International Scientific Conference on Contemporary Tourism – Traditions and Innovations, 19–21 October 2017, Sofia University* (pp. 1–9).

Ivanov, S., Webster, C., & Berezina, K. (2017). Adoption of robots and service automation by tourism and hospitality companies. *Revista Turismo and Desenvolvimento*, *27*(28), 1501–1517.

Ivanov, S., Webster, C., & Seyyedi, P. (2018). Consumers' attitudes towards the introduction of robots in accommodation establishments. *Tourism*, *66*(3), 302–317.

Khaliq, A., Waqas, A., Nisar, Q. A., Haider, S., & Asghar, Z. (2022). Application of AI and robotics in hospitality sector: A resource gain and resource loss perspective. *Technology in Society*, *68*, 101807.

Knani, M., Echckakoui, S., & Ladhari, R. (2022). Artificial intelligence in tourism and hospitality: Bibliometric analysis and research agenda. *International Journal of Hospitality Management*, *107*, 103317.

Kshetri, N. (2012). Cloud computing in developing economies. *Computer*, *43*(10), 47–55.

Kuo, C.-M., Chen, C.-H., Lee, Y.-C., Xu, G., Li, F., & Zhao, X. (2017). Investigating an innovative service with hospitality robots. *International Journal of Contemporary Hospitality Management*, *29*(5), 1305–1321.

Lee, M., Yun, J. J., Pyka, A., Won, D., Kodama, F., Schiuma, G., Park, H., Jeon, J., Park, K., Jung, K., Yan, M.-R., Lee, S., & Zhao, X. (2018). How to respond to the fourth industrial revolution, or the second information technology revolution? Dynamic new combinations between technology, market, and society through open innovation. *Journal of Open Innovation: Technology, Market, and Complexity*, *4*(3), 1–24.

Li, Y., Hu, C., Huang, C., & Duan, L. (2017). The concept of smart tourism in the context of tourism information services. *Tourism Management*, *58*, 293–300.

Lin, T. Y., Wu, K. R., Chen, Y. S., Huang, W. H., & Chen, Y. T. (2021). Takeout service automation with trained robots in the pandemic-transformed catering business. *IEEE Robotics and Automation Letters*, *6*(2), 903–910.

Loureiro, A. (2018). There is a fourth industrial revolution: The digital revolution. *Worldwide Hospitality and Tourism Themes*, *10*(6), 740–744.

McLean, G., & Barhorst, J. B. (2022). Living the experience before you go...but did it meet expectations? The role of virtual reality during hotel bookings. *Journal of Travel Research*, *61*(6), 1233–1251.

Ndhlovu, E., Dube, K., & Kifworo, C. M. (2024a). Tourism and hospitality trends and sustainable development: Emerging issues in the digital era. In *Tourism and hospitality for sustainable development: Volume two: Emerging trends and global issues* (pp. 1–21). Springer Nature Switzerland.

Ndhlovu, E., Dube, K., & Makuyana, T. (2024b). Tourism and hospitality for sustainable development in the digital era: An assessment of the impacts on customers and employees in tourism enterprises. In *Tourism and hospitality for sustainable development: Volume three: Implications for customers and employees of tourism businesses* (pp. 1–19). Springer Nature Switzerland.

Osei, B. A., Ragavan, N. A., & Mensah, H. K. (2020). Prospects of the fourth industrial revolution for the hospitality industry: A literature review. *Journal of Hospitality and Tourism Technology*, *11*(3), 479–494.

Parvez, M. O., Öztüren, A., Cobanoglu, C., Arasli, H., & Eluwole, K. K. (2022). Employees' perception of robots and robot-induced unemployment in hospitality industry under COVID-19 pandemic. *International Journal of Hospitality Management*, *107*, 103336.

Pereira, V., Hadjielias, E., Christofi, M., & Vrontis, D. (2021). A systematic literature review on the impact of artificial intelligence on workplace outcomes: A multi-process perspective. *Human Resource Management Review*, *33*, 100857.

Pillai, R., & Sivathanu, B. (2020). Adoption of AI-based chatbots for hospitality and tourism. *International Journal of Contemporary Hospitality Management*, *32*(10), 3199–3226.

Saulat, A. (2018). Four ways AI is re-imagining the future of travel. Available at: www.mindtree.com/blog/four-ways-ai-re-imagining-future-travel. Retrieved on March 28, 2023.

Shamim, S., Cang, S., Yu, H., & Li, Y. (2017). Examining the feasibilities of industry 4.0 for the hospitality sector with the lens of management practice. *Energies*, *10*(4), 1–19.

Sharma, R., Sachdeva, T., Singh, A., & Nadda, V. (2024). A new era of engagement and satisfaction: Transforming customer experience with AI-driven technologies. In *AI innovations in service and tourism marketing* (pp. 1–16). IGI Global.

Singh, A., & Jaykumar, P. (2019). On the road to consensus: Key soft skills required for youth employment in the service sector. *Worldwide Hospitality and Tourism Themes*, *11*(1), 10–24.

Tatwany, L., & Ouertani, H. C. (2017). A review on using augmented reality in text translation. *2017 6th International Conference on Information and Communication Technology and Accessibility (ICTA)*. IEEE.

Tussyadiah, I. (2020). A review of research into automation in tourism: Launching the annals of tourism research curated collection on artificial intelligence and robotics in tourism. *Annals of Tourism Research*, *81*, 102883.

UNCTAD. (2022). Frontier technology adoption in developing countries A measurement framework and proposed questionnaire. *United Nations Conference on Trade and Development. UNCTAD/DTL/STICT/2021/5*. https://unctad.org/system/files/official-document/dtlstict2021d5_en.pdf

Vecchio, P. D., Mele, G., Ndou, V., & Secundo, G. (2018). Creating value from social big data: Implications for smart tourism destinations. *Information Processing & Management*, *54*(5), 847–860.

Wang, X., Li, X. R., Zhen, F., & Zhang, J. (2016). How smart is your tourist attraction? Measuring tourist preferences of smart tourism attractions via a FCEM-AHP and IPA approach. *Tourism Management*, *54*, 309–320.

World Travel and Tourism Council. (2023). *Economic impact reports*. Retrieved on 8th August, 2025 at https://wttc.org/research/economic-impact

Xiao, A., Chen, R., Li, D., Chen, Y., & Wu, D. (2018). An indoor positioning system based on static objects in large indoor scenes by using smartphone cameras. *Sensors*, *18*(7), 2229.

Xu, M., David, J. M., & Kim, S. H. (2018). The fourth industrial revolution: Opportunities and challenges. *International Journal of Financial Research*, *9*(2), 90–95.

Yilmazdogan, O. C. (2024). Elevating workforce stability: Augmented reality and artificial intelligence solutions for overcoming employee turnover challenges in hospitality and tourism. *Worldwide Hospitality and Tourism Themes*, *16*(5), 598–610.

Chapter 7

Emerging Use of Artificial Intelligence (AI) and Robotics in the Hotel Sub-Sector of the Tourism Industry: Exploring Awareness, Preferred Operational Use, Expectations and Concerns

Victor Anderson Hodibert[a] *and Eudora Hagan*[a]

[a]Takoradi Technical University, Ghana

Abstract

Recent technological advancements in the fields of Artificial Intelligence (AI) and robotics in developed economies have intrinsically pervaded social economic and political platforms across the globe. This chapter investigates the awareness, preparedness, expectations and concerns of hotel managers of the emerging technologies, with a particular focus on hotel industry players in the Western Region of Ghana. Drawing on recent empirical and theoretical studies, the chapter critically examines how varying levels of knowledge, technological readiness and ethical considerations shape stakeholder responses. The analysis reveals a high level of awareness mostly sourced from social media, the internet and television. Data indicate that the use of AI and robotics technologies would be preferred in certain operational areas in the hotel sub-sector of tourism and hospitality industry. However, there are major perceived concerns regarding detrimental impacts on the operations of the hotel sub-sector even though positive impacts, especially on efficiency in operations, are expected. The study recommends the institution of a policy to drive public education on the subject to improve public awareness and knowledge about AI and Robotics technologies. Further, the need to foster synergy among technical experts, academics, policymakers and industry players ought to be prioritized to develop, if not enhance, regulatory frameworks for the adoption of AI and

Artificial Intelligence in Hospitality and Tourism in Africa, 113–128

doi:10.1108/978-1-80686-169-920261007

Robotics technologies in the hotel sub-sector to enhance operations to maximize benefits in sector for economic development.

Keywords: Artificial Intelligence; robotics; technological readiness; hospitality industry; ethics

Introduction

This chapter situates the subject of AI and Robotics technologies within a global context and critically examines the technological divide between developed and emerging economies while addressing the ethical considerations surrounding AI and robotics. It also draws on a case study approach to assess the level of awareness among industry stakeholders of the hotel sub-sector of the tourism and hospitality industry in Ghana.

Over the past decade, scholarly literature on robotics and Artificial Intelligence (AI) has grown in volume and in diversity of perspectives. The International Organization for Standardization (2012) defines a robot as 'an actuated mechanism programmable in two or more axes with a degree of autonomy, enabling it to move within its environment and perform intended tasks'. While robotics is thus framed in terms of its mechanical and operational capabilities, AI has been defined more broadly and variably. Wolfgang (2017) conceptualises AI as an interdisciplinary body of knowledge emerging from multiple domains, including logic, operations research, statistics, control engineering, image processing, linguistics, philosophy, psychology and neurobiology. This definition underscores AI's nature as a convergence of diverse scientific traditions. In contrast, Haenlein et al. (2019) offer a more functional view, describing AI as an autonomous system capable of correctly interpreting external data, learning from such data and applying acquired knowledge to achieve specific goals through adaptive decision-making.

Beyond definitional debates, scholars have examined the evolution and emerging trends of AI and robotics in the tourism and hospitality industry. Murphy et al. (2017) emphasise the growing necessity of incorporating robotics and AI into tourism and hospitality education. They categorise robotics applications into industrial, professional and personal service domains and highlight the urgency for dedicated research in this field. Their argument provides a conceptual springboard for subsequent inquiries into the operational, strategic and pedagogical implications of these technologies.

Tung and Law (2017) argue that the era of robotics and AI is here and now. AI and robotics are increasingly embedded in revenue management, property administration, customer relations and performance analytics, as well as in entertainment and other service functions. However, the success of these technologies depends on their availability, industry acceptance and the effective integration of human and non-human interactions in service delivery.

Ivanov and Webster (2020) observe that, despite extensive academic attention to robotics in tourism, the economic dimension has been underexplored. They stress that adoption will inevitably affect business models, operations and human resource management and thus requires systematic evaluation before implementation. From their perspective, economic impacts should be assessed in terms of demand, supply and destination management, while acknowledging that mobility, customer acceptance and ownership patterns will influence adoption levels.

Drexler and Lapré (2019), in *For Better or for Worse: Shaping the Hospitality Industry through Robotics and Artificial Intelligence*, position technological change as a continuation of the industrial revolution, framing the 'rise of the machines' as both an opportunity and a challenge. They urge the sector to welcome these advancements but caution that adoption decisions must be informed and strategic.

In the African context, Aikins (2021), in *Seek Ye First the Digital Kingdom? Between Data Extractivism and Digital Self-Determinism*, highlights Ghana's adoption of AI in health services, particularly through Zipline's use of drones for medical deliveries to remote areas. He raises concerns about the tension between digital sovereignty and digital neo-colonialism, calling for policy frameworks that respond to the sociopolitical and economic realities of rapid technological change.

While advanced economies lead in AI and robotics adoption, little is known about awareness, preparedness and concerns among industry players in Ghana's tourism sector. This gap underscores the need for context-specific research to capture perspectives from the Global South, address ethical implications and ensure that legal and regulatory frameworks are in place for equitable governance of emerging technologies.

Globalisation and the Technological Divide

Since the Industrial Revolution of the 18th century, advances in technology have consistently reflected global imbalances in origin, accessibility, availability and impact. While technological change continues to transform sectors of the world economy, the divide between the Global North and the Global South has remained persistent – often to the latter's disadvantage – reinforced by neoliberal economic principles. These disparities are shaped by differences in investment flows, trade and technological know-how. UNESCO's (2021) *Artificial Intelligence Needs Assessment for Africa* highlights that the benefits and risks of emerging technologies, including AI, are unevenly distributed across regions.

Bridging this divide requires meaningful technology transfer in AI and robotics. However, transfer mechanisms have often been undermined by structural misrepresentations and discriminatory practices, prompting repeated calls – often through United Nations interventions – for equitable sharing. Although some scholars point to changing dynamics through South–South collaborations (Raslan, 2021), core inequalities remain, extending beyond economic and social differences to political ramifications. Fierce competition among developing countries for scarce investment, coupled with budgetary constraints in industrialised nations, has reduced official development assistance. Private investors are increasingly favouring either developed markets or wealthier newly industrialised states over the least developed economies.

Access to technology also hinges on the usability of digital knowledge and the availability of managerial and administrative know-how resources, frequently left to market forces. Globalisation and neoliberal economic frameworks enable the transmission of technology from advanced to emerging economies, but at a pace and scale dictated by market priorities rather than equity. Modern technologies, often intangible and rapidly evolving, risk becoming obsolete by the time developing economies acquire the skills to use them effectively. This 'technology lag' perpetuates dependence and constrains the Global South's competitiveness, even in the era of AI and robotics, where diffusion is theoretically faster through online connectivity.

Nonetheless, transformative examples exist. In Ghana, for instance, drones have been deployed to deliver essential medical supplies to remote areas, enhancing healthcare access (Aikins, 2021). Yet, global technology giants Google, Amazon, Apple, Facebook and Netflix retain dominance over data and digital infrastructure, reinforcing asymmetries in access and control. While digitalisation may offer opportunities to strengthen financial and economic systems in the Global South, it simultaneously raises cybersecurity vulnerabilities that require proactive, context-specific policy responses.

Aikins (2021) draws on Kwame Nkrumah's vision that the Global South must 'seek first the technological kingdom' to achieve true independence. AI and robotics present both a promise and a paradox: the potential to bridge the divide, yet the risk of deepening it if ethical governance, equitable access and strategic capacity-building are not prioritised. This raises a critical question – what ethical frameworks and governance models are needed to ensure AI and robotics serve as tools for empowerment rather than instruments of exclusion?

Ethical Issues

Ethical concerns surrounding AI and robotics remain pressing, particularly for emerging economies. Core challenges include unequal accessibility, data privacy, protection, infrastructural investment and technology transfer mechanisms. Because these technologies largely originate in advanced economies, developing countries face additional barriers such as limited data storage capacity, high operational costs and restricted access to secure servers. For much of Africa, the high cost of data alone can impede adoption at both macro and micro levels, threatening to keep AI and robotics integration more aspirational than practical.

Without globally coordinated ethical policies and enforceable governance frameworks, this technological divide is likely to persist. Notably, even in the Global North, AI and robotics raise serious ethical debates. Prominent figures such as Elon Musk have warned that uncontrolled AI could be more dangerous than nuclear weapons, likening its misuse to 'summoning the demon'. Similarly, Geoffrey Hinton – often called the 'godfather of AI' – resigned from Google, cautioning against unchecked reliance on AI. In the United States, OpenAI CEO

Sam Altman testified before the Senate on the urgent need for regulation, warning of risks such as electoral interference and threats to national security.

Despite these warnings, AI and robotics are rapidly entering service industries, including hospitality and tourism, delivering measurable gains in efficiency, service quality and financial management, particularly in countries like Japan and China (Allman, 2014). This trend is also evident in Ghana, where international service standards incentivise industry players to adopt emerging technologies to enhance competitiveness. Ghana is among 18 African countries with active AI development initiatives and one of 21 that have prioritised AI in national development plans. It has launched relevant strategies and policies, established AI centres of excellence and aligned AI with broader development goals. However, as UNESCO (2021) reports, Ghana has yet to issue formal ethical guidelines or enact legislation to govern AI and robotics deployment, leaving a critical gap between ambition and ethical safeguards.

Current Trends

Global interest in AI continues to rise rapidly. According to a McKinsey survey, AI adoption increased from 50% in 2020 to 56% in 2021, and 64–76% of organisations now prioritise AI over other IT initiatives (https://www.mckinsey.com/featured-insights/2021-year-in-review). Adoption momentum remains strong: AI investment in hospitality is projected to grow by 60% annually through 2033, and travel executives increasingly view AI as essential for delivering personalised guest experiences (https://www.netsuite.com/portal/resource/articles/business-strategy/ai-hospitality.shtml).

The AI in the tourism market is expanding dramatically from USD 3.37 billion in 2024 to a projected USD 13.87 billion by 2030 at a CAGR of 26.7%, highlighting its growing commercial importance (https://www.grandviewresearch.com/industry-analysis/infrastructure-as-code-market-report). Similarly, the broader global AI market is expected to surge from USD 2.95 billion in 2024 to over USD 13.3 billion by 2030, reflecting a CAGR of 28.7% (https://artsmart.ai/).

In the hospitality and tourism sector, AI's footprint extends across operational layers. Applications such as personalised chatbots, virtual assistants, dynamic revenue management and automated check-in systems are increasingly commonplace (Thaichon, 2024, 2025; https://hoteltechreport.com/news/best-hotel-tech-list/2025). Service robots are now ubiquitous in hotels, managing functions traditionally handled by humans, from environmental controls in 'smart rooms' to concierge services (Drexler & Lapré, 2019).

Recent innovations add further texture to this landscape. Studies highlight the rise of social robots that enhance customer engagement through empathetic and interactive design (Skubis, 2024), and real-time language translation tools are poised to break down travel barriers, enabling more immersive global tourism (An & Abukhalifeh, 2025). Generative AI is being deployed innovatively, such as Italy's 'zIA' chatbot, a friendly virtual 'auntie' providing personalised travel support (Cassani et al., 2024). Experiments with AI concierge systems utilising wearables and IoT data also signal growing real-time personalisation capabilities (Manos et al., 2024).

Preparedness

Adopting AI and robotics in tourism and hospitality has evolved from an option to an imperative. These technologies are reshaping industry standards, prompting businesses to prepare strategically or risk becoming obsolete. Drexler and Lapré (2019) emphasise that adoption is motivated by convenience, efficiency and economic advantage. Recent global events accelerated this shift: COVID-19 catalysed unprecedented digital transformation, with AI systems sustaining essential services, driving digital consumption and elevating data as a strategic asset.

Emerging research confirms that technological readiness is foundational for successful AI adoption factors, such as infrastructure, organisational capability and dynamic adaptability are pivotal (Alam, 2025). The pivotal role of education and workforce empowerment is gaining recognition, with researchers calling for AI-integrated training programmes to elevate ICT literacy and sustainable practices in the hospitality sector, especially among small-scale operators (Lukose & Agbeyangi, 2024).

Expectations and Concerns

The promise of AI and robotics centres on efficiency, cost reduction and improved service consistency (Drexler & Lapré, 2019). However, the reality often falls short. Practical trials – such as robotic waiters – have faced failure due to technical shortcomings, poor service performance and unmet expectations (Drexler & Lapré, 2019). Beyond operational constraints, service delivery in tourism remains deeply human-centred; impersonal machine interactions risk undermining guest satisfaction unless guest-host dynamics are thoughtfully reimagined (Murphy et al., 2017).

Human–robot collaboration introduces cultural and emotional complexity. For personnel, Human–Robot Interaction (HRI) may lead to feelings of isolation and diminished morale if not governed by inclusive workplace strategies (Osawa et al., 2017). To address these shortcomings and concern, Siegel et al. (1997) suggest that hospitality organizations would require well formulated and intentional policies with attention to staff retraining programmes, role realignment, and clear career pathways for both human and robotic workers.

Methodology

This study employed the quantitative methodological approach with the use of a survey. A questionnaire was developed using Google Forms, and a purposive sampling method was adopted. The questionnaire was widely circulated among the target population for the study, comprising CEOs, managers and supervisors of hotels operating in the Western Region of Ghana. The questionnaire was administered mainly through WhatsApp platforms of the Ghana Hotelier's Association of the Western Region. Thus, data were collected electronically through Google via WhatsApp platforms. The coverage was limited to managers, supervisors and chief executive officers of hotels from within the Western Region on the basis that they are decision makers in the sector. Data were analysed with descriptive statistical inferences from bar charts and pie charts. In addition, Likert scale applications were also used to make meaning of some responses. Out of the analyses, conclusions have been drawn to provide significant pointers for further research.

The Western Region, in general, boasts 125 star-rated hotels. Out of this number, 3 are of 4-star status, 5 are of 3-star status, 26 are of 2-star status and 91 are of 1-star status. The star-rated hotels considered for this study range from 1-star to 4-star hotels. In this regard, it was expected that at least 250 respondents would respond to the survey. However, the total number of responses received after circulation of the questionnaire was 176.

Findings and Discussion

Respondents and Hotel Star Rating

Though the questionnaire was posted on an active WhatsApp platform of the Hotelier Association of the Western Region, targeting managers, supervisors and CEOs of hotels operating within the Western Region, the expected response was below expectations. Attributable reasons and assumptions are that the majority of the target group may not have had the time to fill up the questionnaire or were ignorant of the processes one needed to go through in filling up the questionnaire on their phones. Another assumption is that the majority of the target group may have found it unimportant or were unconcerned about emerging technologies in the hotel sub-sector of the tourism industry. It is notable that the majority of the responses came from 1-star-rated hotels because, apparently, the hotels of this star rate rank the highest in the region, as indicated in Table 1.

Table 1. Respondents and Their Rated Hotels.

Star Rated	Frequency (N = 176)	Percentage (%)
1 Star Hotel	120	68
2 Star Hotel	40	23
3 Star Hotel	10	6
4 Star Hotel	6	3
Total	*176*	*100*

Source: Field Survey, 2023–2024.

Sex of Respondents

The sex of respondents shows a relatively high number of males dominating managerial positions in the hotel sub-sector of the tourism industry in the Western Region. Even though women play roles in the sector, there seems to be a gender disparity at high levels of decision-making and the management echelon of the hotel sub-sector. Out of the total number of respondents, 60% were male, while 40% represented female respondents. Arguably, the data shows that men are mostly placed in high-level management positions.

Job Function of Respondents

Data indicate that 74% of the 176 respondents are managers, 23% are supervisors, while 3% are chief executive officers. These positions represent the decision-making body of most organisations and, for that matter, the hotels from which responses were received. This is indicative that the majority of the hotels are being managed by managers rather than chief executive officers, as indicated by the data in Table 2.

Age of Respondents

The age status of respondents indicates that the majority of respondents are below 55 years old. This shows that most hotels in the region are being managed by a much younger population and therefore are people who are in their active years, as indicated in Table 3. Given these data, it would be interesting to conduct future research to understand the motivations leading to the high number of people in active years choosing to work in the hotel sub-sector of the tourism industry.

Years of Experience

Data on years of experience of respondents in the hotel industry indicate that the majority have been in the industry for 10 years and above. This shows that most of the respondents are highly experienced, as represented in Fig. 1. The high

Table 2. Job Functions.

Job Functions	**Frequency (N = 176)**	**Percentage (%)**
Manager	130	74
Supervisors	40	23
CEOs	6	3

Source: Field Survey, 2023–2024.

Table 3. Age of Respondents.

Age	**Frequency (*N* = 176)**	**Percentage (%)**
Below 55	120	68
Above 55	56	32

Source: Field Survey, 2023–2024.

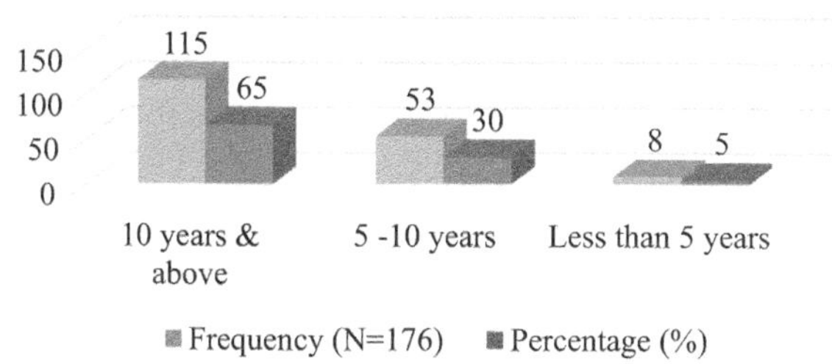

Fig. 1. Years of Experience. *Source:* Fieldwork, 2023–2024.

number of years of experience is indicative of a knowledgeable population in managing positions in the industry.

Awareness of Emerging AI Technologies

Table 4 data indicate that 50% of respondents are highly aware of emerging AI technologies in the tourism industry, while 40% are aware, followed by 10% of the respondents who are partially aware. Awareness of the emerging use of AI, as per the data, is indicative of the fact that respondents are not oblivious to the changes taking place in the use of AI technologies in the hotel sub-sector of the tourism industry and therefore cannot be ignorant.

Table 4. Level of Awareness of Emerging AI and Robotics Technologies.

Variable	**Frequency (*N* = 176)**	**Percentage (%)**
Highly Aware	88	50
Aware	70	40
Partial awareness	18	10

Source: Field Survey, 2023–2024.

Source of Awareness of AI Technologies

Data on the question of the sources from which respondents became aware of the emerging use of AI technologies in the hotel sub-sector of the tourism industry suggests that social media is highly sourced as an awareness platform. Thus, it is a major means by which respondents have become aware of the use of AI technologies in the hotel sub-sector of the tourism industry, as it accounts for 45% of the total responses. Television and the internet follow as a pair, accounting 23% each of the responses, with newsmagazines as the least source of awareness, as presented in Table 5. The assumptions here are that the respondents may be comfortable with accessing information from their technological gadgets, such as phones, rather than reading materials such as newsmagazines. Also, the nonavailability or irregular access to newsmagazines could be a possible factor.

Sources of Awareness of Robotics Technology

On the sources of awareness of robotics technologies, it is inferred that social media accounts for 43% and thus it is the major source of awareness, followed by television, accounting for 34% of responses. This is followed by internet with 17% and lastly, 6% in relation to news magazines. The data are therefore indicative of the fact that the majority resort to the use of technology in general for information, and specifically social media, television and the internet, as represented in Table 6.

Preferred Use of AI Technologies

Responding to the question of operational areas where the use of AI technologies is preferred, respondents, amidst a range of operational areas spanning the bar, lounge, restaurant, kitchen, administration, front office, housekeeping and room service, indicated a high preference for the use of AI in administrative operations. This choice accounted for 34% of the responses, followed by use for front office operations, which is 23% and subsequently, the restaurant 17%, Housekeeping 9%, the lounge 6% and lastly 3% for room service respectively, as presented in Table 7.

Table 5. Sources of AI Technologies Awareness.

Sources	**Frequency (N = 176)**	**Percentage (%)**
TV	40	23
Social media	80	45
Internet	40	23
Newsmagazine	16	9

Source: Field Survey, 2023–2024.

Table 6. Sources of Robotics Technology Awareness.

Variables	Frequency (N = 176)	Percentage (%)
TV	60	34
Social media	76	43
Internet	30	17
Newsmagazine	10	6

Source: Field Survey, 2023–2024.

Table 7. Preferred Operational Areas to Use AI.

Areas of Operations	Frequency (N = 176)	Percentage (%)
Bar	6	3
Lounge	10	6
Restaurant	30	17
Kitchen	10	6
Administration	60	34
Front Office	40	23
House Keeping	15	9
Room Service	5	3

Source: Field Survey, 2023–2024.

Expected Impact of AI in Operations

Respondents gave varied views on the expected impact of the use of AI in hotel operations. Altogether, the responses point to perceived outcomes of the use of AI technologies. The range of expected impact as projected in Fig. 2 indicates that, the highest expected positive outcome is efficiency in general operations, accounting for 38% of the responses. This is followed by 17% indicating improved revenue generation, 11% indicating a reduction in cost of operations and lastly 11% indicating a reduction in expenditure on labour. On the other hand, respondents also perceived negative impacts by indicating that the use of AI could pose electronic challenges and also negatively impact on human resources. These accounted for 17% and 6%, respectively.

Preferred Operational Areas to Use Robotics

Responding to the question of the use of robotics technology in hotel operations, respondents preferred to use this technology in a range of operational areas, including the kitchen, accounting for 34% and the highest operational area of preference. This is followed by housekeeping 23%, with use in restaurant

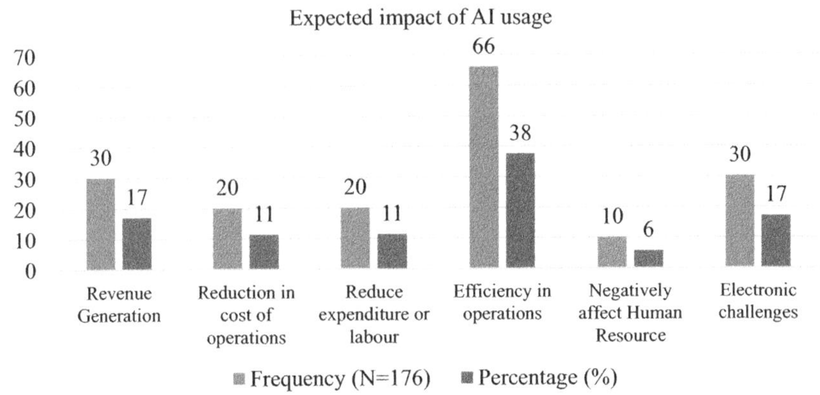

Fig. 2. Expected Impact of the Use of AI. *Source:* Fieldwork, 2023–2024.

operations accounting for 18%. Trailing these are the Front Office (9%), Administration (6%), Lounge (5%) and lastly 3% for Bar and Room service operations as presented in Table 8.

Expected Impact of Use of Robotics in Hotel Operations

Responding to the question of expected impacts, respondents were of the view that the use of robotics in hotel operations would reduce the cost of operations. This view or opinion accounts for 65.3% of the responses. 22.7% indicated that the use of robotic technologies would improve the general use of technology in hotel operations. Improvement in human resource and efficiency in operations accounted for 6.3% and 5.7%, respectively (See Table 9).

Table 8. Preferred Areas of Robotics in Hotel Operations.

Variables	Frequency (N = 176)	Percentage (%)
Bar	6	3
Lounge	8	5
Restaurant	32	18
Kitchen	60	34
Administration	10	6
Front Office	15	9
House Keeping	40	23
Room Service	5	3

Source: Field Survey, 2023–2024.

Table 9. Expected Positive Impact of Robotics.

Variables	Frequency (*N* = 176)	Percentage (%)
Reduce the cost of operations	115	65.3
Improve technology	40	22.7
Improve human resources	11	6.3
Efficiency in operations	10	5.7

Source: Field Survey, 2023–2024.

Respondents Concern About AI and Robotics

Although respondents have high expectations for the use of AI and robotics technologies, they raise concerns that are perceived to be detrimental to operations in the hotel sub-sector in particular and the tourism and hospitality industry as a whole. Table 10 shows the list of concerns raised by respondents.

Significantly, these concerns are also marked by collective responses where 20% represent the view that the use of AI and robotics technologies would have a detrimental impact on human relations. Seven percent raised the concern that technological transformations in these technologies would be difficult to cope with, while another 17% are of the view that AI and robotics technologies have cost implications. 11% indicate that these technologies would change work ethics and human behaviour, and 11% also show that the use of these technologies could make them loose customers, as represented in Table 11.

Table 10. List of Concerns.

S. No	Use Artificial Intelligence and Robotics Technology
1.	Takes away the tangible experience.
2.	The guest might lose the service experience.
3.	Human-to-human relationships would be lost.
4.	Cost implications.
5.	Certainly, there would be areas that would need the human touch.
6.	Change in the working behaviour of workers.
7.	There will be no human experience.
8.	Lead to loss of customers.

Source: Authors' compilation from data 2023–2024.

Table 11. Concerns About Use of AI and Robotics.

Variables	Frequency (N = 176)	Percentage (%)
Will take away tangible experience.	15	9
Guest will lose the service experience	25	14
Lack of human relations.	36	20
Cost implications.	30	17
Change in work ethics/behaviour.	20	11
Loose customers.	20	11
Technological transformations are difficult to cope with.	30	17

Source: Field Survey, 2023–2024.

Conclusion

Managers, supervisors and CEOs of hotels in the Western Region of Ghana are aware of emerging robotics and AI technologies in the tourism and hospitality industry. Primarily, they generated their awareness from sources such as social media, the internet and television. There is a relatively high level of acceptance with regard to the use of these technologies; however, there are clear concerns as to the detrimental impact these technologies may have on the industry even though there are impacts that are expected to be positive, for instance, efficiency in operations. Also, the study suggests that there are preferred areas of operations where the industry players would like to have and use AI and robotics technologies. These are mainly the kitchen, restaurant and housekeeping for robotics and administration, front office and restaurant for AI technologies.

Recommendation

Even though the questionnaire was widely circulated using a dedicated WhatsApp platform, the expected number of responses was not achieved. This may be due to lack of access to internet connectivity, lack of data and time constraints. The limited sample size may not reflect the general attribute, but the data provides information on aspects of characteristics of sample population in relation to AI and robotics technologies in hotel operations. Future studies should employ alternative designs, preferably mixed methods, with longer data collection periods to capture a broader and more representative sample. Replicating the study in other major Ghanaian cities through a national baseline survey would provide valuable comparative insights into the awareness, preferences and major concerns of the tourism and hospitality sector about the use of AI and robotics technologies. Such research would strengthen evidence for both policy and practice.

To improve awareness, policy should prioritise public education through targeted industry seminars and mass media campaigns. Monitoring social media narratives will also help policymakers address misinformation on emerging technologies. Integrating AI and robotics training into tourism and hospitality education would be a strategic approach to prepare future professionals to embrace the use of AI and robotics technologies and technological changes in general.

Ghana's proactive AI policy direction, as noted by UNESCO (2021), highlights government recognition of the technologies' economic potential. Building on this momentum and developing collaboration networks among policymakers, industry players, experts, academics and researchers would lead to the development of ethical frameworks, practical guidelines and strategic synergies that could maximise the use of emerging AI and robotics technologies for economic growth and social benefits while safeguarding tourism and hospitality industry standards.

References

Aikins, J. K. (2021). *Seek ye first the digital kingdom? Between data extractivism and digital self-determinism*. Africa Policy Research Institute. http://afripoli.org

Alam, S. S. (2025). Relationship between technology readiness, AI adoption, dynamic capabilities, sustainable competitive advantage, and technological innovation. *Journal of Business Research*. https://doi.org/10.1016/j.jbusres.2025.114567

Allman, T. (2014, December 13). China restaurant introduces robot waiters. *BBC News*. http://www.bbc.com/news/av/world-asia-30460737

An, Q., & Abukhalifeh, A. N. M. (2025). Technological interventions in overcoming language barriers and facilitating travel experiences of international students. *Journal of Tourism and Cultural Change*, *23*(2–3), 172–188.

Cassani, A., Ruberl, M., Salis, A., Giannese, G., & Boanelli, G. (2024). *zIA: A GenAI-powered local auntie assists tourists in Italy*. https://arxiv.org/pdf/2407.11830

Drexler, N., & Lapré, V. B. (2019). For better or for worse: Shaping the hospitality industry through robotics and artificial intelligence. *Research in Hospitality Management*, *9*(2), 117–120. https://doi.org/10.1080/22243534.2019.1689700

Haenlein, M., Kaplan, A., Tan, C. W., & Zhang, P. (2019). A brief history of artificial intelligence: On the past, present, and future of artificial intelligence. *California Management Review*, *61*(4), 5–14. https://doi.org/10.1177/0008125619864925

International Organization for Standardization. (2012). *ISO 8373:2012(en) Robots and robotic devices – Vocabulary*. https://www.iso.org/standard/55890.html

Ivanov, S., & Webster, C. (2020). Robots in tourism: A research agenda for tourism economics. *Tourism Economics*, *26*(7), 1065–1085.

Lukose, J., & Agbeyangi, A. (2024). Enhancing ICT literacy and sustainable practices in the hospitality industry: Insights from Mnquma Municipality. *Hospitality Research Journal*. https://doi.org/10.48550/arXiv.2410.02781

Manos, A., Filipidou, D. E., Deliyannis, I., Pavlidis, N., Argyros, V., & Mazi, I. (2024). *Personalized travel recommendations using wearables and AI: The INDIANA platform*. https://doi.org/10.48550/arXiv.2411.12227

Murphy, J., Hofacker, C., & Gretzel, U. (2017). Dawning of the age of robots in hospitality and tourism: Challenges for teaching and research. *European Journal of Tourism Research*, *15*, 104–111.

Osawa, H., Ema, A., Hattori, H., Akiya, N., Kanzaki, N., Kubo, A., Koyama, T., & Ichise, R. (2017, March 6–9). What is real risk and benefit on work with robots? From the analysis of a robot hotel. In *Proceedings of the companion of the 2017 ACM/IEEE international conference on human-robot interaction* (pp. 241–242). Vienna, Austria. https://doi.org/10.1145/3029798.3038312

Raslan, R. (2021). Transfer of technology: A North–South debate? *Queen Mary Journal of Intellectual Property*, *11*(3), 339–361. https://doi.org/10.4337/qmjip.2021.03.06

Siegel, D. S., Waldman, D. A., & Youngdahl, W. E. (1997). The adoption of advanced manufacturing technologies: Human resource management implications. *IEEE Transactions on Engineering Management*, *44*(3), 288–298. https://doi.org/10.1109/17.618170

Skubis, I. (2024). Exploring the potential and perceptions of social robots in tourism and hospitality: Insights from industry executives and technology evaluation. *International Journal of Social Robotics*, *17*(2025), 59–72. https://doi.org/10.1007/s12369-024-01197-z

Thaichon, P., Dutta, P. K., Chelliah, P. R., & Gupta, S. (Eds.). (2024). *Technology and luxury hospitality: AI blockchain and the metaverse*. Routledge.

Thaichon, P., Dutta, P. K., Haghi, A. K., & Dutta, S. (Eds.). (2025). *Digital disruption in hospitality: AI and emerging technologies*. Emerald Publishing Limited.

Tung, V. W. S., & Law, R. (2017). The potential for tourism and hospitality experience research in human–robot interactions. *International Journal of Contemporary Hospitality Management*, *29*(10), 2498–2513. https://doi.org/10.1108/IJCHM-10-2015-0618

UNESCO. (2021). *Artificial intelligence needs assessment survey in Africa*. UNESCO Publishing.

Wolfgang, E. (2017). *Introduction to artificial intelligence*. Springer International Publishing.

Chapter 8

Evaluating the Role of AI in Promoting Responsible and Sustainable Tourism Development

Nandipha David

University of South Africa, South Africa

Abstract

The Fourth Industrial Revolution is characterised by rapidly evolving technologies, with Artificial Intelligence (AI) being a transformative innovation across global industries. AI is defined as computer systems capable of performing tasks requiring human intelligence. In tourism, various AI applications, including facial recognition, virtual reality, chatbots and voice-activated conversational AI like Siri and Alexa, are enhancing tourist experiences through features such as language translation, audio tours and personalised recommendations. Beyond marketing, AI holds significant potential as a persuasive tool to influence consumer choices and promote responsible travel behaviour, thereby supporting sustainable tourism development. This chapter defines AI, responsible and sustainable tourism, evaluates different AI types for their role in sustainable tourism development and discusses the economic, social and environmental implications.

Keywords: Artificial Intelligence; developing countries; emerging economies; responsible tourism; sustainable tourism; environmental impacts

Introduction

Tourism is a thriving industry with a significant impact on economies worldwide (Ferràs et al., 2020). Despite facing challenges, such as global crises, the tourism sector has managed to generate revenue and employment opportunities. The

Artificial Intelligence in Hospitality and Tourism in Africa, 129–145

doi:10.1108/978-1-80686-169-920261008

integration of information and communication technology has revolutionised international tourism, offering avenues for innovation and ensuring sustained competitiveness and growth. Notably, Artificial Intelligence (AI) technology has emerged as a game-changer, transforming the customer experience and management systems within the tourism industry (Ding, 2021). From personalisation and recommendation systems to robotics and intelligent travel agents, AI has permeated various aspects of travel and tourism (Zhang, 2022).

The advancement of AI can be attributed to progress in computational power, machine learning, deep learning, artificial vision, and voice and speech recognition (Zhang, 2022). In the tourism sector, AI enables efficient analysis of large customer datasets and facilitates voice interactions with users, fundamentally altering the dynamics of the industry. Furthermore, the proliferation of cloud computing capabilities and the integration of diverse sensors in physical environments have created a holistic tourist experience, resulting in unprecedented transformations in the field (Ferràs et al., 2020). AI technologies, such as face recognition, voice recognition, language translation, image consolidation and tourist information sorting and transmission, have found extensive applications in the tourism industry, attracting an increasingly wider audience (Ding, 2021, p. 2).

In developing countries, where tourism has gained absolute and relative importance, achieving social benefits, inclusive development and environmental conservation is a priority. Leveraging the advantages of AI can inject fresh momentum into the growth of developing countries, while also addressing sustainability concerns. Sustainable tourism development, especially in developing countries, necessitates a stronger emphasis on the role of AI in promoting responsible and sustainable practices (Li et al., 2022).

The integration of AI in the tourism industry has ushered in a new era of possibilities, transforming customer experiences and management practices. While presenting both benefits and challenges, AI has the potential to drive sustainable tourism development, particularly in African countries. By harnessing AI's power, the tourism sector can achieve social, economic and environmental objectives, fostering a more responsible and enjoyable travel experience.

Literature Review

Researchers have started to recognise the benefits of AI in promoting responsible and sustainable tourism (Tussyadiah & Miller, 2019; Tussyadiah, 2020), and as such, AI adoption is being studied extensively with the opportunities and challenges being highlighted in different contexts (Buhalis et al., 2019; Ivanov, 2020; Ukpabi et al., 2018). Despite extensive research, there is, however, still a lack of research on the influence of AI in responsible and sustainable tourism development in the context of emerging and developing countries. Therefore, this chapter intends to explore the potential of AI in developing countries and identify the opportunities and challenges for responsible and sustainable tourism development.

AI in Developing countries

As research on AI becomes more widespread, its definition is often linked to the discipline in which the research is being conducted. The findings in recent studies conducted by Tussyadiah (2020) and Tuo et al. (2021) indicate that most definitions of AI centre around it being a subfield of computer science or how machines can imitate human intelligence. The term 'artificial intelligence' was first coined by John McCarthy, who used the term to describe computer programs that, on the face of it, exhibit intelligence (McCarthy, 2007; Rajaraman, 2014). AI is defined as 'the ability of a digital computer or computer-controlled robot to perform tasks commonly associated with intelligent beings' (Zielinski et al., 2023, p. 7). Essentially, AI involves the development of computers to perform intelligent tasks or solve problems that require reasoning and human intelligence. Therefore, AI is generally regarded as a 'family of technologies' that can recognise, analyse, act, learn and demonstrate enhanced features of human intelligence (Wang et al., 2022, p. 956).

AI can be classified into three categories (see Fig. 1): Weak AI, Strong AI and Super-intelligence AI. The primary focus of Weak AI, also known as Narrow AI, is on performing specific tasks. Strong AI aims to create systems that can perform human-like tasks. Superintelligence AI is defined as any comprehension that surpasses human intellectual activities in any domain (Wang et al., 2022). According to Tuo et al. (2021), the tourism industry is witnessing the growth of AI from Weak AI to Strong AI. To exhibit human behaviour, machines require six capabilities, which represent different subdisciplines of AI. These capabilities include natural language processing, knowledge representation, automated reasoning, machine learning, computer vision and robotics (Tussyadiah, 2020).

Emerging economies like India have explored the potential of AI through the successful use of a robot waitress in a restaurant (in Gujarat, India), which demonstrated the appeal of robotics in the hospitality industry by attracting customers from all over India. This success story demonstrates the vast potential for further AI-powered technologies in the tourism industry of India, enhancing customer experiences and boosting economic growth. Krishnan et al. (2022) predict that by 2028, the proper implementation of AI could increase India's GDP by 9.9%, resulting in significant economic and sustainable growth for the country. The research concludes that technological advancements are crucial for the development of India's economy and sustainability as a developing nation.

Responsible and Sustainable Tourism Development

How does AI link with responsible and sustainable tourism? To answer this question, we must first understand what responsible and sustainable tourism is. Responsible and sustainable tourism has been studied since the 1980s, with the Bruntland Report serving as the starting point of the sustainability debate in tourism (Brundtland, 1987). Published in 1987, the Brundtland Report increased awareness of sustainability and aimed to address the negative impacts of development on the environment. The idea of a more responsible form of

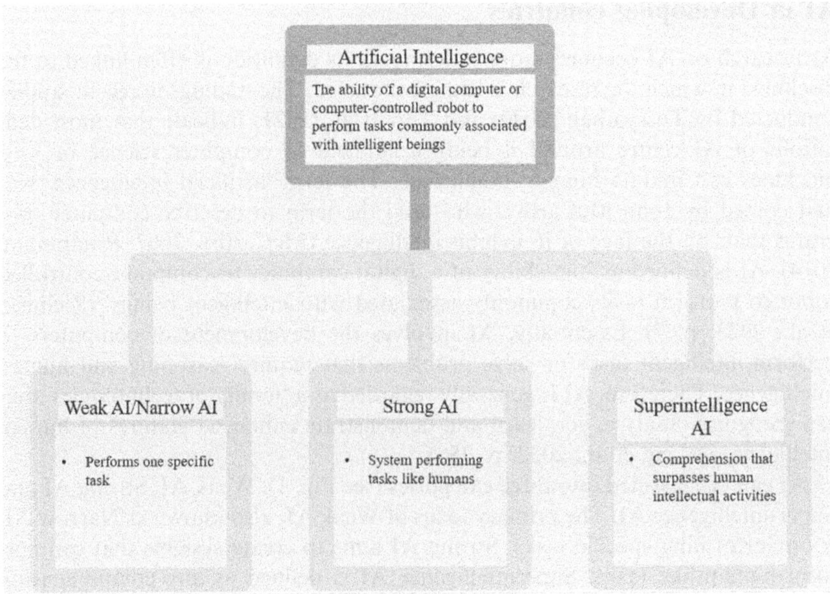

Fig. 1. Artificial Intelligence Classification. *Source*: Author, Adapted From Wang et al., 2022.

tourism was discussed and became an important element within the emerging concept of sustainable tourism. In the last two decades, combining the concepts of responsible and sustainable development with tourism has been the most effective approach to reducing the vulnerabilities of tourism-led developments (Eyisi et al., 2021).

Dávid (2011) suggests that numerous approaches have been put forward to ensure the sustainable management of tourism. However, regardless of the specific sustainability framework employed, it is important to note that sustainability in tourism encompasses more than just environmental aspects. It encompasses the interconnected dimensions of the environment, society and economy. Achieving a balance between these three components is crucial for sustainable tourism, irrespective of the strategic framework adopted. This is because the relationship between tourists, host communities, businesses, attractions and nature is complex yet mutually beneficial, with interactions that are both interconnected and symbiotic (Dávid, 2011). Destinations that prioritise responsible and sustainable tourism can manage resources in a way that meets economic, social and aesthetic needs while also preserving essential ecological processes, biodiversity, life-supporting systems and cultural integrity of diverse communities.

Several studies focusing on tourism sustainability have primarily examined community-based and pro-poor tourism, as well as the positive and negative effects of tourism on various aspects such as the environment, economic development, inequality, income distribution and poverty reduction (Sfodera et al., 2022). Despite decades of academic and practical discussions on the topic, implementing tourism sustainability remains challenging for developing nations. Emerging economies face obstacles such as inadequate infrastructure, limited skill levels, high levels of foreign ownership leading to a loss of control over local resources, limited integration with other domestic economic sectors, uneven distribution of development opportunities, fluctuating earnings due to seasonality and global economic downturns, environmental degradation with the depletion of non-renewable resources, growing detachment among local communities, conflicts over limited resources, increasing crime rates, overcrowding, strained infrastructure, rising prices of goods, services and property, and loss of cultural identity (Sfodera et al., 2022). These factors make the achievement of responsible and sustainable tourism appear unattainable. However, despite these challenges, there is still hope for progress.

To address the challenges and achieve the standards of responsible and sustainable tourism, it is essential for Developing Nations or Emerging Economies to prioritise compliance with and implementation of the United Nations Sustainable Development Goals (SDGs) (Sfodera et al., 2022).

United Nations SDGs

In 2015, the United Nations Sustainable Development Summit approved 17 SDGs, which serve as a blueprint for global development by tackling issues such as poverty, inequality, healthcare, education, gender equality, water and energy access, climate change and environmental sustainability both on land and in the oceans (Kostoska & Kocarev, 2019). Research indicates that tourism can contribute to the attainment of the SDGs in various ways (Gössling, 2021). Tourism contributes to generating income and employment opportunities, particularly in rural areas, where it contributes to poverty alleviation. Tourism can also promote the consumption of locally produced food, support wellness tourism and healthy lifestyles, provide educational opportunities, create economic opportunities for women and reduce inequalities. Additionally, tourism can support the development of sustainable tourism infrastructure, promote responsible tourism practices, conserve marine and terrestrial biodiversity, contribute to reducing greenhouse gas emissions by applying the principles of ecotourism and promote intercultural understanding and peaceful societies through cultural tourism initiatives. Finally, tourism can support partnerships and collaborations between the public and private sectors, civil society and local communities to achieve sustainable tourism development (Kostoska & Kocarev, 2019).

In recent years, there has been an increasing interest in the implementation of the United Nations SDGs. What sets the SDGs apart from previous initiatives is their universal nature, calling for action from both developed and developing countries. They urge policymakers to formulate tourism policies that address the dimensions of economic, social and environmental sustainability. The 17 SDGs are integrated and considered indivisible, aiming to strike a balance among these three aspects of sustainable development (Kostoska & Kocarev, 2019). Technology plays a crucial role in leveraging tourism as a driving force for achieving the SDGs. Advancements in technologies such as AI enable the production and efficient use of resources, contributing significantly to the attainment of the SDGs (Balsalobre-Lorente et al., 2023; Sfodera et al., 2022). In the context of sustainable tourism in developing regions, the key question revolves around how technology can assist in addressing negative environmental and sociocultural impacts while fostering economic growth.

Different Types of AI and Their Potential for Responsible and Sustainable Tourism Development

While there are existing studies exploring the role of various technologies in destination development within the tourism field, the focus on developing countries remains limited. This section of the chapter aims to address this gap by contributing to the literature on AI and sustainability in developing countries. It proposes different types of AI applications that can be considered for the responsible and sustainable development of tourism.

As developing countries tap into new global markets, tourism destinations are adopting new measures to ensure responsible and sustainable tourism practices while remaining competitive. Intelligent systems, including AI technologies, have the potential to influence consumer choices not just from a marketing standpoint but also from a social perspective, by encouraging socially desirable behaviours among tourists. Within the realm of AI, several emerging technologies have evolved in the tourism industry, which can contribute to the realization of responsible and sustainable tourism. Examples of such technologies include Virtual Reality (VR), Virtual Guide applications, Robots and Language Translator applications, and Chatbots (Krishnan et al., 2022; Pillai & Sivathanu, 2020; Samala et al., 2020; Tussyadiah & Miller, 2019; Tussyadiah, 2020). Let us delve further into these AI technologies to understand their potential application.

Virtual Reality

VR is an immersive technology that has recently revolutionised tourist experiences by combining physical and virtual elements (Loureiro et al., 2020). VR replicates real or imagined environments and allows users to interact within them, creating a sense of presence (Loureiro et al., 2020). This enhanced immersion provides users with a more vivid sensory experience, leading to a stronger feeling of being present in the virtual space. During travel, tourists engage with VR applications designed for entertainment and educational purposes (Bideci & Bideci, 2023). VR's potential as a preservation tool lies in its ability to offer virtual experiences that tourists can perceive as substitutes for physically visiting endangered sites (Guttentag, 2010a, 2010b). Particularly in protected areas with sensitive natural and cultural heritage sites, where visitor limitations are desired, VR is regarded as a positive contribution to environmental sustainability (Tussyadiah, 2020). As an example, VR enables tourists to explore delicate marine and terrestrial habitats without physically being present at the location, a concept known as avatar tourism (Ivanov, 2020, p. 357). Avatar tourism involves tourists connecting with robots at the destination, eliminating the need for physical travel and mitigating environmental pressures such as overcrowding.

The advancement of AI presents significant opportunities for tourism destinations to employ AI to influence responsible travel behaviour and achieve sustainability goals through social marketing (Tussyadiah, 2020). Tailoring behaviour change interventions to specific consumer groups based on factors that support the desired behaviours can enhance their effectiveness. For example, Millennials, a popular tourist segment (Sharma et al., 2021), have been found to have a significant interest in virtual tours (Kurniasari et al., 2022). This generation values meaningful experiences but also considers the environmental impact of their actions (Kurniasari et al., 2022). As a result, virtual tours can be incorporated into sustainable travel practices.

China, as one of the largest emerging economies, has already embraced VR tours as a means of preserving natural heritage sites. As early as 2013, Chen et al. (2013, p. 1) developed a digital tour guiding system called 'TelePort' that allowed users to virtually explore the Mogao Caves in Dunhuang City, China, using mobile devices. This system enabled users to view Buddhist cave artwork, including pieces that were damaged or lost, as if they were physically present. Through VR, responsible and sustainable heritage tourism is achieved by promoting environmental protection and heritage conservation through the revitalisation and preservation of these sites (Poetry, 2021). The sustainable nature of VR tours helps ensure that the present generation's needs are met without compromising the ability of future generations to meet their own needs (Bausch et al., 2022).

Virtual Tour Guide

In the tourism industry, AI has predominantly been developed and utilised by tourism suppliers. There is, however, a recent shift towards exploring the use of AI by consumers, in this case, the use of digital tour guides by tourists (Chiao et al., 2018). This development has led to the availability of various AI technologies that offer self-service options to tourists, such as electronic tour guides. With the e-tour guide function, visitors can access relevant information regardless of the specific scenic spot they visit. These e-guides use satellite positioning to guide visitors, providing accurate introductions to the historical stories associated with each location while also avoiding environmentally sensitive areas. Interactive tour guide applications play a crucial role in enhancing each visitor's experience by tailoring the route and information displayed based on individual preferences. Moreover, they contribute to improved predictions of tourist numbers, enhancing route planning and the overall quality of scenic spot management.

Interestingly, tourism destinations with limited technological infrastructure can still benefit from virtual tour guides that are specifically designed to promote responsible and sustainable travel experiences. These virtual tour guides provide an alternative solution, leveraging AI technology to enhance the visitor experience and ensure sustainable practices are followed. By incorporating AI-powered virtual guides, these destinations can offer engaging and informative experiences while minimising negative environmental impacts. This approach contributes to the overall sustainability and responsible management of the tourism industry.

Robots

Robots, as AI-driven assistants, utilise the capabilities of the Internet of Things (IoT) to perform assigned tasks. Unlike other automation technologies, such as chatbots that exist solely in the virtual realm, robots have a physical embodiment. In the context of responsible and sustainable tourism, innovative underwater robots and drones play a significant role. Furthermore, robots can assist in managing tourism activities in environmentally sensitive areas (Ivanov et al., 2023).

From an economic standpoint, robots have an enhancing effect by improving the productivity of tourism employees. The Freedom Park Heritage Site in South Africa has the potential to benefit from the introduction of robots. By automating tasks that are dull or repetitive, robots can contribute to a better-quality work environment for tourism professionals (Ivanov et al., 2023) employed at the heritage site.

Language Translator Applications

The introduction of AI technology for language translation has transformed tourism by enhancing accessibility and breaking down communication barriers, thereby facilitating more meaningful interactions between tourists and locals. When travelling to foreign countries, language barriers can pose challenges; therefore, applications that assist with language translation have emerged as powerful tools that can translate multiple languages, enabling tourists to communicate with locals without the need for expensive language translation services or local guides (Krishnan et al., 2022; Samala et al., 2020). The Samsung Galaxy AI smartphone offers users built-in language translation applications that provide interpretation and translation services during face-to-face conversations and text messaging (Samsung, 2024). Google Translate also offers a 'conversation mode' feature, allowing for seamless back-and-forth dialogue, with the translator detecting and translating languages in real time (Krishnan et al., 2022, p. 295). One notable advantage of this application is its ability to operate offline by downloading languages, making it particularly valuable with limited telecommunications infrastructure and unreliable internet connectivity.

Breaking down language barriers in tourism holds social, economic and environmental benefits. Language translation applications positively impact responsible and sustainable tourism by facilitating more meaningful social interactions between tourists and locals. For instance, when visiting rural areas where Indigenous languages are spoken, travellers can engage with local communities in their native language, fostering authentic cultural exchanges and providing a unique experience in unfamiliar surroundings. Consider the scenario of a Mandarin-speaking tourist from China visiting a rural homestead in KwaZulu Natal, South Africa, and being able to communicate with locals in Zulu while locals respond in Mandarin. Such applications also have economic advantages as they enable tourists to explore destinations that were previously inaccessible due to language barriers. Additionally, the integration of camera functionality in applications like Google Translate allows for the translation of written signage, including environmental laws and educational information about local flora and fauna in nature reserves and protected areas (Samala et al., 2020).

By leveraging AI-based language translation applications, tourism experiences become more inclusive, fostering social connections, supporting local economies and promoting environmental awareness in diverse destinations.

Chatbots

Chatbots, short for chat robots, utilise AI technology and a built-in computer program to establish communication with humans (Pillai & Sivathanu, 2020). There are two main types of AI-based chatbots: text message-based chatbots and voice-based chatbots. Text message-based chatbots rely on pre-loaded answers to frequently asked customer questions, while voice-based chatbots use voice messages to address customer queries. The interface for chatbots can be accessed through various devices such as computers and smartphones (Apple's Siri, and Amazon's Alexa).

In the tourism industry, chatbots play a significant role in travel planning, customer booking, customer support, and providing recommendations to customers regarding travel-related matters. To foster responsible and sustainable tourism development, chatbots can be designed as persuasive agents in efforts to modify behaviour and intervene with travel consumers. By programming chatbots to offer recommendations and suggestions that encourage responsible travel behaviour, they can contribute to promoting sustainability (Tussyadiah & Miller, 2019).

As tourists increasingly rely on VR, chatbots, virtual guides, robots, and language translator applications to meet their daily life and travel needs, it is crucial to evaluate the potential of AI in addressing economic, social and environmental challenges. Tussyadiah (2020) emphasises the need for a fundamental shift in how we perceive intelligent technology, moving beyond considering them mere tools and recognising their complex role as significant social actors.

Opportunities and Challenges of AI on The Economic, Social and Environmental Aspects of Responsible and Sustainable Tourism Development

The next step after obtaining knowledge of the different types of AI and their potential for responsible and sustainable tourism development is recognising the range of opportunities and challenges resulting from the implementation of intelligent automation.

The economic dimension of responsible and sustainable tourism encompasses both positive and negative impacts on emerging economies. On one hand, the implementation of language translating applications can open up previously inaccessible destinations to a larger number of visitors, potentially increasing income opportunities. On the other hand, the widespread use of AI and robots may result in job losses and reduced salaries for human employees and ultimately the revenue of countries in the long run. The massive introduction of robots, in particular, poses a risk of decreasing the income tax base and subsequently leading to a significant drop in income tax revenue (Sfodera et al., 2022).

The social dimension of responsible and sustainable tourism focuses on the sociocultural effects on local communities. Local community participation is widely recognised as an important criterion for responsible and sustainable tourism. Technological innovations like language translator applications are considered favourable for their potential to respect the sociocultural authenticity of host communities, preserve cultural heritage and traditional values, and foster intercultural understanding and tolerance between tourists and locals. However, the dominance of AI-enabled technologies, such as VR and chatbots, may reduce the need for personal, face-to-face interactions between tourists and residents, posing a challenge to local communities. Access to AI-enabled technologies is often limited for emerging economies, hindering full participation and potentially reducing entry-level jobs in the tourism industry for locals, which can negatively impact their well-being (Krishnan et al., 2022; Pillai & Sivathanu, 2020; Tussyadiah & Miller, 2019; Tussyadiah, 2020).

The environmental dimension of responsible and sustainable tourism focuses on the conservation of natural resources and cultural heritage. Understanding the diverse motivations of tourists is crucial, as visitors have different behaviours and attitudes towards destinations (Dávid, 2011). Ideally, tourists should actively participate in environmental protection while maintaining responsible behaviour throughout their stay. AI-enabled solutions, such as enhanced virtual interactions and robots, have the potential to promote tourism products and services while influencing responsible travel behaviour to support sustainability. Research suggests that AI can be designed to guide, inform and mentor tourists, raising awareness and encouraging responsible and sustainable practices (Tussyadiah, 2020; Tussyadiah & Miller, 2019).

While robots hold promise for responsible and sustainable tourism, their manufacturing, operation, recycling and disposal processes consume significant amounts of resources and can contribute to pollution. Language translator applications and virtual tour guides also raise concerns about the conservation and preservation of natural resources and cultural heritage, as overcrowding and increased pollution can result from their widespread use (Sfodera et al., 2022).

Tourism is viewed as a vital element for economic development, poverty alleviation and achieving the SDGs in developing economies. However, the effectiveness of using tourism as a sustainable tool against poverty hinges on the extent to which tourism development policies are integrated with economic, social, and environmental policies. Moreover, ensuring the sustainability of tourism development necessitates the integration of advanced technological innovations such as AI. While the adoption of advanced technologies holds potential benefits for both the industry and society, further research is required to understand the requirements and appropriate application of AI systems. The evaluation of the uses of AI should be accompanied by impact assessments to ensure that the implementation of AI supports the attainment of SDGs through tourism (Kostoska & Kocarev, 2019).

The role of technologies like AI is considered crucial in stimulating economic growth and is subject to extensive deliberation regarding their contribution to poverty alleviation and the pursuit of environmentally and socially sustainable development. Responsible and sustainable tourism positively impacts destination competitiveness and tourism development. Intelligent automation not only facilitates economic diversification for developing countries but also serves as a means to actively involve the local population. Through tourism activities, locals can benefit from economic returns on investments, the creation of local job opportunities and the long-term preservation of environmental, cultural and social resources in the area, provided that these aspects are properly addressed (Krishnan et al., 2022; Pillai & Sivathanu, 2020; Tussyadiah & Miller, 2019; Tussyadiah, 2020).

Case Study

The empirical study by Zeng et al. (2022) investigated how VR tourism experiences could stimulate tourists' cultural dissemination behaviour. Cultural dissemination behaviour refers to the likelihood of individuals promoting or spreading a destination's culture through recommendation, sharing, product-buying and revisiting intentions (Zeng et al., 2022, p. 317). Dunhuang UNESCO Global Geopark (DHGG) in China was the focus of the study.

UNESCO Global Geoparks are designated areas of international significance, where the geological sites and landscapes are centrally managed. The holistic management of these sites includes protection, education and sustainable development (UNESCO, 2024). These areas utilise their geological heritage in conjunction with other aspects of the region's natural and cultural heritage to increase awareness of societal issues such as sustainable resource use, climate change mitigation and natural hazard risk reduction (UNESCO, 2024). According to UNESCO (2024), the success of the global geoparks lies in their *'bottom-up approach of combining conservation with sustainable development while involving local communities'*. As of 2024, 213 Geoparks are located across 48 countries. China is one of the emerging economies where several UNESCO Global Geoparks are found. Dunhuang UNESCO Global Geopark (DHGG) is located in Gansu Province, Northwest China, at the western end of the Hexi Corridor. The DHGG is a rural site situated along the ancient Silk Road, and it holds considerable cultural and heritage significance.

China has recently paid significant attention to the development of Global Geoparks in remote rural areas, as observed by UNESCO (2024). This attention was prompted by the recognition that environmental vulnerability arises as local economies develop. As a result, interventions that address economic, social and environmental challenges are necessary. According to the research by Zeng et al. (2022), the 'Digital Dunhuang' project is such an intervention where AI is used to protect Dunhuang culture. This project utilises VR, augmented reality (AR), and interactive reality to conduct a comprehensive digital collection, processing and storage of Dunhuang Grottoes and related cultural relics. The project also creates a digital resource library of the Grottoes' cultural relics. High-definition digital images and panoramic views of the caves in the Dunhuang are freely accessible to the public via the Internet. Visitors from all over the world can now explore the Dunhuang caves through the 'Digital Dunhuang' project. Visitors can immerse themselves in a virtual space that covers 30 caves and an area of 4,430 square metres of murals, spanning 10 different dynasties. Zeng et al. (2022) postulate that the 'Digital Dunhuang' project transcends time and space limitations, catering to people's desires for travel, appreciation and research. Users can engage in interactive activities like cultural preservation and can invite friends to join in these activities. The research findings by Zeng et al. (2022) assert that these innovative interactive methods enhance users' sense of participation and facilitate the dissemination of Dunhuang culture through interpersonal communication channels. As evidenced in the literature, VR tourism enables tourists to admire the cultural, historical and artistic accomplishments that represent national collective achievements, thereby fostering a sense of collective pride in tourists. When tourists feel proud of these collective achievements, they are more inclined to share and propagate the culture, thus fostering sustainable tourism development of protected areas. This research further demonstrates how AI can be used to protect the environment by reducing visitor numbers while at the same time providing tourists with engaged and enhanced tourism experiences.

Emerging Issues

The implementation of responsible and sustainable tourism presents various challenges and opportunities. The economic dimension of tourism sustainability involves balancing the positive aspects of increased income and accessibility with the potential negative impacts on job opportunities and economic decline due to the rise of AI and robots. The social dimension emphasises the importance of preserving sociocultural authenticity and promoting local community participation, while also considering the potential drawbacks of reduced personal interactions and limited access to AI technologies. The environmental dimension highlights the need for conserving natural resources and cultural heritage, acknowledging the potential environmental consequences of technology-driven tourism practices.

To address these challenges and maximise the benefits of technology in responsible and sustainable tourism, it is crucial to consider the integration of AI-enabled solutions within a comprehensive framework. This framework should prioritise community engagement, cultural preservation and environmental conservation, while also addressing the potential environmental footprint and societal implications of technology implementation. Policymakers, industry stakeholders and local communities must collaborate to strike a balance between technological advancements and the preservation of sociocultural and environmental integrity.

Government policies play a crucial role in effectively managing the potential negative impacts of intelligent automation in the tourism industry and society at large. These policies can include educational and training programs aimed at bridging skill gaps for AI-related jobs or preventing skill erosion due to heavy reliance on automation. Furthermore, incentives can be provided to support labour-intensive sectors like hospitality, while the implementation of a universal basic income can address the potential challenge of widespread unemployment resulting from automation. Additionally, tourism organisations and stakeholders can adopt various intervention strategies to promote responsible behaviours among both tourists and employees.

We have just explored the tip of the iceberg regarding the role of AI in promoting responsible and sustainable tourism development, and this needs to be explored further. This should include detailed consideration of the potential challenges and opportunities associated with technologies such as AI. For instance, proper policy planning should be undertaken, such as the establishment of robust management systems to mitigate issues like overcrowding during peak periods. It is important to carefully manage visitor flows and, when necessary, implement controls on visitor usage in natural and cultural tourist attractions to prevent congestion and environmental degradation. Such measures can effectively preserve and promote local traditions (Sfodera et al., 2022).

Conclusion

Tourism plays a significant role in the economic development and poverty alleviation efforts of developing economies, particularly when it is integrated with comprehensive economic, social and environmental policies. Achieving sustainable tourism development requires the incorporation of advanced technological innovations, such as AI. However, further research is needed to determine the necessary requirements for AI systems and their appropriate application to ensure they support the attainment of SDGs through tourism.

The role of technologies like AI is crucial in stimulating economic growth and addressing poverty while pursuing environmentally and socially sustainable development. Responsible and sustainable tourism practices have a positive impact on destination competitiveness and tourism development. Intelligent automation not only promotes economic diversification but also facilitates greater involvement of the local population. Through responsible tourism activities, local communities can benefit from economic returns, job opportunities and the long-term protection of environmental, cultural and social resources.

Despite challenges, the implementation of AI-supported responsible and sustainable tourism development holds immense potential for poverty alleviation in developing countries. Therefore, it is imperative for tourism researchers and professionals to gain a deeper understanding of the opportunities and challenges presented by AI in the economic, social and environmental aspects of responsible and sustainable tourism development. By doing so, they can effectively address challenges and leverage the opportunities that AI brings forth for the benefit of sustainable tourism development.

Limitations and Recommendations for Future Research

AI has emerged as a highly transformative and innovative technology within the tourism industry (Filieri et al., 2021). As advancements in AI and related technologies continue to progress, the use of intelligent automation in travel and tourism is expected to grow (Tussyadiah, 2020). However, there remains a significant research gap in understanding how these technologies are applied, utilised and impact responsible and sustainable tourism in developing countries.

Despite the increasing volume of research on AI, there is still a lack of comprehensive exploration regarding the implications, including opportunities and challenges, of AI on the economic, social and environmental dimensions of responsible and sustainable tourism development. To harness the potential of AI systems for fostering more responsible tourism, it is crucial to first understand consumers' perceptions of AI. This understanding is essential in designing effective behaviour change strategies that target travel consumers (Tussyadiah, 2020; Van et al., 2020).

Developing countries hold significant importance in achieving the objectives of the SDGs, particularly in terms of poverty reduction and reducing inequality. The adoption of AI-enabled technologies, such as VR, Virtual Guides, Robots, Language Translators and Chatbots, presents both challenges and opportunities for emerging economies, directly impacting the pursuit of the SDGs. One major challenge is the potential threat to jobs in the tourism sector, which can have economic and social consequences. However, it is important to recognise that these devices should not be seen as direct replacements for employees. Human labour will always be essential, as tourists value the traditional human touch and social interaction that the service industry provides (Van et al., 2020).

Moreover, it is crucial to highlight the significance of research and ongoing monitoring in evaluating the impacts of technology-driven tourism and refining strategies accordingly. By aligning the development and application of AI technologies with the United Nations SDGs, emerging economies can strive towards achieving responsible and sustainable tourism practices. While challenges and concerns exist, careful consideration and responsible implementation of technology can act as a catalyst for positive change and contribute to the realization of sustainable tourism.

Despite the challenges involved, the integration of AI into responsible and sustainable tourism development is considered a key driver of poverty alleviation in developing countries. Therefore, it is crucial for researchers and professionals in the tourism industry to enhance their understanding of the opportunities and challenges associated with AI in the economic, social and environmental dimensions of responsible and sustainable tourism development. This understanding will help mitigate challenges and capitalize on the opportunities presented by AI.

References

Balsalobre-Lorente, D., Abbas, J., He, C., Pilař, L., & Shah, S. A. R. (2023). Tourism, urbanization and natural resources rents matter for environmental sustainability: The leading role of AI and ICT on sustainable development goals in the digital era. *Resources Policy*, *82*, 103445.

Bausch, T., Schröder, T., & Tauber, V. (2022). What is to be sustained? The polysemy of sustainability and sustainable tourism across languages and cultures. *Journal of Sustainable Tourism*, *32*(1), 108–131.

Bideci, M., & Bideci, C. (2023, January). Back in time with immersive heritage tourism experience: A study of virtual reality in archaeological sites. In *Information and Communication Technologies in Tourism 2023: Proceedings of the ENTER 2023 eTourism Conference, January 18–20, 2023* (pp. 312–317). Springer Nature Switzerland.

Brundtland, G. H. (1987). What is sustainable development. *Our Common Future*, *8*(9), 1–12.

Buhalis, D., Harwood, T., Bogicevic, V., Viglia, G., Beldona, S., & Hofacker, C. (2019). Technological disruptions in services: Lessons from tourism and hospitality. *Journal of Service Management*, *30*(4), 484–506.

Chen, S. C., Hsu, C. W., Huang, D. Y., Lin, S. Y., & Hung, Y. P. (2013, July). TelePort: Virtual touring of Dun-Huang with a mobile device. In *2013 IEEE International Conference on Multimedia and Expo Workshops (ICMEW)* (pp. 1–6). IEEE.

Chiao, H. M., Chen, Y. L., & Huang, W. H. (2018). Examining the usability of an online virtual tour-guiding platform for cultural tourism education. *Journal of Hospitality, Leisure, Sport & Tourism Education*, *23*, 29–38.

Dávid, L. (2011). Tourism ecology: Towards the responsible, sustainable tourism future. *Worldwide Hospitality and Tourism Themes*, *3*(3), 210–216.

Ding, M. (2021). Research on tourism route planning based on artificial intelligence technology. *Wireless Communications and Mobile Computing*, *2021*, 1–7.

Eyisi, A., Lee, D., & Trees, K. (2021). Developing responsible tourism in emerging economies: The case of Nigeria. *Journal of Tourism and Cultural Change*, *21*(1), 94–109.

Ferràs, X., Hitchen, E. L., Tarrats-Pons, E., & Arimany-Serrat, N. (2020). Smart tourism empowered by artificial intelligence: The case of Lanzarote. *Journal of Cases on Information Technology*, *22*(1), 1–13.

Filieri, R., D'Amico, E., Destefanis, A., Paolucci, E., & Raguseo, E. (2021). Artificial intelligence (AI) for tourism: An European-based study on successful AI tourism start-ups. *International Journal of Contemporary Hospitality Management*, *33*(11), 4099–4125.

Gössling, S. (2021). Tourism, technology and ICT: A critical review of affordances and concessions. *Journal of Sustainable Tourism*, *29*(5), 733–750.

Guttentag, D. A. (2010a). Virtual reality: Applications and implications for tourism. *Tourism Management*, *31*(5), 637–651.

Guttentag, D. A. (2010b). Virtual reality: Applications and implications for tourism. *Tourism Management*, *31*(5), 637–651.

Ivanov, S. (2020). The impact of automation on tourism and hospitality jobs. *Information Technology & Tourism*, *22*, 205–215.

Ivanov, S., Duglio, S., & Beltramo, R. (2023). Robots in tourism and sustainable development goals: Tourism agenda 2030 perspective article. *Tourism Review*, *78* (2), 352–360.

Kostoska, O., & Kocarev, L. (2019). A novel ICT framework for sustainable development goals. *Sustainability*, *11*(7), 1961.

Krishnan, C., Goel, R., & Garg, V. (2022). Role of artificial intelligence and its impact on the tourism industry of India. In *Handbook of research on innovative management using AI in industry 5.0* (pp. 291–302). IGI Global.

Kurniasari, K. K., Ayu, J. P., & Octavanny, V. (2022). Understanding tourists' motivation in virtual tour. *International Journal of Applied Sciences in Tourism and Events*, *6*(1), 31–41.

Li, D., Du, P., & He, H. (2022). Artificial intelligence-based sustainable development of smart heritage tourism. *Wireless Communications and Mobile Computing*, *2022*, 1–12.

Loureiro, S. M. C., Guerreiro, J., & Ali, F. (2020). 20 years of research on virtual reality and augmented reality in tourism context: A text-mining approach. *Tourism Management*, *77*, 104028.

McCarthy, J. (2007). From here to human-level AI. *Artificial Intelligence*, *171*(18), 1174–1182.

Pillai, R., & Sivathanu, B. (2020). Adoption of AI-based chatbots for hospitality and tourism. *International Journal of Contemporary Hospitality Management*, *32*(10), 3199–3226.

Poetry, F. (2021). Virtual tour-an alternative to responsible heritage tourism?. In *ARTEPOLIS 8-the 8th Biannual International Conference (ARTEPOLIS 2020)* (pp. 66–72). Atlantis Press.

Rajaraman, V. (2014). JohnMcCarthy—Father of artificial intelligence. *Resonance*, *19*, 198–207.

Samala, N., Katkam, B. S., Bellamkonda, R. S., & Rodriguez, R. V. (2020). Impact of AI and robotics in the tourism sector: A critical insight. *Journal of Tourism Futures*, *8*(1), 73–87.

Samsung. (2024). How to use Live translate for phone calls on the Galaxy S24. Available at: https://www.samsung.com/latin_en/support/mobile-devices/how-to-use-live-translate-for-phone-calls-on-the-galaxy-s24/ (Accessed May 10, 2024).

Sfodera, F., Cain, L. N., & Di Leo, A. (2022). Is technology everywhere? Exploring generation Z's perceptions of sustainable tourism in developing countries. *International Hospitality Review*, *38*(1), 28–53.

Sharma, K., Jain, M., & Dhir, S. (2021). Analysing the impact of artificial intelligence on the competitiveness of tourism firms: A modified total interpretive structural modeling (m-TISM) approach. *International Journal of Emerging Markets*, *17*(4), 1067–1084.

Tuo, Y., Ning, L., & Zhu, A. (2021). How artificial intelligence will change the future of tourism industry: The practice in China. In *Information and Communication Technologies in Tourism 2021: Proceedings of the ENTER 2021 eTourism Conference, January 19–22, 2021* (pp. 83–94). Springer International Publishing.

Tussyadiah, I. (2020). A review of research into automation in tourism: Launching the annals of tourism research curated collection on artificial intelligence and robotics in tourism. *Annals of Tourism Research*, *81*, 102883.

Tussyadiah, I., & Miller, G. (2019). Perceived impacts of artificial intelligence and responses to positive behaviour change intervention. In *Information and Communication Technologies in Tourism 2019: Proceedings of the International Conference in Nicosia, Cyprus, January 30–February 1, 2019* (pp. 359–370). Springer International Publishing.

Ukpabi, D., Karjaluoto, H., Olaleye, S. A., & Mogaji, E. (2018). Dual perspectives on the role of artificially intelligent robotic virtual agents in the tourism, travel and hospitality industries. In *EuroMed Academy of Business Conference Book of Proceedings*. EuroMed Press.

UNESCO. (2024). UNESCO global geoparks. Available at: https://www.unesco.org/en/iggp/geoparks/about?hub=67817 (Accessed February 24, 2023).

Van, N. T. T., Vrana, V., Duy, N. T., Minh, D. X. H., Dzung, P. T., Mondal, S. R., & Das, S. (2020). The role of human–machine interactive devices for post-COVID-19 innovative sustainable tourism in Ho Chi Minh City, Vietnam. *Sustainability*, *12*(22), 9523.

Wang, K., Kong, H., Bu, N., Xiao, H., Qiu, X., & Li, J. (2022). AI in health tourism: Developing a measurement scale. *Asia Pacific Journal of Tourism Research*, *27*(9), 954–966.

Zeng, Y., Liu, L., & Xu, R. (2022). The effects of a virtual reality tourism experience on tourist's cultural dissemination behavior. *Tourism and Hospitality*, *3*(1), 314–329.

Zhang, L. (2022). Artificial intelligence assisted cyber threat assessment and applications for the tourism industry. *Journal of Computer Virology and Hacking Techniques*, *19*, 1–17.

Zielinski, C., Winker, M. A., Aggarwal, R., Ferris, L. E., Heinemann, M., Lapeña, J. F., Pai, S. A., Ing, E., Citrome, L., Alam, M., Voight, M., & Habibzadeh, F. (2023). Chatbots, generative AI, and scholarly manuscripts: WAME recommendations on chatbots and generative artificial intelligence in relation to scholarly Philippine. *Journal of Otolaryngology Head and Neck Surgery*, *38*(1), 7.

Chapter 9

Artificial Intelligence: A Driving Force of Ghana's Tourism and Hospitality Industry to Foster Sustainability

Stephen Owusu Afriyie[a], *Joseph Akwasi Nkyi*[a], *Gertrude Amoakohene*[a] *and Peter Yao Lartey*[b]

[a]Ghana Communication Technology University, Ghana
[b]Brock University, Canada

Abstract

Artificial Intelligence (AI) has significantly transformed hotel operations by simplifying routine tasks such as reservations and electronic check-in processes, allowing staff to concentrate on delivering customised services for clients. This study aims to examine the role of AI in transforming Ghana's tourism industry and determine the key drivers of sustainability in the industry. The investigation uses a sample size of 103 firms operating in Ghana's tourism and hospitality sector. The empirical analysis relies on primary data gathered through survey instruments from actively operating industry players with valid licences. Respondents include hotel managers, staff, resort operators, restaurant workers and tour guides at various tourist and recreational facilities, waterfalls and mountain resorts. The investigation employs Structural Equation Modelling (SEM) to conduct the statistical estimation and determine the direct and indirect relationships among the multiple factors that explain AI adoption in the context of Ghana's tourism and hospitality industry. It was revealed that AI adoption in Ghana has a significant effect on the sustainability of the tourism and hospitality industry. The study recommends that smart services should be operationalised to help clients locate their desired facilities, select preferred services and accurately complete their paperwork without hitches.

Artificial Intelligence in Hospitality and Tourism in Africa, 147–159

Published under exclusive licence by Emerald Publishing Limited
doi:10.1108/978-1-80686-169-920261009

Keywords: Artificial Intelligence; tourism; hospitality sustainability; technology; Structural Equation Modelling (SEM)

Introduction

Artificial Intelligence (AI) has been defined by many authors as a set of technologies that makes use of human intelligence processes in solving problems (Fogel, 2022). In other words, AI seeks to replace human beings with machines where possible. This technology has successfully been introduced to the tourism industry. Bulchand-Gidumal (2022) gave several reasons why AI is relevant to travel and tourism. Tourists make several decisions based on their choice of destination. These include transportation, accommodation and activities, among others. This is where AI plays a significant role in ensuring tourists have satisfactory trips. Filiopoulos and Poulaki (2023) emphasised that AI provides various tools that have brought about a total transformation and resounding change in the tourism industry operating in a way that presents a satisfactory travel experience. As AI keeps improving, it makes it more reliable and attractive in providing the business solutions required by the tourism and hospitality industry. With AI, the ability to perform tasks that formerly human cognitive would have been required to do makes it useful for the tourism and hospitality industry. This has saved many businesses in tourism and hospitality such as hotels, airlines and resorts, which rely heavily on AI to deliver excellent customer service, save money, time and also, to a large extent, eliminate human error. AI technology also helps the industrial players to build a good reputation for themselves. AI's presence in almost every area of the tourism industry makes it significant in different types of applications such as personalisation, recommender systems, robots, prediction and forecasting, language translation applications and voice recognition, and natural language processing systems. The tourism industry in Ghana has seen significant improvement in the past decade. A report published by Statista (2023) indicated that in the West Africa region, Ghana is the major destination for tourists. It explained that in the year 2020, Ghana received about 355,000 tourists. Ghana was able to manage these tourists with the help of AI. The adoption of AI is critical for embracing innovation in the industry. However, its implementation and acceptance have been confronted with some challenges; hence, the adoption rate has been somewhat lower in Ghana. The lack of strong internet across most of the tourism centres has been a major challenge to the use of AI. This study aims to examine the role of AI in changing the tourism and hospitality industry of Ghana and determine the key drivers of sustainability in the industry.

Literature Review

Development of AI

AI is the study and implementation of techniques to programme computers to mimic human intelligence in areas such as problem-solving, learning and decision-making (Verma, 2023). Machine learning, natural language processing and computer vision are all examples of specialised applications of AI technology. The advancement of AI over the past few decades has enabled cutting-edge uses in many fields (Kapoor et al., 2018). AI has the potential to improve several aspects of the tourist and hospitality industry, including customer service, marketing, revenue management and operational efficiency (Buhalis & Moldavska, 2021). Worldwide, AI has been revolutionising the hospitality and tourism sector by making previously impossible feats of efficiency and individualisation possible. Instantaneous responses to client questions are just one way that AI-powered chatbots have boosted customer service (Gretzel et al., 2017). Revenue management and variable pricing methods are two areas where machine learning algorithms have been implemented to maximise profits (Ivanov & Webster, 2017). The ability to analyse customer data for patterns and preferences has also allowed AI to assist more focused marketing initiatives (Xiang et al., 2015). Several case studies show how AI has been successfully implemented in the hospitality and tourism industry to advance CSR and environmental friendliness. The Marriott hotel group, for one, employs AI-driven systems to optimise energy consumption and cut carbon footprints. Like Hilton's AI-powered 'Connie' robot, which replaces paper brochures with digital ones and offers customised suggestions to visitors, Marriott's AI systems also help the environment (Altaş, 2022).

AI Adoption and Barriers in Ghana's Tourism and Hospitality Industry

While AI could significantly improve the tourism and hospitality sector in Ghana, its use is still in its infancy (Preko & Anyigba, 2022). Lack of infrastructure, competent labour and finance are all stumbling blocks in the way of widespread AI use (Chitturu et al., 2017). These problems are made worse by a lack of international cooperation and government policies that promote them (Adu-Ampong, 2017; Saufi et al., 2014). Capacity-building initiatives could be created to help the workforce acquire the essential skills to overcome these obstacles (Kimbu et al., 2019). Furthermore, the government could introduce policies to incentivise AI adoption and foster partnerships with international organisations to facilitate technology transfer (Amegadzie et al., 2021). Researchers have used a wide range of approaches to examine the effects of AI adoption on sustainability in the hospitality and tourism sector. One common statistical method for investigating the interrelationships of various aspects of AI adoption is Structural Equation Modelling (SEM) (Khan et al., 2019). However, surveys allow scientists to collect first-hand information from professionals and other relevant parties in the field (Veal, 2017). Case studies shed light on the application of AI technology in real-world settings (Yin, 2018). There are benefits and drawbacks to each of these approaches. For instance, SEM enables the concurrent investigation of intricate correlations, but calls for a sizeable sample and reliable data (Hair et al., 2017). While surveys facilitate standardised data gathering, they are not immune to response bias. Although case studies provide a wealth of specific details, they may not be applicable beyond their setting (Yin, 2018). This review of the relevant literature has explored AI's function in the international hospitality and tourist sector, demonstrating its potential to improve sustainability in Ghana's tourism industry. The importance of AI in improving customer service, marketing, revenue management and operational efficiency is one of the key conclusions. Furthermore, international best practises show how AI technology can be successfully integrated to further CSR and environmental protection. In order to fully realise its promise, Amankwah-Amoah and Lu (2022) affirmed that AI must overcome obstacles such as Ghana's inadequate infrastructure, trained workforce and finance.

Sustainability of Ghana's Tourism and Hospitality Industry

The hospitality and tourist industry is just one of several that have seen revolutionary changes thanks to the advent of AI. The use of AI has the potential to elevate service standards and green policies in Ghana's hotel and tourism sector (Akom Ankobrey, 2023). The purpose of this literature review is to look at how AI is used in Ghana's tourism business, discuss some good examples from across the world, find some roadblocks to AI adoption and find some ways to make it more sustainable. The ability to provide for present needs without jeopardising future generations' capability to do the same is what is meant by the term 'sustainability' (WCED, 1987). Sustainability in the hospitality sector requires coping with issues relating to the environment, society and the economy (Buckley et al., 2019). The tourism industry in Ghana is struggling with a number of sustainability issues, such as waste management, energy usage and community engagement. By improving efficiency, decreasing resource use and promoting more ethical decision-making, AI can help promote sustainability (Benckendorff et al., 2019).

Methodology

The purpose of this research is to investigate how AI is revolutionising Ghana's tourism industry and identify the primary factors that promote sustainability within it. The research was conducted using the questionnaire approach. This method was selected since the questionnaire is less expensive and time-consuming, and it allows for the collection of data from a large number of respondents. The respondents of this study were managers of hotels, guest houses, resorts, restaurants, cafeterias and tourist sites in Ghana. A number of difficulties came up while collecting the data since some staff members were unwilling to provide the needed information. They were then convinced that the research was purely for academic purposes.

The technique of random sampling was used to get a sample size of 500 from these sectors. A total of 120 questionnaires were randomly distributed to the participants, but 103 (representing 85.83%) of the total responses were complete, acceptable and useful. A five-point Likert scale was used for the quantitative items (1 being strongly disagree, 2 being disagree, 3 being neutral, 4 being agree and 5 being strongly agree). Thc survey also had a few open-ended questions to let participants share their thoughts on how AI can be a driving force in Ghana's tourism and hospitality industry in order to foster sustainability. The survey was short, taking about 7 minutes to complete, so as not to load responders with too many questions. Respondents were asked at the end of the survey if they would be open to participating in other similar research projects in the future. Out of the 103 valid answers, 94 gave their permission to take part in further studies and were marked to be contacted for follow-up tasks. The investigation employed SEM to conduct the statistical estimation of AI implementation by Ghana's tourism and hospitality industry.

Findings

See Table 1 for the research variables.

To validate the research measurement model, factor estimations, reliability and validity analyses were performed (see Table 2). All the item loadings were higher than the 0.70 effective threshold values. According to Cronbach's claim, the test rule for confirming the reliability and internal consistency of the chosen variables should have a value greater than 0.70 (Cronbach, 1951). To meet the convergent validity condition, however, the variance in the explicit variables should have AVE estimates larger than 0.50 (Fornell & Larcker, 1981). According to the statistics in Table 2, every variable in this study had a Cronbach

Table 1. Research Variables.

Latent Variables	**Observable Variables**
Innovation adoption	Mobile Technology (INNO1)
	Internet of Things (INNO2)
	Information Advancement (INNO3)
	Digital Marketing (INNO4)
Service automation	Self-Service Check-in Kiosks (SETO1)
	Self-Service Check-out Kiosks (SETO2)
Robotic technologies	Delivery Robot (ROBO1)
	Drones (ROBO2)
Artificial intelligence	Chatbots (ARTI1)
	Language Translators (ARTE2)
	Biometric Technologies (ARTE3)
Business sustainability	Financial Improvement (BSUS1)
	Reduced Labour Cost (BSUS2)

Table 2. Factor Loadings, Cronbach's Alpha, AVE and CR of the Variables.

Construct	Indicator	Factor Loading	Cronbach's Alpha	AVE	CR	Reliability/ Validity TESTS
Innovation adoption	INNO1	0.728	0.901	0.723	0.907	Established
	INNO2	0.893				
	INNO3	0.914				
	INNO4	0.855				
Service automation	SETO1	0.817	0.764	0.655	0.792	Established
	SETO2	0.802				
Robotic technologies	ROBO1	0.908	0.820	0.796	0.886	Established
	ROBO2	0.876				
Artificial intelligence	ARTE1	0.938	0.917	0.830	0.936	Established
	ARTE2	0.932				
	ARTE3	0.861				
Business sustainability	BSUS1	0.833	0.832	0.753	0.859	Established
	BSUS2	0.901				

alpha test value better than 0.70, and every AVE had a value greater than 0.50. As a result, the study's data possessed convergent validity and adequate dependability for the research. For outputs to meet composite reliability (CR) requirements, they must be more than 0.70 (Cronbach, 1951). Nonetheless, all of the components' discriminant validity test (CR) measurements fell between 0.801 and 0.922 (Table 2), indicating highly reliable data.

The structural model assessment used to determine how endogenous and exogenous factors relate to one another is shown in Fig. 1. Path coefficients are included in the assessment to determine the significant influence of the exogenous variable on an endogenous variable and to determine the importance of the relationships within the structural model. According to Fig. 1, Innovation Adoption had a positive relationship with Service Automation, Robotic Technologies and Business Sustainability, using AI as the driving force (Hu et al., 2020). The results obtained from the impact of the implicit (latent) factors are 0.755, 0.868 and 0.781 for Service Automation, Robotic Technologies and AI, respectively. Given that Innovation Adoption has positive effects on the other variables, the tourism and hospitality industry must embrace it and make sure that all facility regulations, guidelines and policies are implemented. Additionally, it was shown that AI positively affects Business Sustainability, which is consistent with the research work of Deri et al. (2023). Service Automation and Robotic Technologies both have positive effects on AI. It means that raising

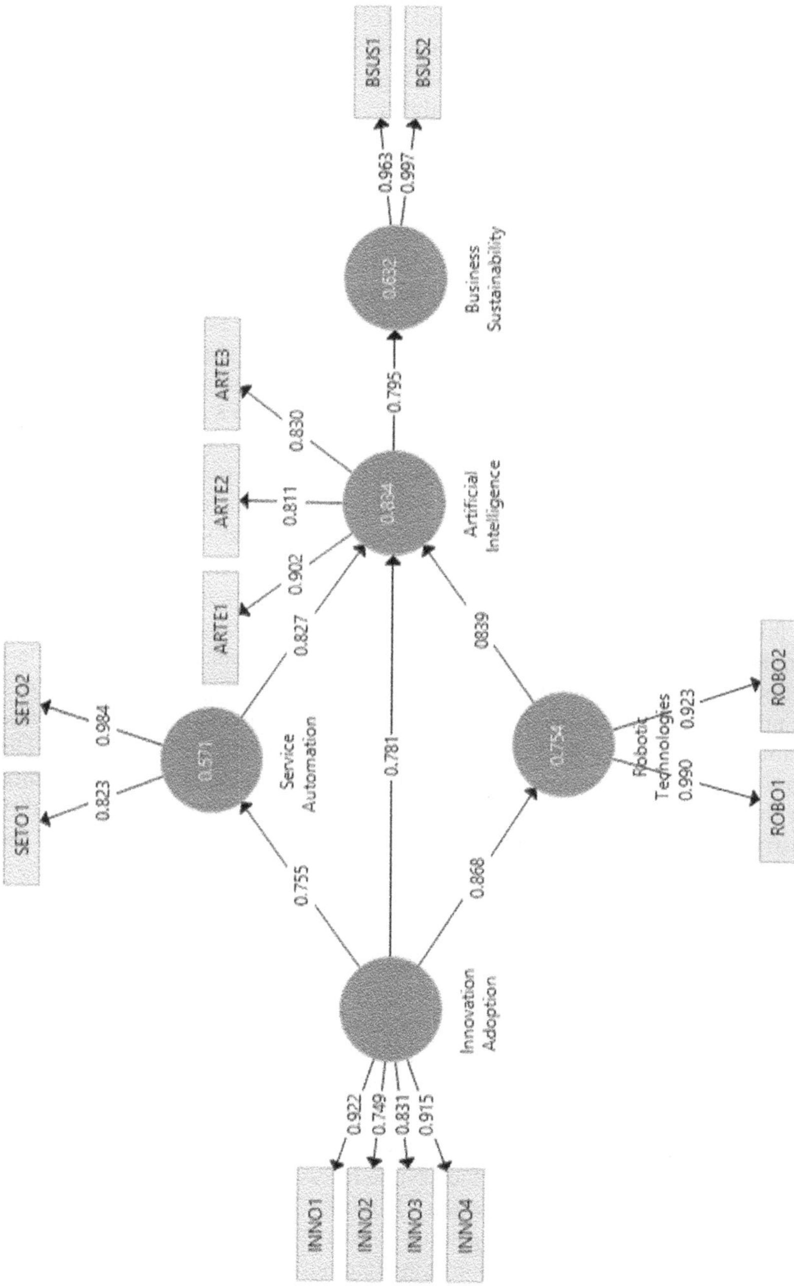

Fig. 1. Structural Model.

levels of Service Automation and Robotic Technologies can boost AI. Our findings align with the research conducted by Tussyadiah (2020), which demonstrated that Service Automation and Robotic Technologies have advantageous effects on AI. The AI – Business Sustainability relationship's path coefficient value (0.795) is positive and high. This demonstrates the high predictive power of AI on the sustainability of businesses in the sector. The endogenous factors utilised in this study, such as Service Automation, Robotic Technologies, Artificial Intelligence, and Business Sustainability, have R^2 values of 0.571, 0.754, 834, and 0.632, respectively. The combined effects of the exogenous variables on the endogenous latent variables are represented by the R^2 values. From Fig. 1, the cross-loadings between the observable and latent variables revealed high scores. Correlation between factors can be compared solely due to cross-loadings. According to Fornell and Larcker (1981), the cross-loading measurement must be more than 0.7. The study's constructs satisfied the inference criteria, meaning that their outer loadings were more than 0.70. Nearly all cross-loadings in the study were around 0.8 and 0.9. This shows that there is a high correlation between the constructs and their indicators. For example, the cross-loadings were 0.908 and 0.917 between Business Sustainability and Financial Improvement (BSUS1) and Reduced Labour Cost (BSUS2). Robotic deployment could prevent thievery and revenue loss at sales locations (Khogali & Mekid, 2023). In today's business environment, workers frequently relocate to other places for a variety of reasons, and business owners may find it challenging to find new employees. Furthermore, employing robotic technology during night shifts when many humans are reluctant to work offers an effective and functionary solution, particularly for lodging establishments. This unfavourable situation would be prevented as the increasing use of robotic technologies produces a labour force that can work around the clock (24/7). The sector offers accommodation, food, drinks, entertainment and catering to clients. Over the years, the quality and quantity of the Ghanaian tourism and hospitality industry have grown at an exponential pace. The industry is regarded as the fourth income-generating sector after gold, cocoa and oil (Preko, 2020).

The study's endogenous variables, including Service Automation, Robotic Technologies, AI and Business Sustainability have R^2 values of 0.571, 0.754, 0.834 and 0.632, respectively. These R^2 values are used to evaluate the structural model and indicate the prediction accuracy of the model. The combined effects of the exogenous variables on the endogenous latent variables are indicated by the R^2 values. They portray the extent to which the exogenous construct associated with the endogenous constructs explains their variance. Business Sustainability, which is the study's dependent variable, has an R^2 value of 0.632. This shows that the associated exogenous constructs account for 63.2% of the variance in the endogenous construct. Nonetheless, 57.1%, 75.4% and 83.4% of the variance in Service Automation, Robotic Technologies, and AI were respectively explained by the exogenous constructs associated with them. This demonstrates the realistic prediction potential and significance of the structural model developed in this work. As it can be seen from Table 3, the endogenous variables had a substantial coefficient of determination (R^2 values falling between

Table 3. Results of R^2 and Q^2.

Endogenous Variables	R^2	Q^2	Effect Size
Service automation	0.571	0.357	Large
Robotic technologies	0.754	0.393	Large
Artificial intelligence	0.834	0.429	Large
Business sustainability	0.632	0.358	Large

Small: $0.0 < Q^2$ effect size < 0.15; Medium: $0.15 < Q^2$ effect size < 0.35; Large: Q^2 effect size > 0.35.

60 and 80%), indicating that they had a good potential for prediction. Service Automation, Robotic Technologies, AI and Business Sustainability had respective Q^2 values of 0.357, 0.393, 0.429 and 0.358. Q^2 statistics exhibit the model's predictive relevance, just as R^2 values indicate the model's predictive accuracy. The Q^2 values, sometimes referred to as 'Stone-Geisser's Q^2 value' (Geisser, 1974; Stone, 1974), show how predictively relevant the route model is for the endogenous latent variables. Q^2 effect size is said to be small if the value is less than 0.15, medium if it is between 0.15 and 0.35, while large if Q^2 effect size is more than 0.35. From Table 3, the Q^2 yielded values ranging from 0.357 to 0.429, all of which are higher than 0.350 as recommended by Stone and Geisser. This suggests that the path model has a strong predictive relevance for the endogenous variables. Large effect sizes are shown by the study's findings for Service Automation, Robotic Technologies, AI and Business Sustainability. This proves that the study's structural model certainly has predictive relevance.

The estimation of the model fitness is displayed in Table 4, which reveals how well the chosen model replicates the observed covariance matrix between the indicator items. Some of the indices that were used in the examination are: Chi-square, χ^2 (CMIN), degrees of freedom (DF), goodness of fit index (GFI), adjusted goodness of fit index (AGFI), normed fit index (NFI), relative fit index (RFI), incremental fit index (IFI), Tucker-Lewis index (TLI), comparative fit index (CFI) and root mean square error of approximation (RMSEA). Table 4 revealed that this study's overall model fitness was appropriate. Even if the model appears to be sound, it is still appropriate to determine the chi-square value (χ^2) divided by the DF, as the χ^2 statistic is typically sample size-sensitive. Nonetheless, χ^2/DF was 1.787, indicating a satisfactory model fit because it is less than the criterion of 5.0. Additionally, the model showed a high degree of significance (0.001). Table 4 shows that the study yielded values of 0.919, 0.942, 0.951, 0.947, 0.939, 0.921 and 0.937 for GFI, AGFI, NFI, RFI, IFI, TLI and CFI, respectively, with recommended cut-offs for the indices set at 0.90. Nonetheless, it was discovered that every index fell within the suggested range, indicating a good fit.

Table 4. Measures of the Model Fitness.

Fit Statistics	Recommended Range	Structural Model
Chi-square, χ^2 (CMIN)	—	31.271
Degrees of freedom (DF)	—	29
χ^2 Significance	Significant ($p \leq 0.05$)	0.001
χ^2/DF	<5.0	1.182
Goodness of Fit Index (GFI)	>0.90	0.919
Adjusted Goodness of Fit Index (AGFI)	>0.90	0.942
Normed Fit Index (NFI)	>0.90	0.951
Relative Fit Index (RFI)	>0.90	0.947
Incremental Fit Index (IFI)	>0.90	0.939
Tucker Lewis Index (TLI)	>0.90	0.921
Comparative Fit Index (CFI)	>0.90	0.937
Root Mean Square Error of Approximation (RMSEA)	≤0.05	0.028

Conclusion

AI technologies could be categorised as chatbots, language interpreters, self-service check-in and check-out kiosks, facial recognition software, drones, virtual assistants, optimisation services, robots (such as robot receptionists, robot bussers, robot bartenders, robot bellboys, robot guides, delivery robots, etc.) and other AI applications. AI technology could be used for meetings and event management, based on the idea that attendees could relax and have a good time. Appreciating participants, especially clients will rise if they are assured of utilising pre-assigned QR codes to join meetings, greet them by SMS or see their names displayed on the screen. The study recommends that smart services be operationalised to assist customers in finding the facilities they want, choosing their preferred service and completing their paperwork swiftly without hustle. Employees are also affected by these technologies. Technologies that can reduce labour turnover which has a rippling effect on employment. Many people believe these technologies can take the position of employees, but in reality, they should be seen as tools that support employees and improve the quality of services they provide for sustenance and growth. Staff should be trained on the assistive as well as useful nature of these technologies and how to use them appropriately to enhance business operations (Ivanov & Webster, 2019). Nevertheless, the issue of how well guests and staff accept new technologies should also be viewed as a serious threat. Potential roadblocks include guests who are not tech-savvy, staff who are reluctant to use these technologies and unwillingness to accept new technologies. The fact that modern internet-based technologies give rise to cybersecurity concerns, ethical considerations like privacy and confidentiality have become another significant challenge. These obstacles to the use of robots and AI applications in the tourism and hospitality industry must be addressed. Staff should be trained on the assistive as well as useful nature of these technologies and how to use them appropriately to enhance business operations. Courses on the positive aspects and potential uses of robotic and artificial intelligence, as well as how to maximise human–robot interaction, should be included in higher education curricula (Özkan & Toz, 2022). This will help students, who are prospective employees of the sector, consider these technologies as auxiliary staff rather than a threat. Industry players, both internal and external must adopt and utilise advanced technology in the future to continually stay in business and improve revenues.

References

Adu-Ampong, E. A. (2017). Divided we stand: Institutional collaboration in tourism planning and development in the Central Region of Ghana. *Current Issues in Tourism*, *20*(3), 295–314. https://doi.org/10.1080/13683500.2014.915795

Akom Ankobrey, G. (2023). Following the 'hype': The role of leisure practices during 'homeland'visits in transnational youth's way of relating to Ghana. *Global Networks*, *23*(1), 262–276.

Altaş, A. (2022). *Digital transformation in restaurants* (pp. 1–23). IGI Global. https://doi.org/10.4018/978-1-7998-6904-7.ch001

Amankwah-Amoah, J., & Lu, Y. (2022). Harnessing AI for business development: A review of drivers and challenges in Africa. *Production Planning & Control*, 1–10.

Amegadzie, J. K., Kanubala, D. D., Cobbina, K. A., & Acquaye, C. (2021). State and future prospects of artificial intelligence (AI) in Ghana. In *Proceedings of the 27th SMART-ISTEAMS-IEEE, April 2021* (pp. 1–10).

Benckendorff, P. J., Xiang, Z., & Sheldon, P. J. (2019). *Tourism information technology* (3rd ed). CABI.

Buckley, R., Zhong, L., Ma, J., Chen, N., Ma, J., Chen, N., . . ., & Shujie, Y. (2019). The principles of sustainable tourism. *Annals of Tourism Research*, *78*, 102743.

Buhalis, D., & Moldavska, I. (2021). Voice assistants in hospitality: Using artificial intelligence for customer service. *Journal of Hospitality and Tourism Technology*, *13*(3), 386–403. https://doi.org/10.1108/JHTT-03-2021-0104

Bulchand-Gidumal, J. (2022). Impact of artificial intelligence in travel, tourism, and hospitality. In *Handbook of e-Tourism* (pp. 1943–1962). Springer International Publishing. https://doi.org/10.1007/978-3-030-48652-5_110

Chitturu, S., Lin, D. Y., Sneader, K., Tonby, O., & Woetzel, J. (2017). *Artificial intelligence and Southeast Asia's future*. Singapore Summit.

Cronbach, L. J. (1951). Coefficient alpha and the internal structure of tests. *Psychometrika*, *16*, 297–334.

Deri, M. N., Ari Ragavan, N., Niber, A., Zaazie, P., Akazire, D. A., Anaba, M., & Andaara, D. (2023). COVID-19 shock in the hospitality industry: Its effect on hotel operations within the Bono region of Ghana. *African Journal of Economic and Management Studies*, *14*(3), 355–378.

Filiopoulos, A., & Poulaki, P. (2023). The development and management of slow tourism through the 'intangible cultural heritage. In *Tourism innovation in the digital era* (pp. 123–135). Emerald Publishing Limited.

Fogel, D. B. (2022). Defining artificial intelligence. *Machine learning and the city: Applications in architecture and urban design* (pp. 91–120). https://doi.org/10.1002/9781119815075.ch7

Fornell, C., & Larcker, D. F. (1981). Evaluating structural equation models with unobservable variables and measurement error. *Journal of Marketing Research*, 39–50.

Geisser, S. (1974). A predictive approach to the random effect model. *Biometrika*, *61*, 101–107.

Gretzel, U., Werthner, H., Koo, C., & Lamsfus, C. (2017). Conceptual foundations for understanding smart tourism ecosystems. *Computers in Human Behavior*, *50*, 558–563.

Hair, J. F., Hult, G. T. M., Ringle, C. M., & Sarstedt, M. (2017). *A primer on partial least squares structural equation modeling (PLS-SEM)*. Sage Publications. https://www.statista.com/topics/9367/tourism-industry-in-ghana/. Accessed on February 11, 2023.

Hu, X., Danso, B. A., Mensah, I. A., & Addai, M. (2020). Does innovation type influence firm performance? A dilemma of star-rated hotels in Ghana. *Sustainability*, *12*(23), 9912.

Ivanov, S. H., & Webster, C. (2017). Adoption of robots, artificial intelligence and service automation by travel, tourism and hospitality companies – A cost-benefit analysis. *International Journal of Tourism Research*, *19*(6), 693–703.

Ivanov, S., & Webster, C. (2019). Economic fundamentals of the use of robots, artificial intelligence, and service automation in travel, tourism, and hospitality. In *Robots, artificial intelligence, and service automation in travel, tourism and hospitality* (pp. 39–55). Emerald Publishing limited. https://doi.org/10.1108/978-1-78756-687-320191002

Kapoor, K. K., Tamilmani, K., Rana, N. P., Patil, P., Dwivedi, Y. K., & Nerur, S. (2018). Advances in social media research: Past, present and future. *Information Systems Frontiers*, *20*(3), 531–558.

Khan, G. F., Sarstedt, M., Shiau, W.-L., Hair, J. F., Ringle, C. M., & Fritze, M. P. (2019). Methodological research on partial least squares structural equation modeling (PLS-SEM): An analysis based on social network approaches. *Internet Research*, *29*(3), 407–429. https://doi.org/10.1108/IntR-12-2017-0509

Khogali, H. O., & Mekid, S. (2023). The blended future of automation and AI: Examining some long-term societal and ethical impact features. *Technology in Society*, *73*, 102232.

Kimbu, A. N., Ngoasong, M. Z., Adeola, O., & Afenyo-Agbe, E. (2019). Collaborative networks for sustainable human capital management in women's tourism entrepreneurship: The role of tourism policy. *Tourism Planning & Development*, *16*(2), 161–178. https://doi.org/10.1080/21568316.2018.1556329

Özkan, S. B., & Toz, M. (2022). A review study on the investigation of the effects of using robots in education on metacognitive behaviors. *Computer Applications in Engineering Education*, *30*(4), 1277–1288.

Preko, A. (2020). Tourism development: National policies and tourism priorities in Ghana. *International Journal of Tourism Policy*, *10*(4), 380–391. https://doi.org/10.1504/IJTP.2020.10034924

Preko, A., & Anyigba, H. (2022). The tourism and hospitality career progression pathway. *International Hospitality Review* (ahead-of-print). https://doi.org/10.1108/IHR-02-2022-0005

Saufi, A., O'Brien, D., & Wilkins, H. (2014). Inhibitors to host community participation in sustainable tourism development in developing countries. *Journal of Sustainable Tourism*, *22*(5), 801–820. https://doi.org/10.1080/09669582.2013.861468

Stone, M. (1974). Cross-validatory choice and assessment of statistical predictions. *Journal of the Royal Statistical Society: Series B*, 111–147.

Tussyadiah, I. (2020). A review of research into automation in tourism: Launching the annals of tourism research curated collection on artificial intelligence and robotics in tourism. *Annals of Tourism Research*, *81*, 102883.

Veal, A. J. (2017). *Research methods for leisure and tourism*. Pearson Education.

Verma, M. (2023). Artificial intelligence role in modern science: Aims, merits, risks and its applications. *Artificial Intelligence*, *7*(5).

WCED (World Commission on Environment and Development). (1987). *Our common future*. Oxford University Press.

Xiang, Z., Du, Q., Ma, Y., & Fan, W. (2015). A comparative analysis of major online review platforms: Implications for social media analytics in hospitality and tourism. *Tourism Management*, *58*, 51–65.

Yin, R. K. (2018). *Case study research and applications: Design and methods*. Sage Publications.

Chapter 10

Utilising AI to Enhance Customer Experience in Tourism and Hospitality in Ghana

Charles Roland Haruna, Maame Gyamfua Asante-Mensah, Michael Ashun, Nyamekesse Samuel, Benedict Jojo Afful and Boamah Charles Ofosu Ofori

University of Cape Coast, Ghana

Abstract

Artificial Intelligence (AI) functionalities have helped improve the working lives of the human population in sectors like the health sector, education sector, industries and tourism. Emerging economies, in particular, have been exploring the potential of AI to transform their tourism and hospitality sectors. This research paper aimed to examine the use of pre-trained AI models in the tourism and hospitality industries in emerging economies. The study presented a literature review of the current state of AI in the tourism and hospitality industries, including its opportunities and challenges. It then proposed the use of a pre-trained AI model, specifically the Bidirectional Encoder Representations from Transformers (BERT) model, to help address some of the challenges facing the tourism and hospitality sectors in emerging economies. BERT is a language model that can be fine-tuned for a range of natural language processing (NLP) tasks such as sentiment analysis, entity recognition and text classification. The paper discussed the potential applications of BERT in the tourism and hospitality sectors, such as analysing customer feedback, enhancing chatbot interactions and improving search engine optimization (SEO) for tourism websites. The Recall-Oriented Understudy for Gisting Evaluation (ROUGE) was used to evaluate the accuracy of the chatbot model that was used in this study. In conclusion, this research paper suggested that pre-trained AI

Artificial Intelligence in Hospitality and Tourism in Africa, 161–182

doi:10.1108/978-1-80686-169-920261010

models, such as BERT, can offer valuable insights and solutions in improving customer satisfaction in the tourism and hospitality industries in emerging economies.

Keywords: Artificial Intelligence; tourism and hospitality; customer experience; natural language processing; BERT model

Introduction

The tourism and hospitality sectors are among the biggest and fastest-growing sectors in the world and have a substantial impact on the economies of many nations, especially emerging economies. The deployment of Artificial Intelligence (AI) technologies to improve customer experience, increase operational effectiveness and spur revenue growth has become increasingly prevalent in the business in recent years. While AI is becoming more popular in rich nations, its uptake and effects in developing economies are still mostly unstudied.

AI refers to the creation of computer systems that are capable of carrying out tasks that typically call for human intelligence. They employ the information gathered in their operations. Data are a crucial part of AI since it helps machine learning algorithms learn and become more accurate (McClelland, 2017). For creating and implementing AI solutions that can enhance customer experiences, operational effectiveness and revenue management, data about tourism and hospitality is crucial. To forecast client preferences and behaviour, offer customised travel itineraries and experiences, and improve pricing and inventory management, for instance, machine learning algorithms can be trained using these data on some tourist and hospitality companies (Mariani & Borghi, 2022). The quality and quantity of data available for AI applications can significantly impact the effectiveness of AI solutions. With the growth of digital technologies and online platforms, vast amounts of data are being generated in the tourism and hospitality industries, including customer reviews, booking patterns, social media interactions and online search behaviour. These data can be analysed and leveraged to gain valuable insights into customer behaviour and preferences, enabling the development of AI solutions that can enhance customer experience and drive business performance (Ataman, 2023).

The tourism and hospitality sectors have grown significantly during the last 10 years because of consumer demand and technical improvements. The industry is characterised by fierce rivalry and a commitment to providing clients with high-quality services. The industry has been embracing new technologies, with AI at the forefront, to remain competitive and meet client expectations (Agrawal, 2021). Chatbots, recommendation engines and customisation algorithms are just a few examples of AI-based systems that have the potential to transform the market by delivering more individualised and effective services, cutting costs and improving the customer experience.

However, the tourism and hospitality industries experienced several difficulties and issues before AI was integrated into those sectors. One of the many issues the sector encountered was the inability to offer personalised services to their clients due to a lack of understanding of their preferences, behaviours and expectations, which made it challenging to adapt their services to suit their needs. Language hurdles in the industry made it difficult to communicate with consumers who didn't understand English, which was another difficulty. Another difficulty the sector encountered was the sluggish adoption of technological innovation by the tourist and hospitality sectors (Raphael & Qureshi, 2010). As a result, outmoded procedures and systems were created. Due to this lack of innovation, the sector found it challenging to keep up with shifting consumer demands and technological improvements. Due to these difficulties, industry leaders came up with the concept of integrating AI into their operations. In the early stages, the introduction of AI in the industry was limited to basic tasks such as automating booking and reservation systems. These early systems were simple rule-based systems that could perform basic functions such as processing reservations and managing guest profiles (Roser, 2022). The application of AI in the sector grew along with technology. The creation of more complex systems that could make predictions and suggestions based on data was made possible by the introduction of machine learning algorithms (Bergoeing et al., 2010). As a result, marketing strategies have become more individualised and focused, and forecasting and resource allocation have also improved.

Natural language processing (NLP) developments in recent years have made it possible to create chatbots and virtual assistants that can communicate with clients in real time. This has improved the customer experience and lightened the pressure on the personnel, allowing them to concentrate on more challenging jobs (Abel et al., 2024).

This takes us to the main goal of this study, which is to investigate how AI is affecting the travel and hospitality sectors in developing nations. The Bidirectional Encoder Representations from Transformers (BERT) AI paradigm will be applied in this work, though. The goal of this research is to apply a pre-trained NLP model created by Google AI Language to analyse customer feedback, improve chatbot interactions, and optimise search engine optimization (SEO) for travel websites. Another aim of this research work will be to delve into the use of sentiment analysis and the role it can play in the tourism and hospitality industry. The study's conclusions will be important in offering perceptions into the potential of AI in the travel and hospitality sectors of emerging nations, which can be utilised to direct decision-making by industry players (Devlin et al., 2019).

Literature Review

The tourism and hospitality industries have been rapidly adopting AI to enhance customer experiences. This literature review aims to explore the impact of AI on customer experiences in the tourism and hospitality industries and associated services.

Impact of AI on Hospitality

How AI technologies are increasingly being used as digital assistants is the focal point of an article written by Limna. The paper also emphasised how AI helps businesses in the hospitality industry in a variety of ways, including improving customer service, expanding operational capability and lowering costs. Some risks associated with AI advancements, such as job loss in low-tech sectors, loss of control due to robot autonomy, and safety, security and privacy concerns, were also discussed (Limna, 2023). AI-powered robots have been developed to automate housekeeping tasks such as cleaning, laundry and room service. Studies have shown that these robots can improve operational efficiency and reduce labour costs while maintaining high levels of cleanliness and service quality (Lee, 2022).

Cozzio et al. (2025) investigated the challenges and opportunities of adopting AI in the hospitality industry. They did so by exploring how personnel at different hierarchical levels within hotels perceive the benefits and obstacles associated with AI adoption. A review of research work by Bisoi et al. (2020) stated the key benefits of using digital technologies. It said that they produce a tremendous amount of data for travel companies. Numerous brands have integrated data-driven tools and advanced analytics into their enterprise solutions to derive contextual insights through their interactions with both existing and potential customers. These tools have played a major role in helping brands deliver a satisfying experience to customers for activities that include booking hotel rooms or leisure services (Bisoi et al., 2020).

A bibliometric analysis of the literature on the impact of AI in the hospitality industry was based on its operations, customer experience and revenue management. The results suggested that AI has a significant impact on operational efficiency, cost savings and quality of service. The use of AI can also help hotels reduce manual labour and streamline processes, leading to significant cost savings. By providing personalised recommendations and experiences, AI can enhance guest satisfaction, loyalty and repeat business. In terms of revenue management, AI has enabled hotels to optimise pricing, forecasting and inventory allocation, leading to increased revenue, occupancy rates and profitability (Kadagidze & Ugrelidze, 2023).

Impact of AI on Tourism

In research dedicated to findings on the applications, risks, and benefits of ChatGPT in tourism, it was discovered that ChatGPT and other similar models are likely to have a profound impact on several tourism processes. They will contribute to further streamlining customer service in front-of-house operations and increasing productivity and efficiency in back-of-house operations. Although negative consequences for human resources are expected, this technology mostly enhances tourism employees (Carvalho & Ivanov, 2024).

Florido-Benítez et al. (2024) studied the impact of AI advancements on smart tourist destinations' (STDs) tourism marketing. The study aimed at enhancing the quality of services and further illustrate their future agenda to improve tourists' experiences. The authors presented real examples of AI technology in a tourism context to better understand the potential of this digital tool. Their findings inferred that AI is a multipurpose tool that helps manage, monitor, and analyse sales information; revenue management; minimise prediction errors; streamline operations; and develop better marketing strategies, optimising economic resources, reducing marketing costs, and responding dynamically to changing needs for tourists and residents in STDs.

AI systems in the tourism industry can be stand-alone systems or embedded in existing applications and systems. These systems include recommender systems, personalisation systems and techniques, conversational systems (chatbots and voice assistants), forecasting tools, autonomous agents, language translation applications and smart tourism destinations. Although each system is analysed separately, it is stated that tourists will usually interact with technologies that integrate several of these systems (Bulchand-Gidumal, 2022).

Critical insight into the impact of AI and robotics in the tourism sector found that AI and robotics have the potential to revolutionise the industry by providing personalised experiences, enhancing operational efficiency, and improving customer service. However, the study also highlighted the need for careful consideration of the ethical and social implications of AI and robotics in the tourism industry (Sigala, 2020).

The Use of Pre-Trained AI Models in Tourism and Hospitality

Jalil et al. (2025) focused on Malaysian SMEs by investigating the relationship between the intention to adopt AI and digital value creation, highlighting a notable lack of prior empirical research on this topic. Their findings demonstrated a significant positive correlation, indicating that AI adoption encourages enhanced digital value creation. Further, the work revealed that this relationship is positively mediated by technology orientation, offering valuable insights for researchers and entrepreneurs seeking to leverage AI for business growth. Recent developments in generative AI have revolutionized personalized travel recommendation systems through a Retrieval-Augmented Generator (RAG) framework. This framework produces user-specific, contextually appropriate suggestions by combining retrieval-based techniques with large language models (LLMs). The authors incorporated the Big Five and Myers-Briggs Type Indicator (MBTI) personality models into this RAG framework to further personalize recommendations based on unique user preferences and behaviors. This personality-driven approach demonstrated how personality insights enhance generative AI's potential in travel planning (Garg et al., 2025). Adeyemi and Chikuta (2024) concluded that chatbots, that are being powered by pre-trained NLP models, can help and have been helping hotels to improve their service efficiencies at the same time reducing labour cost at the same time and are able to 24/7, deliver multilingual customer support, in some parts of Southeast Asia and Africa.

Talukder et al. (2025) inferred that relying on AI presented a significant opportunity for emerging markets to accelerate tourism development and improve destination marketing. AI-enabled advancements allowed these markets to make intelligent decisions regarding resource distribution, ability to forecast tourist behavior, and provide tailored experiences, thereby increasing their competitiveness. In addition, AI applications could help local enterprises to enhance productivity, to improve marketing management, and offer successful lessons in innovative marketing and customer care solutions. Kırtıl et al. (2024) analyzed methods for adapting AI chatbots to meet the specific requirements of the tourism sector. They proposed enhancing the abilities of chatbots to interpret tourist queries and present more precise, tailored responses by customizing general AI models. The proposed strategy aimed to bridge the divide between standard AI and the complexities of tourism, thereby improving customer service.

In the work by (Frenette, 2025), the article discussed how the implementation of AI technologies could effectively be deployed in assisting with curation of ethical travel, especially in regards to cruise and resort services. This paper further investigated the relationship between AI and responsible tourism, with references to such technical issues as bias, underrepresentation of the cultures represented through tourism (mostly at the margins), the necessity to have humans oversee automated itinerary planning.

Furthermore (Christou et al., 2025), conducted a study by conceptually exploring how Generative AI (GenAI) reshaped value co-creation, destination governance, and responsible innovation within the tourism sector by positioning GenAI as an active tourism participant. Using an integrative, theory-building approach, the research proposed a "Synthetic Experience System" that clarified how value emerged and identified potential co-destruction points. The framework provided a roadmap for stakeholders to manage GenAI ethically and sustainably, offering a shared vocabulary and research propositions to guide future empirical investigations.

In conclusion, the literature suggests that AI has a significant impact on customer experiences in the tourism and hospitality industries. AI is being used to personalise travel experiences, provide recommendations, optimise pricing and revenue management and enhance operational efficiency. However, the factors that drive customers' AI acceptance decisions in the hospitality sector remain inadequately explored. Further research is needed to explore the ethical and social implications of AI in the tourism industry.

Contributions of the Work

This section describes the methods and models applied to achieve the research objectives, from concept development to implementation. In this research, the BERT-based AI models were used to create an AI chatbot that helps users gain knowledge about various tourist attractions in Ghana while suggesting some key points to consider when visiting. It also emphasised a sentiment analysis, which is used to generate a bar chart based on user reactions generated from their comments on services provided at these tourist sites and hotels.

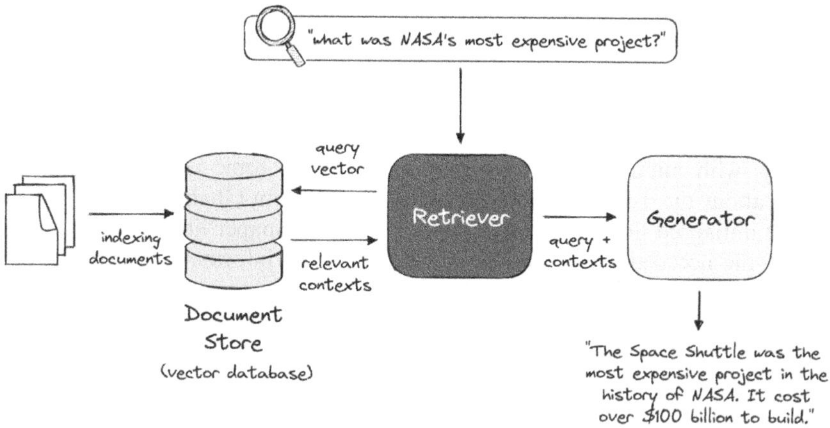

Fig. 1. Structure of Open-Book Abstractive QA Pipeline. *Source:* Pinecone, n.d., Open-Book Abstractive QA Pipeline.

In an era characterised by rapid advances in AI and NLP, the combination of chatbots and sentiment analysis marks a critical step towards the development of more intelligent and emotionally responsive conversational systems. The goal of this work is to combine the capabilities of chatbots, which excel at interactive communication, with sentiment analysis, which can accurately detect the emotional overtones of human language. The combination of these technologies not only improves user engagement but also enables the system to detect and respond to users' emotional states.

Long Form Question and Answering: Chatbot

There are two all-encompassing ways to deal with Question Answers (QA), abstractive (generative) and extractive. The distinction between the two lies in how the response is built. For abstractive QA, a response is produced by an NLP generator model, normally found on outer records. Extractive QA varies from this methodology. As opposed to creating replies, it utilises a reader model to extricate them straightforwardly from outer reports, like removing scraps from a paper (Pinecone, n.d.). In this research work, we are utilising external sources to feed the generator/reader models in the two cases. This is known as an open-book QA as it copies open-book tests where understudies (the models) can allude to a book (outer records) during the test. In our situation, the void of unstructured information turns into our open book. Fig. 1 illustrates what an open-book abstractive QA pipeline appears to be.

Also, the Long Form Question and Answering, which is a form of open-book abstractive QA called Long-Form Question-Answering (LFQA), is utilised. LFQA centres around the generation of multi-sentence replies to open questions

(Fan et al., 2019). In gathering data for the LFQA model, the method adopted was Web scraping. Web scraping is a powerful tool for collecting data from the web. It involves extracting information from websites using automated tools and scripts, such as Python or R but in our case, we used Python for our scripts. This process was used to gather large amounts of structured and unstructured data quickly, with minimal manual effort. The targeted topic used was sites that talked about the Tourism and Hospitality industries in Ghana.

The initialised links were then passed to the newspaper library in Python to extract the necessary texts and titles. The extracted information was split into chunks of paragraphs for further cleaning and pre-processing. The cleaned data was then stored in the document store in this case PineconeDocumentStore was used as the document store.

Retriever

The QA pipeline uses a vector database, a document store that stores vectors addressing a solitary document's text content. The retriever model encodes message content into a vector embedding, mathematically addressing its unique significance. The vector database stores these vectors, and similarity metrics measure the closeness of new query vectors to existing vectors. The top k most comparative vectors are returned, guaranteeing the most semantically comparable settings are recognised.

The 'flax-sentence-embeddings/all_datasets_v3_mpnet-base' was used as the retriever model for this project.

Generator

Generators are a type of sequence-to-sequence (Seq2Seq) model used in LFQA systems or applications. In LFQA, the generator is responsible for building the answer (Long Form Question Answering in Haystack | Pinecone, n.d.), also shown in Fig. 2.

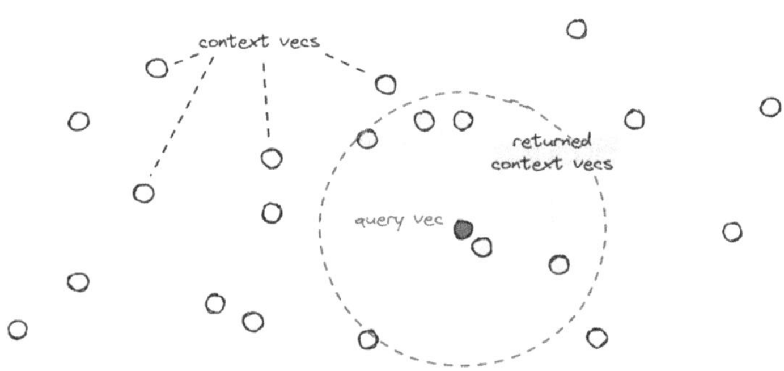

Fig. 2. Similar Context Vectors to Query Vector. *Source*: Pinecone, n.d., Top *k* Vectors Using Euclidean (or L2) Distance.

Shown in Fig. 3, the generator model used for this research project was to initialise the vblagoje/bart_lfqa, which is a model trained specifically for LFQA, with the help of Haystack's Seq2SeqGenerator (Vblagoje/Bart_Lfqa · vblagoje, 2021).

Querying

The generator model, a crucial component of machine learning, is trained on a dataset that includes information about a particular topic. However, if the model has not been trained on a topic, it may not have memorised the necessary information within its model weights. Additionally, the generator may not have returned any contexts containing the answer, indicating a lack of reliable external sources of information. To improve the accuracy of the generator's answer, it is recommended to increase the number of contexts retrieved. For general knowledge queries, the generator model can often retrieve the answer directly from its own 'memory', which is optimised during training. Larger models are better at direct answer generation.

Sentiment Analysis

Sentiment analysis is a language classification task that aims to classify positive, negative and neutral sentiments of a topic, on web forums, feedback portals, social media etc. The process involves tokenising raw text data, feeding it into a sentiment model and outputting a set of values representing the correct sentiment class. The argmax of this output array is used to determine the winning sentiment classification. The model used for this research project is the 'cardiffnlp/twitter-roberta-base-sentiment-latest'. The model is a sentiment analysis tool that utilises a

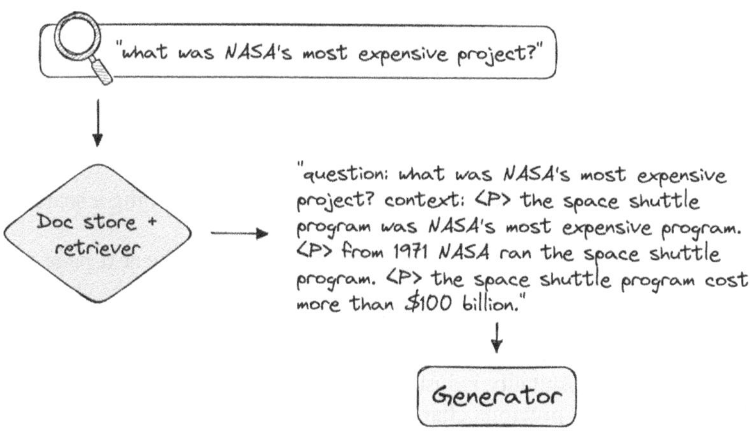

Fig. 3. Diagram of Retrieved Content Fed to a Generator. *Source*: Pinecone, n.d., Retrieved Content Fed to Generator Model.

RoBERTa-base model prepared on 124 million tweets from January 2018 to December 2021. The model is calibrated for sentiment analysis utilising the TweetEval benchmark. It is appropriate for English and has three marks: 0 for negative, 1 for unbiased and 2 for positive sentiment. The model is incorporated into TweetNLP and can be utilised to utilise the transformers pipeline. The base dataset for English is the brought-together TweetEval rendition of the Semeval-2017 dataset (Cardiffnlp/Twitter-roberta-base-sentiment-latest · Hugging Face, 2023).

Most sentiment analysis model assigns sentiment scores to each text, providing a quantitative measure of sentiment. The scores range from −1 (indicating negative sentiment) to 1 (indicating positive sentiment). These sentiment scores enable the calculation of descriptive statistics, such as mean sentiment scores, sentiment distribution and sentiment trends over time.

Sentiment analysis data undergoes analysis using statistics. These statistical measurements provide an overview of the sentiment conveyed in the gathered texts, allowing for the identification of trends and patterns in sentiment. We calculate average sentiment scores to gain insight into the sentiment within the dataset, while analysing sentiment distribution helps us understand how prevalent positive, negative and neutral sentiments are across the data.

Project Design

Every project has a user interface (UI) that makes user navigation easy. This section is to provide a brief description of how the UI of both models will be viewed. It will also provide knowledge on how they will operate.

Web Chat Interface (Tourist)

- *Create an account, log in and log out of the account*
  The user (tourist) in question has to be able to log into the system with the necessary login details that they got from creating an account on the chatbot platform before they can get access to the chatbot. This was very necessary in the building of the bot because it provides confidentiality when it comes to the chat that the user had with the bot.
- The user should be able to interact with the bot by performing a search to get information about various hotels and tourist sites.
  After the user logs into his account, it should take them to the next page, which is the chat page. This is where they will be able to interact with the chatbot.

  A chat box was developed so that the user could interact with the chatbot. The chatbot was only programmed to provide answers based on questions related to the tourism and hospitality industries.
- The user can view previous chats
  The user has the right to view their previous chats with the bot. This was done to prevent the user from wasting time having another conversation with the bot about things they've already discussed.

Web Dashboard for the Semantic Analysis (Staff Management)

- Login
  The staff member who has been permitted to use the sentiment analysis has the right to log into the system by providing the appropriate login details that are known to the system.
- Upload a CSV file containing reviews for sentiment analysis.
  The user can upload CSV files that contain the comments made by users who have experienced the services provided by staff members of the tourist site or the hotel. This CSV file can be found on the hotel or tour website, where users are allowed to share their views and rate their experiences.
- View the Chart form of sentiment reviews.
  The results after the sentiment analysis have finished processing the CSV file are then displayed as a bar chart, Fig. 4, which can be viewed by the logged-in staff member. The results were converted into a bar chart because it's easy to read and understand for most people.
- Download the sentiment feedback.
  The provided results can be downloaded into another CSV file, which can be used by the hotel or tourist company to improve their services.

System Requirements

The system requirements are the technical blueprints that convert the project's vision into a concrete and functioning reality. The system requirements, which must be aligned with the project's aims and user requirements, specify the precise functionality, technical capabilities and performance standards that the project

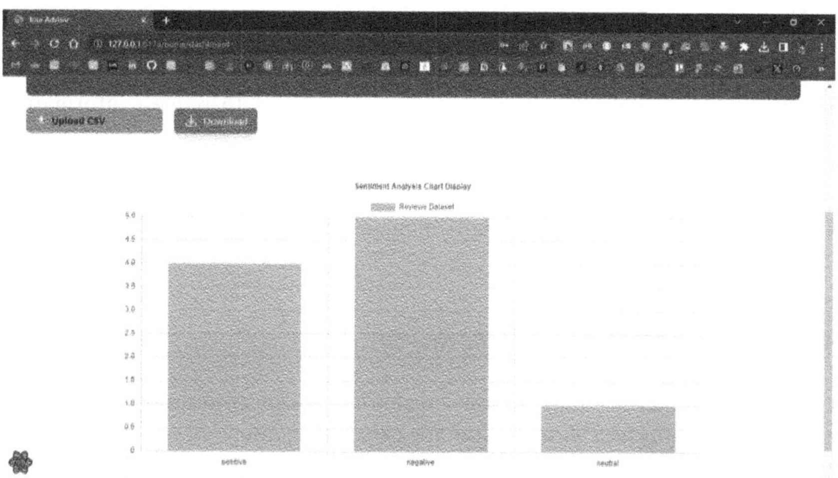

Fig. 4. Sentiment Analysis.

must achieve. These requirements operate as a link between the conceptual design of the project and its practical implementation, helping the development team construct a system that serves its intended purpose. The system requirements establish the specifications for both the chatbot and the sentiment analysis modules in the context of the chatbot and sentiment analysis integration projects, ensuring that they create a holistic user experience. These requirements can be grouped into hardware requirements and software requirements.

Hardware Requirements

Hardware requirements are requirements for a hardware device. The application server will therefore be able to run on any hardware capable of running Ubuntu Server 20.04 LTS 'Focal Fossa' and a Graphical Accelerated Unit (GPU). Since the server is responsible for responding to requests sent by the user, a persistent Internet connection is required before the user can use the programme since it is a web application.

Software Requirements

The web dashboard can only be accessed using a computer or mobile device with a web browser function that supports JavaScript and also supports HTML5. The user must have a Web browser that is up-to-date and supports the features of the application.

Functional Requirements of the System

- The system must require an email and password to access the UI based on the logged-in role type, and access is granted only after the user has been authenticated.
- The system must use error detection.
- The system must be up-and-depth 24 hours a day and accessible in real time.
- The system's data must be highly secure.
- The system should allow tourists to type in queries to request information about various tourist sites.
- The system should allow the staff management to upload the CSV files for sentiment analysis.
- The system should allow the staff management to generate charts from the results obtained.

Non-Functional Requirements of the System

- The system interface must follow appropriate design conventions.
- The system interface should allow for easy navigation.
- Users will receive appropriate feedback on the actions they take on the system.
- The system will consume fewer computer resources.

Experiments and Results

This chapter discusses the metrics that we will use in NLP for the comparison of generative or extractive tasks, wherein two texts are to be compared. Specifically, the ROUGE, which stands for Recall Oriented Understudy for Gisting Evaluation metrics, was used for our testing and evaluation of our question-and-answering model, and label decoding or label mapping was adopted for the Sentiment Analysis accuracy and testing.

Chatbot Test with ROUGE Metric

ROUGE stands for Recall-Oriented Understudy for Gisting Evaluation. The name is deceptively complicated, because this is not a difficult metric to understand, and it's incredibly easy to implement. ROUGE is a set of metrics, rather than just one, used to evaluate the performance of a question-and-answering model.

There are several variants of ROUGE metrics, including ROUGE-N, which measures the number of matching n-grams between the model-generated text and the reference text, and ROUGE-L, which measures the longest common subsequence (LCS) between the two texts. ROUGE scores consider both recall and precision and are typically calculated for a set of predictions and references. ROUGE metrics are widely used in evaluating the performance of text summarisation models.

ROUGE-N

ROUGE-N measures the number of matchings '*n*-grams' between our model-predicted answer and a 'reference'. An *n*-gram is a grouping of tokens or words. A unigram (1-gram) would consist of a single word. A bigram (2-gram) consists of two consecutive words:

Original: 'the quick brown fox jumps over'

> *Unigrams: ['the', 'quick', 'brown', 'fox', 'jumps', 'over']*
>
> *Bigrams: ['the quick', 'quick brown', 'brown fox', 'fox jumps', 'jumps over']*
>
> *Trigrams: ['the quick brown', 'quick brown fox', 'brown fox jumps', 'fox jumps over']*

The reference in this case is the true answer.

With ROUGE-N, the N represents the n-gram that is being used. For ROUGE-1, it measures the match rate of unigrams between a model output and a reference.

ROUGE-2 and ROUGE-3 use bigrams and trigrams, respectively. Once the type of N is decided, a decision is made on whether to calculate the ROUGE recall, precision or F1 score.

RECALL

The recall counts the number of overlapping n-grams found in both the model output and reference and then divides this number by the total number of n-grams in the reference, Eqs. (1) and (2). It looks like this:

$$\frac{\text{number of } n - \text{grams found in model and reference}}{\text{number of } n - \text{grams in reference}} \tag{1}$$

$$\frac{\text{count}_{\text{gram}}(\text{gram}_n)}{\text{count}(\text{gram}_n)} \tag{2}$$

The recall calculation ensures that the model is capturing all of the information contained in the reference, but this isn't so great at ensuring a model is not just pushing out a huge number of words to game the recall score.

Precision

The job of the generator top k is to output the top 'k' values that have been collected by the retriever "top k." This then becomes the final output or result that the user sees when he queries his question to the chatbot.

$$\frac{\text{number of } n - \text{grams found in model and reference}}{\text{number of } n - \text{grams in model}} \tag{3}$$

Applying the precision calculation, Eq. (3), to the previous example, the result obtained will be 43%.

F1-Score

The F1 score is a machine learning evaluation metric that measures the accuracy of a model. It combines the precision and recall scores of a model, leading to its widespread use in recent literature. The F1 score is calculated as the harmonic mean of the precision and recall scores and ranges from 0 to 100%. A higher F1 score denotes a better-quality classifier. F1 score is a much more comprehensive evaluation metric in comparison to accuracy since it maximises two competing objectives simultaneously. F1 score, Eq. (4), can be used for both class-wise and overall evaluations. Furthermore, the other variations of the F1 score, specifically the Fβ score, allow for finer control and prioritisation of precision or recall.

$$2 * \frac{\text{precision} * \text{recall}}{\text{precision} + \text{recall}} \tag{4}$$

ROUGE-L

ROUGE-L is a variant of the ROUGE metric that stands for LCS based statistics. It is used to evaluate the performance of text summarisation models by measuring the similarity between the model-generated summary and the reference summary based on the length of the LCS between them. ROUGE-L is considered to be more effective than ROUGE-1 and ROUGE-2 as it captures sentence-level structure similarity more accurately and does not depend on consecutive n-gram matches. The ROUGE-L score ranges from 0 to 1, where a higher score indicates a better-quality summary. Equations (5)–(7) are the methods for calculating ROUGE-L

$$R_{lsc} = \frac{LSC\,(X, Y)}{m} \tag{5}$$

$$P_{lsc} = \frac{LSC\,(X, Y)}{n} \tag{6}$$

$$F_{lcs} = \frac{(1 + \beta^2)\, R_{lsc} P_{lsc}}{R_{lsc} + \beta^2 P_{lsc}} \tag{7}$$

ROUGE-S

ROUGE-S is a variant of the ROUGE metric that stands for Skip-Bigram-based Co-Occurrence Statistics. It is used to evaluate the performance of text summarisation models by measuring the similarity between the model-generated summary and the reference summary based on the skip bigrams (pairs of non-consecutive words) that occur in both texts. ROUGE-S is considered to be more effective than ROUGE-1 and ROUGE-2 as it captures the semantic similarity between the two texts more accurately. The ROUGE-S score ranges from 0 to 1, where a higher score indicates a better-quality summary.

ROUGE-S allows us to add a degree of leniency to our n-gram matching. For our bigram example, we could match by using a skip-bigram measure.

Test and Results with ROUGE Metric

To begin implementing the ROUGE metric, testing the question and answering model used, the experiment started by initialising it and defining the necessary models. The model pipeline was initialised and the six (6) sets of questions were placed inside a list. The set of questions was lopped and fed to the model, and for every set of questions, the model output was appended to the model out list, and the reference it used was appended to the reference list.

The output results of the model were then cleaned up using regex to avoid any unwanted characters and symbols, since punctuation differences can cause the ROUGE score to view the words as not matching. To fix this, the re library in Python was imported and was used to remove any characters that are not spaces, letters, or numbers by defining a regular expression rule.

The prediction scores for each prediction the model made, but to get the average or general performance of the model, an average calculation was used on the scores by using the **avg = True** flag.

The model had an average prediction performance of 0.77, which is a good rating it between 0 and 1. Representing it in a percentage form, we have a 77% correct prediction score.

Sentiment Analysis Accuracy Test and Results

For the model test for sentiment analysis, a set of known sentences or reviews was initialised together with their labels and was passed to the model to make predictions of the reviews.

A set of test datasets together with label examples of text inputs and their corresponding sentiment labels of known reviews were gathered. The dataset covers a diverse range of sentiments and is representative of the target domain. The sentiment labels were random and made sure that they contained positive, negative, or neutral or neutral sentiments.

The test datasets were pre-processed to match the format expected by the model. This was done by tokenising the text inputs, encoding them into numerical representations, and formatting them according to the model's requirements. This implies that the same pre-processing steps that were used during the training of the model were used here to avoid errors and wrong interpretations.

The model was loaded into memory using the Hugging Face's transformers library (Hugging Face, n.d.). This model is pre-trained on a large corpus of Twitter data for sentiment analysis. The loaded model was then used to make predictions on the pre-processed test dataset. The pre-processed inputs were passed to the model to obtain the predicted sentiment labels by executing it.

By default, the model will output label indices representing the predicted sentiments, but to obtain a human-readable format for further analysis, the predicted label indices were mapped back to their corresponding sentiment labels. This step involved creating a label mapping that associates each label index with its sentiment label. The label mapping was then applied to convert the predicted indices into human-readable sentiment labels.

Evaluations of the Experiments Conducted

NLP tools are indispensable in a wide range of applications, from social media analysis to customer service, in the era of rapid technological advancement. Two key components of NLP are chatbots and sentiment analysis, both of which play pivotal roles in interpreting and engaging with human language. The research aimed to assess the accuracy of a chatbot utilising ROUGE and evaluate the accuracy of sentiment analysis.

A thorough understanding of a chatbot's performance in producing human-like responses was acquired thanks to the evaluation of its correctness using ROUGE measures. The chatbot's capacity for producing coherent, contextually relevant responses, thanks to ROUGE, a tool that is often employed in the context of text summarisation and machine translation, was assessed. We obtained quantitative insights about the chatbot's competence by concentrating on metrics like precision, recall and F1 score. The findings demonstrated that the chatbot did a good job of producing responses that were semantically relevant to user inputs, but there were still several areas that might require improvement, particularly in handling ambiguous requests and keeping a constant conversational context.

On the other hand, the goal of our assessment of the sentiment analysis was to see how accurate it was at identifying the sentiment contained in the text. Sentiment analysis is widely used in business, marketing and the social sciences because it helps firms comprehend user input and public opinion. Our testing showed that the sentiment analysis distinguished among positive, neutral and negative emotions in a range of texts, from product reviews to social media comments. It did, however, occasionally have problems understanding irony, sophisticated language and input from many languages. Despite this, sentiment analysis was a useful tool for automating sentiment analysis activities and drawing insightful conclusions from enormous amounts of textual data.

In summary, the research has illuminated the potential and constraints of NLP tools, particularly a chatbot and a sentiment analysis. Although the chatbot proved it could produce meaningful responses, there is still potential for improvement in how it responds to confusing questions and keeps the context during lengthy chats. On the other hand, the sentiment analysis demonstrated its efficiency in classifying sentiment despite having difficulties with sophisticated language.

This study's importance goes beyond simple performance indicators. It highlights the dynamic nature of NLP technologies and the requirement for ongoing improvement and development. The accuracy and adaptability of chatbots and sentiment analysis are of the utmost importance as they continue to play crucial roles in numerous domains. This research has provided insightful information about the effectiveness of NLP tools.

Conclusion and Recommendations

This research aimed to delve into the fascinating convergence of improved performance and accurate functionality of chatbots. Specifically investigated the use of ROUGE to test for the accuracy of chatbots and the exceptional precision displayed by sentiment analysis in the tourism and hospitality industry. This study contributed to the expanding landscape of AI-powered applications by thoroughly studying the accuracy of a chatbot by employing the ROUGE metric and evaluating the nuanced effectiveness of sentiment analysis algorithms.

Importance of the Research in the Tourism and Hospitality Industry

The incorporation of technology has brought about transformational changes in the dynamic world of modern tourism, influencing the way tourists explore new places and interact with hospitality services. The deployment of AI-driven chatbots meant to provide detailed information about tourist locations and assist in locating the best hotels is one outstanding innovation in this landscape.

With the introduction of these intelligent chatbots, a new era of tailored travel counselling has begun. These chatbots function as digital travel companions, providing tourists with real-time insights about historical sites, cultural attractions and hidden gems thanks to their capacity to quickly access enormous databases of information. These chatbots have proven essential in assisting travellers in identifying and booking hotels that match their preferences and price limits, in addition to their position as digital guides. Tourists can now make well-informed decisions and experience a hassle-free travel planning process thanks to the seamless integration of AI and a user-friendly UI.

Furthermore, the use of sentiment analysis technology in the hotel industry has resulted in significant benefits for both visitors and service providers. Establishments can acquire significant insights into the quality of their services by using sentiment analysis to examine feedback and ratings from hotel staff members. This allows them to make informed modifications, resulting in a more pleasant and gratifying tourist experience.

The positive influence of sentiment analysis extends beyond individual companies to the entire tourism and hospitality sectors. Tourists are more likely to enjoy extraordinary care as hotels attempt to improve their services based on data-driven insights, resulting in higher satisfaction and favourable ratings. This virtuous loop not only creates an outstanding culture but also helps the growth and reputation of the tourism industry as a whole.

Finally, the confluence of AI-driven chatbots and sentiment analysis has transformed the way travellers discover new places and interact with hospitality services. These technological innovations have increased passenger engagement and happiness by providing accurate information and personalised recommendations. Simultaneously, sentiment analysis has raised service standards throughout the hospitality industry, encouraging a culture of continual improvement. As these developments progress, the future of tourism is bright, with seamless digital companionship and extraordinary guest experiences at the forefront.

Recommendations for Future Work

The use of chatbots and sentiment analysis has opened up transformative opportunities for the tourism and hospitality industries, improving client experiences and optimising service delivery. As we move towards a more digital and customer-centric landscape, various opportunities for future research and innovation emerge. Some enhancements that are suggested to keep the bot and analysis up-to-date are as follows:

- Improve chatbot algorithms to provide customised recommendations based on user preferences and previous encounters. Chatbots may generate customised itineraries, restaurant recommendations and travel tips using AI-driven personalisation, enhancing the user experience.

- Extend chatbot capabilities to support many languages, allowing them to effectively communicate with a broad global audience. Language-specific sentiment analysis can also help improve services by providing useful insights into cross-cultural experiences.
- Create a dynamic feedback framework that allows sentiment analysis to process real-time comments from travellers and employees. This loop allows for quick responses to issues and fosters continual improvement in service quality.
- Emotional recognition skills should be added to sentiment analysis. Detecting emotions other than basic sentiment (such as enthusiasm or irritation) can provide a more in-depth insight into client experiences.

Limitations

The completion of a project focused on the adoption of a chatbot and a sentiment analysis within the tourism and hospitality industries reveals several intricate restrictions that require careful attention. Because this technological integration has the potential to transform customer contacts and improve service quality, it is critical to recognise the obstacles that may develop when crafting the final remarks of such an endeavour. In this setting, a thorough understanding of the limits encountered throughout the development and implementation of these technologies is critical for reaching complete conclusions that encompass both accomplishments and future improvement options. This conversation will go into the numerous constraints experienced while working on the project's completion, throwing light on technological, ethical and practical issues.

- Finding enough data to feed the chatbot was hard to come by, and this limited the chatbot's capabilities to provide rich responses to user questions.
- Limited computational resources were also another factor that hindered both models from reaching their maximum potential. The computer used in creating both projects was not powerful enough to contain more functionalities.
- Lacking a stable internet connection was another limitation that hindered the fast development of both projects. Both projects needed to access the internet during their runtime processes, and this was a bit of a headache since getting a stable network became an issue.
- The sentiment analysis had problems detecting the feelings attached to some responses due to the language barrier.
- The sentiment analysis was a bit biased in its responses.
- Keeping the chatbot updated was a bit of a worry too, since a bit of such data wasn't available at our disposal.

Conclusion

Finally, the use of a chatbot and a sentiment analysis in the tourism and hospitality industries marks a significant innovation that has the potential to revolutionise consumer interactions and service quality. This study project set out to investigate the integration of various technologies and shed light on their consequences, benefits and limitations in the dynamic landscape of travel and hospitality.

While the installation of a chatbot introduces streamlined interactions and provides quick access to information, comprehensive analysis revealed that there are hurdles to overcome. Language nuances, a lack of rich data and limited computational resources surfaced as important challenges that require continued development and refining. The ability to handle several languages, manage complex queries and provide real-time results is critical to providing a great user experience.

Furthermore, while sentiment analysis has enormous potential for assessing client satisfaction, it has its own set of restrictions. Accurate emotion detection across languages and cultures, bias mitigation and understanding of subtle emotional cues remain areas of concern that require ongoing study and progress.

Because the tourism and hospitality industries are ever-changing, the research emphasised the need for adaptation. Rapid changes in travel rules, destination popularity and consumer preferences highlighted the importance of keeping the chatbot and sentiment analysis up-to-date and ensuring the information provided is current and credible.

In conclusion, this study sheds light on the potentially revolutionary impact of adopting a chatbot and sentiment analysis in the tourism and hospitality industries. It highlighted the advances made in improving customer experience and service efficiency while also highlighting the complexity that necessitates ongoing innovation and attention. Finally, the convergence of these technologies, led by ethical considerations and a dedication to continuous development, has the potential to transform the future of consumer interactions in the lively world of tourism and hospitality.

References

Abel, U., Emmanuel, C., & Pascal, U. O. (2024). Leveraging AI-powered chatbots to enhance customer service efficiency and future opportunities in automated support. *Computer Science*, *5*(10), 2485–2510. https://doi.org/10.51594/csitrj.v5i10.1676

Adeyemi, B., & Chikuta, O. (2024). Adoption of AI chatbots for customer service in African hotels: Opportunities and challenges. *Journal of Hospitality Management and Tourism*, *18*(2), 45–58. https://doi.org/10.1234/jhmt.2024.4567

Agrawal, M. (2021, June 22). The new normal: Reimagine the transformation of industries with AI. *Forbes*. https://www.forbes.com/sites/forbesbusinesscouncil/2021/06/22/the-new-normal-reimagine-the-transformation-of-industries-with-ai/?sh=1800301f179d

Ataman, A. (2023, April 7). *Data quality in AI: Challenges, importance & best practices*. AIMultiple. https://research.aimultiple.com/data-qualityai/

Bergoeing, R., Loayza, N., & Piguillem, F. (2010). Why are developing countries so macro volatile? *Journal of Development Economics*, *97*(2), 314–321. https://doi.org/10.1016/j.jdeveco.2011.04.001

Bisoi, S., Roy, M., & Samal, A. (2020). Impact of artificial intelligence in the hospitality industry. *International Journal of Advanced Science and Technology*, *29*(5), 4265–4276. https://www.researchgate.net/profile/Mou-Roy-2/publication/343180745_Impact_of_Artificial_Intelligence_in_the_Hospitality_Industry/links/5f1a9c8b92851cd5fa421ba3/Impact-of-Artificial-Intelligence-in-the-Hospitality-Industry.pdf

Bulchand-Gidumal, J. (2022). Impact of artificial intelligence in travel, tourism, and hospitality. In *Handbook of e-Tourism* (pp. 1943–1962). Springer International Publishing. https://link.springer.com/rwe/10.1007/978-3-030-48652-5_110

Carvalho, I., & Ivanov, S. (2024). ChatGPT for tourism: Applications, benefits and risks. *Tourism Review*, *79*(2), 290–303. https://doi.org/10.1108/TR-02-2023-0088

Christou, E., Fotiadis, A., & Giannopoulos, A. (2025). Generative AI as a tourism actor: Reconceptualising experience co-creation, destination governance and responsible innovation in the synthetic experience economy. *Journal of Tourism, Heritage & Services Marketing (JTHSM)*, *11*(2), 16–41. https://doi.org/10.5281/zenodo.16562067

Cozzio, C., Santos Arteaga, F. J., & Maurer, O. (2025). Artificial intelligence adoption in hospitality: Challenges and opportunities across hierarchical levels. *Tourism Review*. https://doi.org/10.1108/TR-10-2024-0913

Devlin, J., Chang, M.-W., Lee, K., & Toutanova, K. (2019). BERT: Pre-training of deep bidirectional transformers for language understanding. In *Proceedings of the 2019 Conference of the North American Chapter of the Association for Computational Linguistics: Human Language Technologies, Volume 1 (Long and Short Papers)* (pp. 4171–4186). Association for Computational Linguistics. https://doi.org/10.48550/arXiv.1810.04805

Fan, A., Jernite, Y., Perez, E., Grangier, D., Weston, J., & Auli, M. (2019). ELI5: Long form question answering. *arXiv*. https://arxiv.org/abs/1907.09190

Florido-Benítez, L., & del Alcázar Martínez, B. (2024). How artificial intelligence (AI) is powering new tourism marketing and the future agenda for smart tourist destinations. *Electronics*, *13*(21), 4151. https://doi.org/10.3390/electronics13214151

Frenette, J. (2025, August 7). *AI for ethical travel curation: Supporting inclusive, culturally sensitive itineraries in global resort and cruise services*. ResearchGate. https://doi.org/10.5281/zenodo.16420133

Garg, A., Verma, D., Pandey, L., Kumar, K. S., Singh, R., & Sharma, A. (2025). Enhancing tailored travel by integrating generative AI with insights driven by personality. In *2025 International Conference on Intelligent Control, Computing and Communications (IC3)* (pp. 404–409). IEEE. https://doi.org/10.1109/IC363308.2025.10957442

Hugging Face. (2023, June 1). Cardiffnlp/Twitter-roberta-base-sentiment-latest [Pre-trained model]. *Hugging Face*. https://huggingface.co/cardiffnlp/twitter-roberta-base-sentiment-latest

Hugging Face. (n.d.). *Flax-sentence-embeddings/All_Datasets_V3_Mpnet-base*. Hugging Face. https://huggingface.co/flax-sentence-embeddings/all_datasets_v3_mpnet-base. Accessed on August 1, 2025.

Jalil, M. F., Lynch, P., Marikan, D. A. B. A., & Isa, A. H. B. M. (2025). The influential role of artificial intelligence (AI) adoption in digital value creation for small and medium enterprises (SMEs): Does technological orientation mediate this relationship? *AI & SOCIETY*, *40*(3), 1875–1896. https://doi.org/10.1007/s00146-024-01969-1

Kadagidze, L., & Ugrelidze, R. (2023). The impact of artificial intelligence on hotel revenue management: Opportunities and challenges. *International Journal of Hospitality Management*, *114*, 103525. https://doi.org/10.1016/j.ijhm.2023.103525
Kırtıl, I. G., Çizel, B., Uzun, S., & Uzut, İ. (2024). Bridging the gap: Fine-tuning artificial intelligence (AI) chatbots for tourism. In *Paper presented at the conference on managing tourism across continents.* stanbul. https://www.researchgate.net/publication/384885151_Bridging_the_Gap_Fine-Tuning_Artificial_Intelligence_AI_Chatbots_for_Tourism
Lee, K. J. (2022). Effects of service robots in the hospitality and tourism sectors: A critical review and future research directions. 관광연구저널, *36*(4), 21–33. https://www.researchgate.net/publication/360737173_Effects_of_service_robots_in_the_hospitality_and_tourism_sectors_A_critical_review_and_future_research_directions#fullTextFileContent
Limna, P. (2023). Artificial intelligence (AI) in the hospitality industry: A review article. *International Journal of Computing Sciences Research*, *7*, 1306–1317. https://doi.org/10.25147/ijcsr.2017.001.1.103
Mariani, M., & Borghi, M. (2022). Big data and analytics in tourism and hospitality: A systematic literature review. *International Journal of Contemporary Hospitality Management*, *34*(3), 1155–1180. https://doi.org/10.1108/IJCHM-06-2021-0739
McClelland, C. (2017). *The difference between artificial intelligence, machine learning, and deep learning*. Medium. https://medium.com/iotforall/the-difference-between-artificial-intelligence-machine-learning-and-deep-learning-3aa67bff5991
Pinecone. (n.d.-a). Integrating Pinecone with Haystack (PineconeDocumentStore). In *Pinecone Documentation*. Retrieved August 1, 2025, from https://docs.pinecone.io/integrations/haystack
Pinecone. (n.d.-b). Long form question answering (LFQA) in Haystack. *Pinecone*. Retrieved August 1, 2025, from https://www.pinecone.io/learn/haystack-lfqa/
Pinecone. (n.d.-c). Long form question answering in Haystack | Pinecone. Retrieved July 12, 2025, from https://www.pinecone.io/learn/haystack-lfqa/#LFQA-in-HaystackP
Pinecone-io. (n.d.-d). examples/integrations/haystack/haystack_lfqa.ipynb [Jupyter notebook]. *GitHub*. https://github.com/pinecone-io/examples/blob/master/integrations/haystack/haystack_lfqa.ipynb
Raphael, C., & Qureshi, S. (2010). Technology adoption in the tourism and hospitality industry: A review of literature and future directions. *International Journal of Hospitality Management*, *29*(3), 512–521.
Roser, M. (2022). Technology adoption. Our world in data. Retrieved August 1, 2025, from https://ourworldindata.org/technology-adoption
Sigala, M. (2020). Tourism and COVID-19: Impacts and implications for advancing and resetting industry and research. *Journal of Business Research*, *117*, 312–321. https://doi.org/10.1016/j.jbusres.2020.06.015
Talukder, M. B., Khan, M. R., Kumar, S., Singh, K., & Lina, F. Y. (2025). AI strategies for tourism development in emerging markets. In *Practical strategies and case studies for online marketing 6.0* (pp. 117–138). IGI Global Scientific Publishing. https://www.igi-global.com/chapter/ai-strategies-for-tourism-development-in-emerging-markets/379278
vblagoje. (2021, October 17). vblagoje/Bart_Lfqa [Large language model]. *Hugging Face*. https://huggingface.co/vblagoje/bart_lfqa

Conclusion: The Adoption of AI in Africa's Hospitality and Tourism Industry – Charting a Path for the Future

Esi Akyere Mensah[a], *Aaron Yankholmes*[b], *Frank Badu-Baiden*[c] *and Nii Longdon Sowah*[d]

[a]International University of Grand Bassam, Cote D'Ivoire
[b]Nottingham Trent University, UK
[c]University of Central Florida, USA
[d]University of Ghana, Ghana

The contributions in this book collectively constitute a wide-reaching attempt on the growing importance of Artificial Intelligence (AI) in Africa, a region historically marginalised within global high-technology domains. Despite the continent's demographic weight and its expanding digital economy, scholarly engagement with the trajectory of AI development in Africa has remained limited when compared with regions such as Asia, Europe or North America (CIPIT, 2025; World Bank, 2021). The paucity of academic attention on the trajectory of AI development in Africa is particularly acute.

A nascent yet expanding body of scholarship on tourism in Africa has concentrated on development dynamics in the continent's most frequently visited destinations, including Egypt, Morocco, Ghana, Kenya, Tanzania, Tunisia, South Africa and Zimbabwe (Timothy, 2023). While this literature offers valuable insights into patterns of tourism growth and policy, far less is known about how the industry is adapting to the transformative changes introduced by AI, or how the continent as a whole will position itself in relation to global AI trends observed in both advanced and emerging markets. The aim of this book has therefore been to illuminate the diverse manifestations of AI adoption in Africa's tourism and hospitality industry and to unpack both the opportunities and challenges that accompany this transformation.

Of course, within the limitations of a single book, it has not been possible to include every dimension of AI adoption, nor to examine every country or unique innovation capability in depth. Nevertheless, the collective effort has succeeded

Artificial Intelligence in Hospitality and Tourism in Africa, 183–193

doi:10.1108/978-1-80686-169-920261011

in highlighting current patterns and trends, outlining opportunities and barriers, and contextualising the socioeconomic and political dynamics that frame Africa's AI landscape. In doing so, the chapters have brought into focus the potential for AI adoption in tourism and hospitality to reshape competitiveness, enhance visitor experiences and contribute to sustainable development.

Charting the Future: Critical Questions Ahead

Current scholarship on the trajectory of AI development in Africa remains predominantly descriptive, highlighting the need for more theoretically grounded and analytically rigorous research to unpack the continent's distinctive dynamics of adoption across diverse sectors, including tourism and hospitality (CIPIT, 2025; PwC, 2023). While balancing AI adoption with the imperative of social, economic and environmental sustainability is a global concern, this challenge is particularly pronounced in Africa, where technological advancement must be carefully aligned with inclusive development objectives and the preservation of both cultural and natural heritage (UNESCO, 2021; World Bank, 2021).

Although this volume has explored numerous facets of AI adoption in Africa's tourism and hospitality industry, it also makes clear that our understanding is still nascent in many areas. There remains a dearth of scholarly knowledge about the complex dynamics of technological innovation in African tourism contexts, especially outside the handful of well-studied countries. Looking ahead, several future directions offer a unique opportunity for scholars and practitioners to shape research agendas that are not only technologically forward-looking but also deeply rooted in Africa's developmental, cultural and sustainability priorities. This section outlines five key areas where research is most urgently needed: (1) AI for sustainable and inclusive tourism development; (2) innovation ecosystems and capacity building; (3) AI policy, ethics and governance in tourism; (4) impact assessment and market readiness; and (5) cross-regional and South–South collaboration. As illustrated in Fig. 1, the journey towards AI adoption should be built on a foundation of human capital. Without addressing the fundamental deficit in digital skills, progress in other areas will be critically limited. This underpins the first research area: 'leveraging AI for sustainable and inclusive tourism development…'

AI for Sustainable Tourism Development

AI holds particular promise for sustainable tourism development on the continent, but this remains underexplored in scholarship. Much of the existing research has emphasised the contribution of AI to efficiency and competitiveness in advanced economies, with less attention to how these technologies might be leveraged to meet Africa's unique challenges. AI-driven platforms could connect local entrepreneurs to global markets, enabling small-scale operators to participate in international supply chains. Predictive models could optimise resource allocation across tourism value chains, ensuring that benefits are distributed

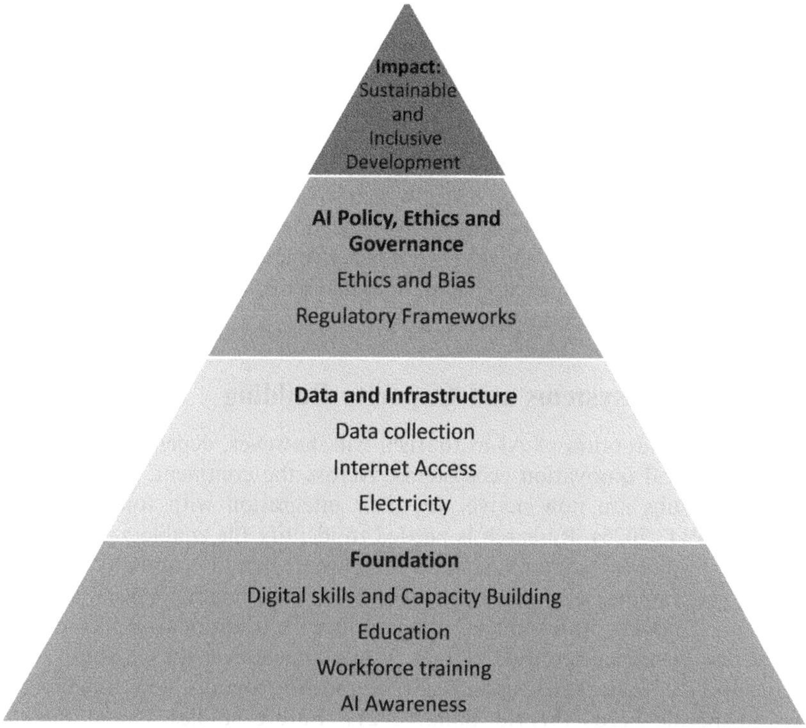

Fig. 1. Priority Pyramid for AI in Hospitality and Tourism in Africa. *Source:* Authors' construct.

more equitably (Gössling & Mei, 2025; Gretzel et al., 2020). Equally, AI tools such as machine learning and natural language processing can preserve and promote cultural heritage by supporting artefact restoration, documenting endangered languages and creating immersive augmented reality experiences that both protect and showcase Africa's tangible and intangible patrimony (UNESCO, 2021). These tools carry immense potential for expanding access while safeguarding authenticity.

In Kenya, for example, safari operators in the Maasai Mara are piloting AI-powered camera traps and predictive analytics to track wildlife movements. These tools optimise safari routes, reduce fuel consumption and enhance visitor satisfaction while also contributing to conservation data (World Wildlife Fund, 2022). Such initiatives illustrate how AI can simultaneously advance environmental sustainability and competitiveness in tourism. However, research is needed to examine whether the economic benefits of these innovations extend meaningfully to local communities, such as the Maasai, who depend heavily on tourism revenues for livelihoods.

The role of AI in diversifying Africa's tourism geography also warrants further exploration. Much of the continent's tourism research has focused on established destinations such as South Africa, Kenya, Morocco, Egypt and Tanzania. Yet less-studied regions – the Sahel, Central Africa or island states like Comoros and Seychelles – stand to benefit significantly from AI-enabled strategies (Mensah et al., 2025). AI systems could forecast niche demand for adventure tourism in Chad, ecotourism in Gabon or cultural tourism in Benin, helping reduce over-concentration in established hotspots. Diversification supported by AI could make the sector more resilient to shocks such as pandemics, conflicts or environmental change, while empowering rural and marginalised communities to participate more fully in tourism economies.

Innovation Ecosystems and Capacity Building

The successful adoption of AI in tourism will, however, depend heavily on the strength of local innovation ecosystems. Across the continent, more than 600 technology hubs are now active, yet their integration with tourism remains limited (CIPIT, 2025). Research is needed to identify the enablers of ecosystem development that can support AI adoption in tourism and hospitality. Skills and training programmes are critical, as digital literacy remains uneven across the continent. Tourism professionals, often trained in traditional service delivery, require new competencies in AI literacy. While some universities in South Africa, Ghana and Kenya are offering data science and AI programs, few are tailored to tourism-specific needs (World Bank, 2021). Future studies should therefore assess how vocational training, online certifications and curriculum reforms can prepare the tourism workforce for AI adoption.

Indeed, there are indications that infrastructure and government policy progress will be critically limited without a concerted focus on building a skilled workforce first and foremost. This reflects a pragmatic, bottom-up understanding that technology is driven by people, and that Africa's AI revolution in tourism must be built on a foundation of education and training.

Equally, incubators and accelerators play an important role in nurturing startups applying AI to travel booking, hospitality management or ecotourism. Kenya's iHub has supported tourism-related digital ventures, while South Africa hosts AI-driven wildlife management startups. Yet their reach and scalability remain limited. Comparative research could explore why certain ecosystems succeed in integrating AI into tourism while others lag.

Rwanda provides a compelling example. Positioned as a regional leader in AI and digital innovation, the country hosts the Centre for the Fourth Industrial Revolution (C4IR) in partnership with the World Economic Forum. While much of Rwanda's focus has been on finance and agriculture, the government has signalled interest in extending AI to tourism and hospitality (Rwanda Ministry of ICT, 2023). Kigali's pilot smart city projects demonstrate how policy alignment, infrastructure investment and public-private partnerships can create enabling conditions for tourism innovation. Examining Rwanda's model could provide transferable lessons for other African countries seeking to build AI-ready tourism ecosystems.

AI Policy, Ethics and Governance in Tourism

Government incentives and supportive policy frameworks are equally vital. Mauritius, for instance, has introduced tax breaks and innovation-friendly policies that position it among the highest-ranking African countries in the Global Innovation Index (GII), alongside South Africa (WIPO, 2024). Comparative analyses between these high performers and lower-ranked states could illuminate best practices for fostering AI innovation in tourism.

Yet as AI adoption expands, questions of ethics, governance and sovereignty become increasingly urgent. Tourism involves the collection and management of sensitive personal and cultural data, raising concerns about ownership, consent and control. If managed primarily by foreign-owned platforms, African countries risk losing sovereignty over data flows central to tourism development. Research is needed to explore governance models that ensure national control while respecting community consent (African Union, 2024).

Morocco illustrates both the potential and the challenges. The Ministry of Tourism has piloted AI-driven platforms to better manage overtourism in heritage-rich cities like Marrakech and Fez. Visitor data is used to manage crowd flows and implement dynamic ticketing systems that protect fragile sites while sustaining revenues (OECD, 2025). While effective for conservation, these practices raise questions about who decides how visitor data is used, who profits from it and how local communities participate in decision-making. Empirical research is critical to address such governance dilemmas and ensure that AI enhances, rather than undermines, cultural integrity.

This concern also extends to cultural narrative ownership. AI can digitise and disseminate cultural heritage, but issues of authenticity and benefit-sharing loom large. For example, a virtual museum powered by AI that curates Maasai cultural traditions prompt questions of who owns the representation, who controls access and how revenues are shared. UNESCO (2021) emphasises that communities must retain agency over their heritage, yet case studies are needed to understand how this principle can be applied in African tourism contexts.

The African Union's Continental AI Strategy (2024) provides a foundation for ethical and inclusive governance, emphasising responsible AI, infrastructure development and harmonised legal frameworks. The challenge lies in translating these continental ambitions into sector-specific strategies for tourism. Scholars should explore how AI governance can prevent algorithmic bias in destination marketing, ensure equitable benefit-sharing and protect cultural assets from digital overexposure (Gull, 2025).

Impact Assessment and Market Readiness

Empirical impact assessment remains another underdeveloped area. While anecdotal reports highlight the benefits of AI-powered chatbots, predictive analytics and translation tools, little systematic evidence exists on how these innovations affect African tourism businesses and customer experiences. In South Africa, for example, high-end hotels in Cape Town and Johannesburg are experimenting with AI-enabled booking systems and predictive maintenance for energy efficiency (Hospitality Net, 2023). These tools have been shown to enhance operational efficiency and customer satisfaction. However, smaller lodges and guesthouses – common in rural areas – struggle with the financial and technical barriers to adoption, deepening the digital divide within the sector. Research is therefore needed to assess how AI affects employment, revenue distribution, customer trust and sustainability outcomes across enterprises of different scales (Tussyadiah, 2020; Xiang et al., 2021).

This issue is particularly pressing given the dominance of small and medium-sized enterprises (SMEs) in African tourism. SMEs often face prohibitive costs, infrastructure constraints and digital trust deficits that hinder adoption (PwC, 2023). Understanding these barriers through market readiness studies is critical for designing targeted interventions, such as microfinance schemes, cooperative AI adoption models or donor-supported capacity-building initiatives. Equally, it is necessary to measure AI's impact not only on financial performance but also on broader indicators of social and environmental sustainability. Does AI help reduce carbon footprints by optimising travel flows? Does it create new forms of employment, or does it exacerbate job displacement? These questions should anchor future empirical research.

Cross-Regional Synergies: South–South and North–South Collaboration for AI in Tourism

Africa's AI and tourism futures will depend on collaborative frameworks both within the continent and across the Global South. Africa shares structural similarities with Asia and Latin America, where AI has been deployed in eco-tourism, smart destinations and community-based tourism models (Castro, 2025; Government of India, 2022). Comparative research could examine how Costa Rica's use of AI in ecotourism or India's smart tourism initiatives might inform African contexts.

At the same time, intra-African collaboration offers significant opportunities. Initiatives such as the Smart Africa Alliance, which involves over 30 countries, are spearheading digital infrastructure and AI governance projects with strong cross-border implications (Dalberg, 2025). While tourism is not yet a central focus, Smart Africa's cross-border data-sharing platforms could be extended to include tourism flows, offering smaller states better access to insights on global and regional travel trends. This could empower countries that have traditionally remained at the periphery of Africa's tourism economy to gain visibility in global markets.

The Deep Learning Indaba network further demonstrates the role of research communities in building collective AI capacity across Africa. Similar models could be adapted to tourism, creating platforms for sharing best practices, pooling expertise and conducting joint research. This aligns with the African Union's vision of collective digital sovereignty, ensuring that AI becomes a tool of empowerment rather than dependency. South–South partnerships could serve not only as mechanisms for resource pooling but also as platforms for shaping global narratives on the ethical and sustainable use of AI in tourism.

There is also considerable potential for North–South partnerships and engagement with countries ranked highly on the GII, such as Switzerland, the United States, Singapore, South Korea and Finland (WIPO, 2024). These nations offer advanced expertise in AI applications for smart cities, sustainable tourism and innovation ecosystems. Collaborative research between African institutions and universities in these countries could facilitate the cross-fertilisation of ideas, ensuring that Africa gains access to frontier AI research while simultaneously contributing its own innovations – such as mobile-driven AI ecosystems in Kenya or Rwanda's smart city pilots – to global debates. Importantly, such partnerships must be structured equitably to avoid reproducing extractive patterns, focusing instead on reciprocal knowledge transfer, joint capacity building and co-creation of solutions tailored to African contexts.

The combination of intra-African collaboration, South–South partnerships and North–South exchanges with high-innovation economies creates fertile ground for shared learning and innovation (see call to action in Table 1). This multi-layered framework would not only accelerate AI adoption in African tourism but also position the continent as an active contributor to the global discourse on ethical, sustainable and inclusive applications of AI in tourism and hospitality. By leveraging Africa's unique strengths while drawing on lessons from both emerging and advanced economies, the continent can ensure that AI becomes a tool of empowerment, resilience and cultural stewardship rather than dependency.

Table 1. A Call to Action: Priorities for Stakeholders.

Stakeholder Group	Immediate Priority	Key Action Points
Researchers & Academics	Shift from descriptive to solutions-oriented research.	1. Develop context-aware AI models for African Hospitality and tourism MSMEs. 2. Create frameworks for assessing AI's social and environmental impact. 3. Pioneer studies on AI ethics, data sovereignty, and cultural narrative ownership.
Policymakers & Government Agencies	Develop supportive, sector-specific policy frameworks.	1. Integrate **digital skills** development into national tourism strategies.

(Continued)

Table 1. *(Continued)*

Stakeholder Group	Immediate Priority	Key Action Points
		2. Incentivise AI adoption for sustainability (e.g. tax breaks for green AI). 3. Establish clear data governance protocols to protect national and community interests.
Industry Practitioners (Hotels, Tour Ops)	Invest in foundational digital literacy and pilot projects.	1. Partner with tech hubs to pilot AI tools in specific areas (e.g. booking, conservation). 2. Advocate for workforce training programmes to upskill employees. 3. Demand transparent and equitable AI solutions from technology providers.
Technology Hubs & Innovators	Move from generic solutions to tourism-specific applications.	1. Develop AI tools that address local problems (e.g. low-bandwidth translation, local content curation). 2. Create incubator programmes focused exclusively on tourism and hospitality tech. 3. Facilitate knowledge transfer between tech experts and tourism professionals.
International Partners & Donors	Move from top-down transfer to equitable co-creation.	1. Fund research and capacity-building programmes focused on **Africa's priorities** (sustainability, inclusion). 2. Support South–South collaboration networks for knowledge sharing. 3. Ensure partnerships are structured to build local IP and skills, not create.

Source: Authors (2025).

Conclusion

Africa remains one of the least visited regions of the world and is persistently underrepresented in global research, science, technology and innovation. Yet, with its youthful population and abundant natural and cultural resources, the continent holds immense potential to harness AI as a driver of tourism development and as a pathway towards the achievement of the United Nations Sustainable Development Goals (SDGs). Africa is not merely a passive recipient of technological transfer but represents a dynamic intellectual frontier, a relatively uncharted space for generating new ideas, testing theories and advancing models of AI adoption that are not only regionally significant but also globally relevant.

Research on AI adoption within the sector in Africa remains at an incipient stage. Where scholarship does exist, it frequently mirrors the trajectories of established 'successful' destinations, leaving vast geographical scope for new work that uncovers the intricacies, complexities and distinct manifestations of AI adoption across diverse African contexts. As we noted in the introduction, some countries have begun experimenting with AI to enhance the industry. In these countries, AI is being deployed to streamline operations, reduce costs, optimise service delivery and enrich customer experiences (World Bank, 2021). Yet, despite these advances, the potential of AI in African tourism remains only partially understood and vastly underexplored. In this context, the continent presents a distinctive intellectual and empirical frontier – a relatively untapped space for generating data, testing paradigms and advancing theories that could not only reshape tourism on the continent but also enrich and challenge global perspectives on AI adoption in hospitality and service industries. While the region continues to grapple with negative imagery and enduring stereotypes that dissuade some visitors, the region's cultural richness and mystique exert a strong allure on others (Timothy, 2023). Indeed, this paradox offers fertile ground for examining how AI may serve to mediate, reproduce or transform prevailing narratives of African destinations within the global tourism marketplace.

Thus, the possibilities for scholarly inquiry are vast. From questions of digital inclusion, data sovereignty and ethical governance to practical applications in cultural heritage preservation, community-based tourism and sustainable development, the avenues for exploration are as diverse as the continent itself. This book positions itself as an opening contribution – a foundation for a broader and deeper scholarly dialogue. Its purpose is not to provide definitive answers but to raise critical questions, set future research agendas and invite meaningful collaboration. If it succeeds in stimulating debate and positioning Africa at the centre of global conversations on AI and tourism, then it will have achieved its aim.

References

African Union. (2024). *Continental strategy for artificial intelligence in Africa.* African Union Commission.

Castro, G. (2025). *Costa Rica is saving forest ecosystems by listening to them.* https://www.wired.com/story/costa-rica-forest-conservation-sounds/. Accessed on November 20, 2025.

Chan, E. S., Okumus, F., & Chan, W. (2020). What hinders hotels' adoption of environmental technologies: A quantitative study. *International Journal of Hospitality Management, 84*, 102324. https://doi.org/10.1016/j.ijhm.2019.102324

Dalberg, A. (2025). *Africa's role in the global AI landscape: AI action summit 2025.* Dalberg.

Gössling, S., & Mei, X. Y. (2025). AI and sustainable tourism: An assessment of risks and opportunities for the SDGs. *Current Issues in Tourism*, 1–14. https://doi.org/10.1080/13683500.2025.2477142

Gretzel, U., Sigala, M., Xiang, Z., & Koo, C. (2020). Smart tourism: Foundations and developments. *Electronic Markets, 30*(1), 1–10. https://doi.org/10.1007/s12525-015-0196-8

Government of India. (2022). *Ministry of Tourism: Report on national digital tourism mission.* https://tourism.gov.in/sites/default/files/2022-09/National%20Digital%20Tourism%20Mission_2022.pdf. Accessed on November 20, 2025.

Gull, S. (2025, January 8). *The African Union has a strategy to make Africa a global leader in AI.* Diplomatic Courier. https://www.diplomaticourier.com/posts/african-union-strategy-make-africa-global-leader-ai#:~:text=The%20strategy%20plans%20to%20utilize,tech–savvy%20populations%20ready%20to. Accessed August 24, 2025.

Hospitality Net. (2023). *AI in hospitality: Transforming service, operational efficiency, and personalization.* https://www.hospitalitynet.org/opinion/4127221.html. Accessed on September 25, 2025.

Mensah, E. A., Odame, D. N. A., Ankrah, I., Obuobisa-Darko, T., & Hinson, R. E. (2025). From reviews to reflections: Understanding tourist sentiments and satisfaction in African destinations through user-generated content. *Annals of Tourism Research Empirical Insights, 6*(1), 100174.

OECD. (2025). *National urban policy review of morocco.* OECD Publishing. https://doi.org/10.1787/af7ee02f-en. Accessed on November 19, 2025.

PwC. (2023). *The economic impact of artificial intelligence in Africa.* PricewaterhouseCoopers.

Rwanda Ministry of ICT. (2023). *The national AI policy.* https://www.ictworks.org/national-artificial-intelligence-policy-rwanda. Accessed on September 25, 2025.

The Centre for Intellectual Property and Information Technology Law (CIPIT). (2025). *The state of ICT in Africa 2022: Digital trends and AI adoption.* https://aiconference.cipit.org/documents/the-state-of-ai-in-africa-report.pdf. Accessed August 24, 2025.

Timothy, D. J. (Ed.). (2023). *Cultural heritage and tourism in Africa.* Taylor & Francis.

Tussyadiah, I. (2020). A review of research into automation in tourism: Launching the annals of tourism research curated collection on AI and robotics in tourism. *Annals of Tourism Research, 81*, 102883. https://doi.org/10.1016/j.annals.2020.102883

UNESCO. (2021). *AI and the futures of learning in Africa: Ensuring inclusion and equity.* UNESCO.

WIPO. (2024). *Global innovation index 2024.* World Intellectual Property Organization.

World Bank. (2021). *The future of work in Africa: Harnessing the potential of digital technologies for all.* World Bank.

World Wildlife Fund. (2022). *Artificial intelligence and conservation*. https://www.worldwildlife.org/our-work/science/artificial-intelligence-and-conservation/. Accessed on September 25, 2025.

Xiang, Z., Stienmetz, J., & Fesenmaier, D. R. (2021). Smart Tourism Design: Launching the annals of tourism research curated collection on designing tourism places. *Annals of Tourism Research*, *86*, 103154.

Printed and bound by CPI Group (UK) Ltd, Croydon, CR0 4YY

17/09/2026

14964600-0001